Excel 2002
Level 2

ESSENTIALS

Excel 2002
Level 2

E
S
S
E
N
T
I
A
L
S

MARIANNE FOX
COLLEGE OF BUSINESS ADMINISTRATION
BUTLER UNIVERSITY

LAWRENCE C. METZELAAR
COLLEGE OF BUSINESS ADMINISTRATION
BUTLER UNIVERSITY

Prentice Hall

Upper Saddle River, New Jersey

LIBRARY OF CONGRESS CATALOGING-IN-PUBLICATION DATA

Fox, Marianne B.
    Essentials Excel 2002 Level 2 / Marianne Fox, Lawrence C. Metzelaar.
        p. cm.—(Essentials 2002 series)
    Includes index.
    ISBN 0-13-092765-1
      1. Microsoft Excel for Windows.   2. Business—Computer programs.   3.
Electronic spreadsheets.   I. Metzelaar, Lawrence C.   II. Title.   III. Series.
    HF5548.4.M523 F67893 2002
    005.369—dc21   2001003765

Publisher and Vice President: Natalie E. Anderson
Executive Editor: Jodi McPherson
Managing Editor: Monica Stipanov
Assistant Editor: Jennifer Cappello
Editorial Assistant: Mary Ann Broadnax
Developmental Editors: Joyce J. Nielsen and Jan Snyder
Media Project Manager: Cathleen Profitko
Executive Marketing Manager: Emily Knight
Manager, Production: Gail Steier de Acevedo
Project Managers: Tim Tate and April Montana
Associate Director, Manufacturing: Vincent Scelta
Manufacturing Buyer: Natacha St. Hill Moore
Design Manager: Pat Smythe
Interior Design: Kim Buckley
Cover Design: Pisaza Design Studio, Ltd.
Production Assistant to Design and Media: Christopher Kossa
Manager, Print Production: Christy Mahon
Full-Service Composition: Impressions Book and Journal Services, Inc.
Printer/Binder: Courier Companies, Inc. Kendallville

Credits and acknowledgments borrowed from other sources and reproduced, with permission, in this textbook appear on the appropriate page within the text.

Microsoft, Windows, Windows NT, MSN, The Microsoft Network, PowerPoint, Outlook, FrontPage, Hotmail, the MSN logo, and/or other Microsoft products referenced herein are either trademarks or registered trademarks of Microsoft Corporation in the United States and/or other countries. Screen shots and icons reprinted with permission from the Microsoft Corporation. This book is not sponsored or endorsed by or affiliated with Microsoft Corporation.

Microsoft and the Microsoft Office User Specialist Logo are either trademarks or registered trademarks of Microsoft Corporation in the United States and/or other countries. Pearson Education is independent from Microsoft Corporation, and is not affiliated with Microsoft in any manner. This text may be used in assisting students to prepare for a Microsoft Office User Specialist (MOUS) Exam. Neither Microsoft, its designated review company, nor Pearson Education warrants that use of this text will ensure passing this exam.

Use of this Microsoft Office User Specialist Approved Courseware Logo on this product signifies that it has been independently reviewed and approved in complying with the following standards:

Acceptable coverage of all content related to the Core and Expert Level Microsoft Office exams entitled "Excel 2002" when used in combination with the following books: essentials Excel 2002 Level 1 and essentials Excel 2002 Level 3.

10 9 8 7 6 5 4 3 2 1
ISBN 0-13-092765-1

What Does This Logo Mean?

It means this courseware has been approved by the Microsoft® Office User Specialist Program to be among the finest available for learning **Microsoft Excel 2002.** It also means that upon completion of this courseware, you may be prepared to become a Microsoft Office User Specialist.

What Is a Microsoft Office User Specialist?

A Microsoft Office User Specialist is an individual who has certified his or her skills in one or more of the Microsoft Office desktop applications of Microsoft Word, Microsoft Excel, Microsoft PowerPoint, Microsoft Outlook, or Microsoft Access, or in Microsoft Project. The Microsoft Office User Specialist Program typically offers certification exams at the "Core" and "Expert" skill levels.* The Microsoft Office User Specialist Program is the only Microsoft-approved program in the world for certifying proficiency in Microsoft Office desktop applications and Microsoft Project. This certification can be a valuable asset in any job search or career advancement.

More Information:

To learn more about becoming a Microsoft Office User Specialist, visit www.mous.net

To purchase a Microsoft Office User Specialist certification exam, visit www.DesktopIQ.com

To learn about other Microsoft Office User Specialist approved courseware from Prentice Hall, visit www.prenhall.com/phit/mous_frame.html

---

* The availability of Microsoft Office User Specialist certification exams varies by application, application version, and language. Visit www.mous.net for exam availability.

Microsoft, the Microsoft Office User Specialist Logo, PowerPoint, and Outlook are either registered trademarks or trademarks of Microsoft Corporation in the United States and/or other countries.

Dedication

We would like to dedicate this book to all who use it, in appreciation of your desire to learn how to learn, and your selection of our book to support those efforts.

Acknowledgments

We want to express our appreciation to the entire *essentials* 2002 team—other authors, editors, production staff, and those in marketing who start and end the process of developing and delivering a quality text. Special thanks go to those with whom we were most involved on a day-to-day basis: **Monica Stipanov**, managing editor; **Joyce Nielsen**, developmental editor; and **April Montana**, project manager. They continue to have our respect and gratitude for the prompt, professional, and always pleasant way in which they manage the creative process.

We also thank several colleagues at Butler University for supporting the collaborative process that was critical to the success of the *essentials* 2002 series: the dean of the College of Business Administration, **Dr. Richard Fetter;** and the executive director of Information Resources, initially **Sondrea Ozolins** and then **Ken Sorenson.** Their combined support enabled us as series editors to host a launch meeting at Butler University, and to coordinate a listserv used by authors and editors to ensure consistency and quality across all titles in the series.

About the Series Editors

Marianne Fox—Series editor and coauthor of *essentials Excel 2002 Level 1, Level 2*, and *Level 3*. Marianne Fox is an Indiana CPA with B.S. and M.B.A. degrees in Accounting from Indiana University. For more than 20 years, she has enjoyed teaching full-time—initially in Indiana University's School of Business; since 1988 in the College of Business Administration at Butler University. As the co-owner of an Indiana-based consulting firm, Marianne has extensive experience consulting and training in the corporate and continuing education environments. Since 1984, she has co-authored more than 35 computer-related books; and has given presentations on accounting, computer applications, and instructional development topics at a variety of seminars and conferences.

Lawrence C. Metzelaar—Series editor and coauthor of *essentials Excel 2002 Level 1, Level 2*, and *Level 3*. Lawrence C. Metzelaar earned a B.S. in Business Administration and Computer Science from the University of Maryland, and an Ed.M. and C.A.G.S. in Human Problem Solving from Boston University. Lawrence has more than 30 years of experience with military and corporate mainframe and microcomputer systems. He has taught computer science and Management Information Systems (MIS) courses at the University of Hawaii, Control Data Institute, Indiana University, and Purdue University; currently, he is a full-time faculty member in the College of Business Administration at Butler University. As the co-owner of an Indiana-based consulting firm, he has extensive experience consulting and training in the corporate and continuing education environments. Since 1984, he has co-authored more than 35 computer-related books; and has given presentations on computer applications and instructional development topics at a variety of seminars and conferences.

About the Series Authors

Linda Bird—Author of *essentials PowerPoint® 2002 Level 1* and *Level 2*. Linda Bird specializes in corporate training and support through her company, Software Solutions. She has successfully trained users representing more than 75 businesses, including several Fortune 500 companies. She custom designs many of her training materials. Her clients include Appalachian Electric Power Co., Goodyear, Pillsbury, Rockwell, and Shell Chemical. Her background also includes teaching at Averett College and overseeing computer training for a business training organization.

Using her training experience as a springboard, Linda has written numerous books on PowerPoint, Word, Excel, Access, and Windows. Additionally, she has written more than 20 instructor's manuals and contributed to books on a variety of desktop application programs. She has also penned more than 150 magazine articles, as well as monthly how-to columns on PowerPoint and Excel for *Smart Computing* magazine.

Linda, a graduate of the University of Wisconsin, lives near the Great Smoky Mountains in Tennessee with her husband, Lonnie, and daughters, Rebecca and Sarah. Besides authoring books, Linda home-educates her daughters. If she's not writing, you can probably find her trekking around the mountains (or horseback riding) with her family.

Keith Mulbery—Author of *essentials Word 2002 Level 1, Level 2*, and *Level 3*. Keith Mulbery is an associate professor in the Information Systems Department at Utah Valley State College, where he teaches computer applications courses and assists with curriculum development. Keith received his B.S. and M.Ed. (majoring in Business Education) from Southwestern Oklahoma State University. Keith has written several Word and WordPerfect textbooks. His previous book, *MOUS essentials Word 2000*, received the Utah Valley State College Board of Trustees Award of Excellence in January 2001. In addition, he was the developmental editor of *essentials Word 2000 intermediate* and *essentials Word 2000 advanced*. Keith also conducts hands-on computer application workshops at the local, state, and national levels, including at the National Business Education Association convention.

Dawn Parrish Wood—Author of *essentials Access 2002 Level 1*, *Level 2*, **and** *Level 3*. Dawn Parrish Wood is an independent contractor, and provides software training through her own business, Software Support. She teaches customized courses to local businesses and individuals in order to upgrade employee skills and knowledge of computers. Dawn has written materials for these specialized courses for her own use. She also provides software consultation to local businesses. Previously, she was the computer coordinator/lead instructor for the Business & Industry Services division at Valdosta Technical Institute in Valdosta, Georgia. The majority of the coursework she taught was in continuing education. Prior to teaching, she worked as a technical support representative and technical writer for a software firm. She lives in Valdosta, Georgia, with her husband, Kenneth, and their two daughters, Micaela (4 1/2 years) and Kendra (2 1/2 years). Both girls have been her superlative students, learning more on the computer every day.

Contents at a Glance

Table of Contents

Introduction

Essentials courseware from Prentice Hall Information Technology is anchored in the practical and professional needs of all types of students.

The *essentials* series has been conceived around a "learning-by-doing" approach that encourages you to grasp application-related concepts as you expand your skills through hands-on tutorials. As such, it consists of modular lessons that are built around a series of numbered, step-by-step procedures that are clear, concise, and easy to review. The end-of-chapter exercises have likewise been carefully graded from the routine Checking Concepts and Terms to tasks in the Discovery Zone that gently prod you into extending what you've learned into areas beyond the explicit scope of the lessons proper. Following, you'll find out more about the rationale behind each book element and how to use each to your maximum benefit.

Key Features

- ❏ **Step-by-Step Tutorials.** Each lesson in a project includes numbered, bold step-by-step instructions that show you how to perform the procedures in a clear, concise, and direct manner. These hands-on tutorials let you "learn by doing." A short paragraph may appear after a step to clarify the results of that step. To review the lesson, you can easily scan the bold numbered steps. Accompanying data files eliminate unnecessary typing.

- ❏ **End-of-Project Exercises.** Check out the extensive end-of-project exercises (generally 20 to 25 percent of the pages in each project) that emphasize hands-on skill development. You'll find three levels of reinforcement: Skill Drill, Challenge, and Discovery Zone. Generally, each exercise is independent of other exercises, so you can complete your choices in any order. Accompanying data files eliminate unnecessary typing.

  Skill Drill Skill Drill exercises reinforce project skills. Each skill reinforced is the same, or nearly the same, as a skill presented in the project. Each exercise includes a brief narrative introduction, followed by detailed instructions in a step-by-step format.

  Challenge Challenge exercises expand on or are somewhat related to skills presented in the lessons. Each exercise provides a brief narrative introduction, followed by instructions in a numbered-step format that are not as detailed as those in the Skill Drill section.

  Discovery Zone Discovery Zone exercises require advanced knowledge of topics presented in lessons, application of skills from multiple lessons, or self-directed learning of new skills. Each exercise provides a brief narrative introduction. Numbered steps are not provided.

  Two other sections precede the end-of-project exercises: **Summary** and **Checking Concepts and Terms**. The Summary provides a brief recap of tasks learned in the project, and guides you to topics or places where you can expand your knowledge. The Checking Concepts and Terms section includes Multiple Choice and Discussion questions that are designed to check your comprehension and assess retention. Projects that introduce a new work area include a Screen ID question.

- ❏ **Notes.** Projects include two types of notes: "If you have problems…" and "To extend your knowledge…" The first type displays between hands-on steps. These short troubleshooting notes help you anticipate or solve common problems quickly and effectively. Many lessons in the projects end with "To extend your knowledge…" notes that provide extra tips, shortcuts, and alternative ways to complete a process, as well as special hints. You may safely ignore these for the moment to focus on the main task at hand, or you may pause to learn and appreciate the additional information.

❐ **Task Guide.** The Task Guide lists common procedures and shortcuts. It can be used in two complementary ways to enhance your learning experience. You can refer to it while progressing through projects to refresh your memory on procedures learned. Or, you can keep it as a handy real-world reference while using the application for your daily work.

❐ **Illustrations.** Multiple illustrations add visual appeal and reinforce learning in each project. An opening section titled "Visual Summary" graphically illustrates the concepts and features included in the project and/or the output you will produce. Each time a new button is introduced, its icon displays in the margin. Screen shots display after key steps for you to check against the results on your monitor. These figures, with ample callouts, make it easy to check your progress.

❐ **Learn-How-to-Learn Focus.** Software has become so rich in features that cater to so many diverse needs that it is no longer possible to anticipate and include everything that you might need to know. Therefore, a learn-how-to-learn component is provided as an "essential" element in the series. Selected lessons and end-of-project exercises include accessing onscreen Help for guidance. References to onscreen Help are also included in selected project summaries and "To extend your knowledge…" notes.

How to Use This Book

Typically, each *essentials* book is divided into seven to eight projects. A project covers one area (or a few closely related areas) of application functionality. Each project consists of six to eight lessons that are related to that topic. Each lesson presents a specific task or closely related set of tasks in a manageable chunk that is easy to assimilate and retain.

Each element in the *essentials* book is designed to maximize your learning experience. Following is a list of the *essentials* project elements and a description of how each element can help you:

❐ **Project Objectives.** Starting with an objective gives you short-term, attainable goals. Using project objectives that closely match the titles of the step-by-step tutorials breaks down the possibly overwhelming prospect of learning several new features of an Office XP application into small, attainable, bite-sized tasks. Look over the objectives on the opening page of the project before you begin, and review them after completing the project to identify the main goals for each project.

❐ **Key Terms.** Key terms introduced in each project are listed, in alphabetical order, immediately after the objectives on the opening page of the project. Each key term is defined during its first use within the text, and is shown in bold italic within that explanation. Definitions of key terms are also included in the Glossary.

❐ **Why Would I Do This?** You are studying Office XP applications so you can accomplish useful tasks. This brief section provides an overview of why these tasks and procedures are important.

❐ **Visual Summary.** This opening section graphically illustrates the concepts and features that you will learn in the project. One or more figures, with ample callouts, show the final result of completing the project.

 ❐ **If You Have Problems…** These short troubleshooting notes help you anticipate or solve common problems quickly and effectively. Even if you do not encounter the problem at this time, make a mental note of it so that you know where to look when you (or others) have difficulty.

 ❐ **To Extend Your Knowledge…** Many lessons end with "To extend your knowledge…" comments. These notes provide extra tips, shortcuts, alternative ways to complete a process, and special hints about using the software.

Typeface Conventions Used in This Book

Essentials 2002 uses the following conventions to make it easier for you to understand the material.

❑ Key terms appear in ***italic and bold*** the first time they are defined in a project.

❑ Monospace type appears frequently and looks `like this`. It is used to indicate text that you are instructed to key in.

❑ *Italic text* indicates text that appears onscreen as (1) warnings, confirmations, or general information; (2) the name of a file to be used in a lesson or exercise; and (3) text from a dialog box that is referenced within a sentence, when that sentence might appear awkward if the dialog box text were not set off.

❑ Hotkeys are indicated by underline. Hotkeys are the underlined letters in menus, toolbars, and dialog boxes that activate commands and options, and are a quick way to choose frequently used commands and options. Hotkeys look like this: File, Save.

Accessing Student Data Files

The data files that students need to work through the projects can be downloaded from the Custom PHIT Web site (www.prenhall.com/customphit). Data files are provided for each project. The filenames correspond to the filenames called for in this book. The files are named in the following manner: The first character indicates the book series (e=essentials); the second character denotes the application (w=Word, e=Excel, and so forth); and the third character indicates the level (1=Level 1, 2=Level 2, and 3=Level 3). The last four digits indicate the project number and the file number within the project. For example, the first file used in Project 3 would be 0301. Therefore, the complete name for the first file in Project 3 in the *Word Level 1* book is ew1-0301. The complete name for the third file in Project 7 in the *Excel Level 2* book is ee2-0703.

Instructor's Resources

❑ **Customize Your Book (www.prenhall.com/customphit).** The Prentice Hall Information Technology Custom PHIT Program gives professors the power to control and customize their books to their course needs. The best part is that it is done completely online using a simple interface.

Professors choose exactly what projects they need in the *essentials* Office XP series, and in what order they appear. The program also allows professors to add their own material anywhere in the text's presentation, and the final product will arrive at each professor's bookstore as a professionally formatted text.

To learn more about this new system for creating the perfect textbook, go to www.prenhall.com/customphit, where you can go through the online walkthrough of how to create a book.

❑ **Instructor's Resource CD-ROM.** This CD-ROM includes the entire *Instructor's Manual* for each application in Microsoft Word format. A computerized testbank is included to create tests, maintain student records, and provide online practice testing. Student data files and completed solutions files are also on this CD-ROM. The *Instructor's Manual* will contain a reference guide of these files for the instructor's convenience. PowerPoint slides, which give more information about each project, are also available for classroom use.

❑ **Test Manager.** Prentice Hall Test Manager is an integrated, PC-compatible test-generation and classroom-management software package. The package permits instructors to design and create tests, maintain student records, and provide online practice testing for students.

Prentice Hall has also formed close alliances with each of the leading online platform providers: WebCT, Blackboard, and our own Pearson CourseCompass.

❑ **WebCT and Blackboard.** This custom-built distance-learning course features exercises, sample quizzes, and tests in a course-management system that provides class administration tools as well as the ability to customize this material at the instructor's discretion.

❑ **CourseCompass.** CourseCompass is a dynamic, interactive online course-management tool powered by Blackboard. It lets professors create their own courses in 15 minutes or less with preloaded quality content that can include quizzes, tests, lecture materials, and interactive exercises.

Training and Assessment (www.prenhall.com/phit)

Prentice Hall
TRAIN Generation **it**

Prentice Hall's Train Generation IT is a computer-based training software a student can use to preview, learn, and review Microsoft® Office application skills. Delivered via intranet, network, CD-ROM, or the Web, Train IT offers interactive, multimedia, computer-based training to augment classroom learning. Built-in prescriptive testing suggests a study path based on not only student test results, but also the specific textbook chosen for the course.

Prentice Hall
ASSESS Generation **it**

Prentice Hall's Assess Generation IT is separate computer-based testing software used to evaluate a student's knowledge about specific topics on Word, Excel, Access, and PowerPoint®. More extensive than the testing in Train IT, Assess IT offers more features for the instructor and many more questions for the student.

Creating Special Effects in a Worksheet

Objectives

In this project, you learn how to

- ✔ Create WordArt
- ✔ Insert and Rotate an AutoShape
- ✔ Create a Text Box
- ✔ Group Objects
- ✔ Add Emphasis with Lines and Arrows
- ✔ Add Emphasis with Callouts
- ✔ Insert Clips
- ✔ Insert a Predefined Diagram

Key terms in this project include

- ❑ adjustment handle
- ❑ AutoShape
- ❑ callout
- ❑ clip
- ❑ clip art
- ❑ Clip Organizer
- ❑ diagram
- ❑ grouped objects
- ❑ text box
- ❑ thumbnail
- ❑ WordArt

Why Would I Do This?

When you design worksheets for others to view, it is essential that they be aesthetically pleasing. Excel provides a variety of tools to help make worksheets look professional, yet be easy to use. Using Excel's special effects tools to enhance your worksheets is as fun as it is essential.

Visual Summary

Excel's toolbox of special effects includes AutoShapes—such as lines, arrows, basic shapes, and callouts—and text boxes, WordArt, pictures, clip art, and predefined diagrams. You can glimpse the power of Excel's special effects tools by viewing Figure 1.1.

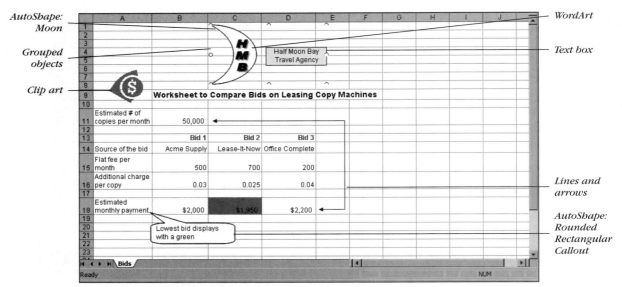

Figure 1.1

In the first seven lessons in this project, you add the special effects shown in Figure 1.1 to a worksheet for the Half Moon Bay Travel Agency. The worksheet computes the expected cost per month of leasing a copy machine—a cost that varies with the expected number of copies made. Consistent with company policy, three bids are being evaluated, each with a different fixed monthly fee and charge per copy. In the last lesson, you create and edit an organizational chart for the Half Moon Bay Travel Agency.

Lesson 1: Creating WordArt

WordArt displays user-specified text in one of 30 predefined styles (see the WordArt Gallery in Figure 1.2). The styles include curved, slanted, and vertical text. Each style has a predefined color scheme.

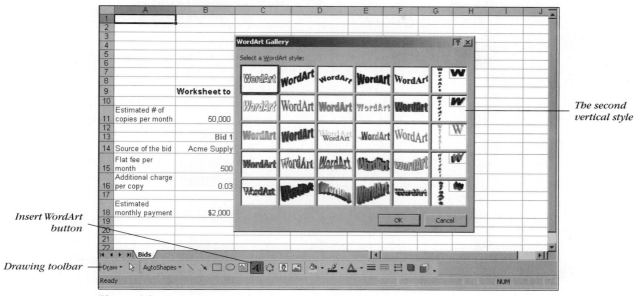

Insert WordArt button

Drawing toolbar

The second vertical style

Figure 1.2

WordArt is not entered in a cell. It is a separate object that can be moved, sized, and edited. For example, you can select a WordArt object and change its color scheme, apply a Shadow or 3-D effect, and edit its text.

In this lesson, you create the Half Moon Bay Travel Agency initials HMB using WordArt. You select a vertical WordArt style and size it appropriately. The result will be part of a three-object logo displayed at the top of the Half Moon Bay Travel Agency's worksheet model to analyze copy machine bids (refer to Figure 1.1). You assemble the logo over the course of Lessons 1 through 4.

To Create WordArt

1 **Open the *ee2-0101* file, and save it as** LeaseOptions.
The file contains a single worksheet named Bids.

2 **If the Drawing toolbar does not appear on your screen, select View, Toolbars and click Drawing.**

3 **Click the Insert WordArt button on the Drawing toolbar.**

4 **Click the second vertical style (refer to Figure 1.2), and click OK.**
The Edit WordArt Text dialog box displays.

5 **Replace *Your Text Here* by typing HMB (see Figure 1.3).**

(Continues)

To Create WordArt (Continued)

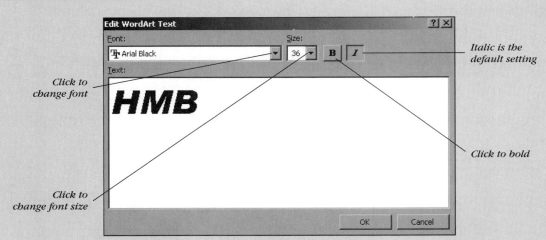

Figure 1.3

6 **Click OK.**

The initials *HMB* display in the selected WordArt style in the middle of the screen. The round sizing handles at the midpoints and corners indicate that the object is selected. The WordArt toolbar displays.

7 **Drag the WordArt object to column B, above row 9.**

8 **Make sure that the WordArt object is still selected and then drag one or more handles to resize the object as shown in Figure 1.4.**

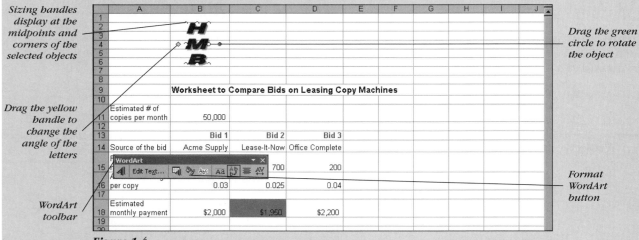

Figure 1.4

This is a temporary adjustment. In Lesson 2, you resize the object to fit within a moon shape.

9 **Make sure that the WordArt object is still selected, and click the Format WordArt button on the WordArt toolbar (refer to Figure 1.4).**

10 **Apply the Blue fill color to the WordArt object.**

11 **Click outside the WordArt object to deselect it, and save your changes to the *LeaseOptions* workbook.**

Keep the *LeaseOptions* workbook open for the next lesson, or close the workbook and exit Excel.

To extend your knowledge...

Deleting an Object

To delete WordArt or any other object, click within the object to select it, and press ⒟ⓔⓛ.

Formatting WordArt

Use the Format WordArt dialog box to format a shape. You can display this dialog box by right-clicking the WordArt object and selecting Format WordArt from the shortcut menu. You can then work with one or more of five tabs: Colors and Lines, Size, Protection, Properties, and Web.

Lesson 2: Inserting and Rotating an AutoShape

An **AutoShape** is a predefined shape that you create using the AutoShape menu from the Drawing toolbar (see Figure 1.5). Categories of AutoShapes include Lines, Connectors, Basic Shapes, Block Arrows, Flowchart, Stars and Banners, and Callouts.

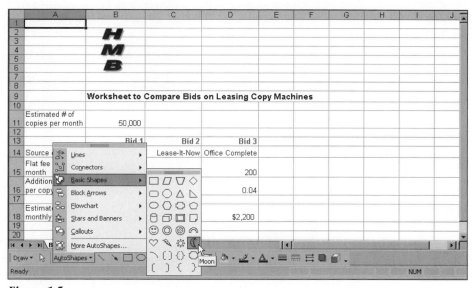

Figure 1.5

To create a shape, select it from the AutoShapes menu, and draw it on the worksheet with the mouse; alternatively, you can click a cell and let Excel draw it for you. You can then move, size, rotate, or flip the shape, and then apply a variety of formats.

If you select a shape with some open space inside of it—a banner, circle, star, block arrow, and so forth—you can insert text. Lines and connectors show relationships and do not allow messages to be attached.

In this lesson, you create Half Moon Bay's corporate symbol, a half-moon. You select a basic shape and flip it.

To Insert and Rotate an AutoShape

❶ **Open the *LeaseOptions* workbook, and display the Drawing toolbar, if necessary.**

❷ **Click the AutoShapes button on the Drawing toolbar, and position the mouse pointer on Basic Shapes.**
A display of shapes, four in each row, appears to the right of the AutoShapes menu (refer to Figure 1.5).

❸ **Click the Moon shape (the last option in the sixth row).**
The shape is a crescent moon curved in the direction of the letter C, or a left parenthesis. The mouse pointer changes to a thin black cross.

❹ **Click cell A1.**
Excel inserts the shape and displays it with sizing handles, indicating the shape is selected.

❺ **Click the Draw button at the left end of the Drawing toolbar, and position the mouse pointer on Rotate or Flip.**
Excel displays the draw options that can be applied to the selected object (see Figure 1.6).

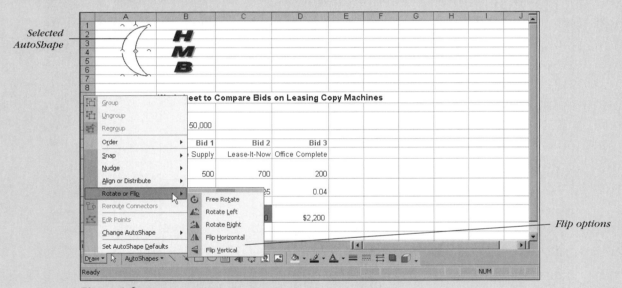

Figure 1.6

❻ **Click Flip Horizontal.**
The crescent moon flips to the opposite direction—that is, it curves similar to a right parenthesis.

❼ **Click outside the object to deselect it, and save your changes to the *LeaseOptions* workbook.**
Keep the *LeaseOptions* workbook open for the next lesson, or close the workbook and exit Excel.

To extend your knowledge...

Formatting AutoShapes

Use the Format AutoShape dialog box to format a shape. You can display this dialog box by right-clicking a shape and then selecting Format AutoShape from the shortcut menu.

Adding Text to an AutoShape

To add text to an AutoShape, right-click the object and then select Add Text from the shortcut menu. Type the text and then select the text. Change the font style or size, and apply other enhancements such as color, and click outside the object to deselect it. If some of the text does not display, select the object and increase its size.

Adding a Fill Color to an AutoShape

You can add a fill (background) color to an AutoShape without using the Format AutoShape dialog box. Select the shape, click the down arrow attached to the Fill Color button in the toolbar, click the desired color, and click outside the object to deselect it.

If a flashing cursor displays when you select an AutoShape, the object includes text, and text edit mode is active. Before you can apply a fill color, you must exit text edit mode by clicking the border of the selected object.

Replacing One AutoShape with Another

You can easily change an AutoShape from one style to another. Click the AutoShape to select it and then click Draw on the Drawing toolbar. Select Change AutoShape, pick a general category, and click the desired style.

Lesson 3: Creating a Text Box

A **text box** is an object, usually shaped like a square or rectangle, that contains words. Text automatically wraps to fit within the boundaries of the box, and you can make the box larger or smaller by dragging a sizing handle. If you create a text box by dragging the mouse pointer, it displays with a solid border; if you click the worksheet to add the box and then resize it or begin typing, the text does not have a border.

You can edit the words in a text box in the same way you would edit text in a word-processing document—select the text to be changed and then type the correction. Some formatting can be done using the Fill Color, Line Color, Font Color, and Line Style toolbar buttons. For other formatting you can choose Format, Text Box, and make selections within the Format Text Box dialog box.

In this lesson, you create a text box containing the name of the Half Moon Bay Travel Agency. You draw the box using the mouse, enter the text using the default font, and apply a light yellow fill (background) to the box (see Figure 1.7).

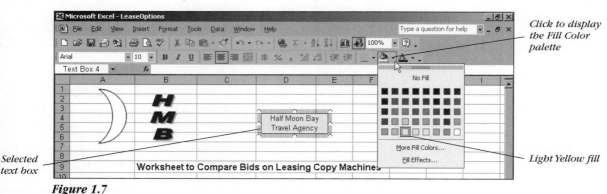

Figure 1.7

To Create a Text Box

❶ Open the *LeaseOptions* workbook, if necessary.

❷ Click the Text Box button on the Drawing toolbar.

(Continues)

To Create a Text Box (Continued)

3 **Drag open the text box beginning in cell D4 (similar in size and position to the box shown in Figure 1.7).**
The text box is selected. A flashing cursor displays in the upper-left corner of the text box.

4 **Click the Center button in the toolbar and then type** Half Moon Bay Travel Agency **in the text box.**

5 **Click the text box border.**

6 **Click the down arrow to the right of the Fill Color button in the Formatting toolbar or the Drawing toolbar. (Figure 1.7 illustrates use of the Formatting toolbar.)**
The Fill Color palette displays.

If you have problems...

If the Fill Color palette is dim, you have not selected the text box border. Text boxes have two selection modes, both of which cause sizing handles to display. A flashing cursor, which indicates text editing mode, displays if you click within a text box. Clicking the border of a text box enables you to edit the text box properties, including fill, border color, and line style.

7 **Select Light Yellow from the Fill Color palette.**

8 **Click outside the text box to deselect it, and save your changes to the *LeaseOptions* workbook.**
Keep the *LeaseOptions* workbook open for the next lesson, or close the workbook and exit Excel.

To extend your knowledge...

Formatting a Text Box

Use the Format Text Box dialog box to format a text box. You can display this dialog box by clicking within the text box, right-clicking a border of the box, and then selecting Format Text Box from the shortcut menu.

Readability and Linking

As you add text color and background fill, be mindful of a reader's ability to see the text. Strive for sharp color contrast. For example, yellow text on a white background is nearly impossible to read, and red on green is a problem for people who are color blind.

If the text you want to enter in a text box or AutoShape already exists in a cell, you can set a link to that cell instead of typing the text. Click within the text box or shape, click the formula bar, type an equal sign, click the cell containing the desired text, and then press ⏎Enter.

Lesson 4: Grouping Objects

Grouped objects consist of two or more objects that can be manipulated as a single object. Prior to grouping, each object has its own set of sizing handles (see Figure 1.8). After grouping, a single set of sizing handles surrounds the objects.

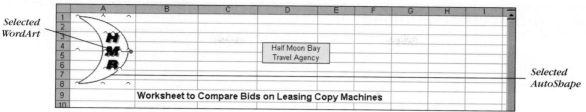

Selected WordArt

Selected AutoShape

Figure 1.8

When objects are grouped, any action applied to the group impacts each object in the group. You can, for example, resize all the objects in a group, rotate and flip them, drag them to a different location, and apply attributes such as text, fill, and line color. If you want to change only one object in the group, you can ungroup the objects, make the change, and then regroup the objects.

Stacked objects, such as the moon and the WordArt shown in Figure 1.8, display in layers. You can change the order in which objects display by using an Order option accessed through the Drawing toolbar, or by right-clicking any object in the group and selecting Order from the shortcut menu. Four options are available on the Order menu. Send to Back or Bring to Front places the selected object at the bottom or top of the stack, respectively. If there are three or more layers, use the Bring Forward and Send Backward options to move an object one layer at a time.

In this lesson, you group the moon and the *HMB* WordArt as one object and then add a third object to the group—the text box containing the company name. You start by adjusting size and order of the individual objects—the WordArt initials must fit within the moon shape, and the initials must display on top of the moon.

To Group Objects

❶ Open the *LeaseOptions* workbook, if necessary.

❷ Drag the WordArt object on top of the moon.
The moon obscures the WordArt object. Now reverse the two objects to get the effect of text inside the moon.

❸ Right-click the moon shape, position the mouse pointer on Order, and select Send to Back.

❹ Resize the moon so that it extends from cell A1 to cell A8.

❺ Click within the WordArt object, and resize it so that the initials *HMB* fit inside the moon.

❻ Hold down (◆Shift), and select both the moon and the WordArt objects.
Each object displays its own set of sizing handles (refer to Figure 1.8).

❼ Right-click the selected objects and position the mouse pointer on Grouping (see Figure 1.9).

(Continues)

To Group Objects (Continued)

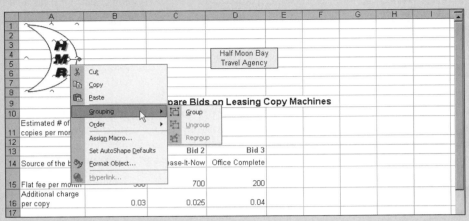

Figure 1.9

8 **Select Group.**
Now only one set of sizing handles appears because grouped objects take on the characteristics of a single object.

9 **Move the grouped objects from column A to column C.**

10 **Repeat the procedures described in steps 6 through 8 to include the text box in a grouping of three objects (see Figure 1.10).**

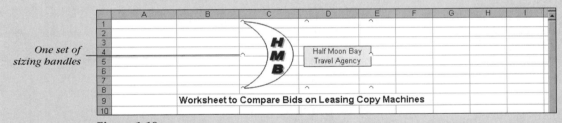

One set of sizing handles →

Figure 1.10

11 **Click outside the grouped objects, and save your changes to the *LeaseOptions* workbook.**
Keep the *LeaseOptions* workbook open for the next lesson, or close the workbook and exit Excel.

To extend your knowledge...

Changing the Order of Stacked Objects

Sometimes an object in a stack is hidden by another object. You can select an object and then press `Tab↹` or `↑Shift`+`Tab↹` to move forward or backward through the objects on a worksheet.

Ungrouping and Regrouping Drawing Objects

To ungroup drawing objects, click within any object in the group, display the Draw menu on the Drawing toolbar, and select Ungroup.

To regroup drawing objects, select any one of the objects previously grouped, display the Draw menu on the Drawing toolbar, and select Regroup.

Limitations of Grouping Objects

Grouping works best on drawing objects. Including other objects, such as text boxes, in the group limits what can be done with the group. You can rotate and flip an AutoShape, for example, but the same actions cannot be applied to a text box. Therefore, if one of the objects in a group is a text box, the group cannot be flipped and rotated. When this happens, the affected menu items or buttons appear dimmed.

Lesson 5: Adding Emphasis with Lines and Arrows

Use arrows to point to a specific location in a worksheet, or to show a connection between two or more related areas or objects on the worksheet. Lines can be used to frame an area, connect or separate areas and objects, or show relationships.

To create an arrow or line, select the object from the Drawing toolbar and then drag the line or arrow in the worksheet using the mouse. You can then apply line styles, such as color, thickness, pattern, and arrow. Figure 1.11 illustrates many of the tools for drawing lines and arrows.

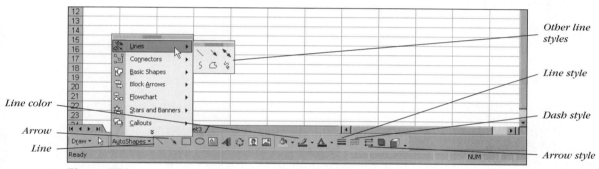

Figure 1.11

Lines and arrows are objects that can be moved, copied, resized, and rotated. Clicking anywhere on a line or arrow selects it and displays sizing handles at each end. To move the object to a new location, position the mouse pointer over it until you see the drag and drop symbol—a four-headed arrow—and drag the line to its new location. To change the length, click a sizing handle, and drag the object longer or shorter, or pivot its angle.

In this lesson, you create objects to show a relationship in the Bids worksheet between the estimated number of copies per month and the estimated monthly payments. You create two left arrows connected with a vertical line (refer to Figure 1.1).

To Add Emphasis with Lines and Arrows

❶ Open the *LeaseOptions* workbook, if necessary.

❷ Scroll down to display row 18, if necessary, and click the Arrow button on the Drawing toolbar.

❸ Click toward the right end of cell E18, and drag left to create a short arrow pointing left (refer to the higher of the two arrows in Figure 1.12).

(Continues)

To Add Emphasis with Lines and Arrows (Continued)

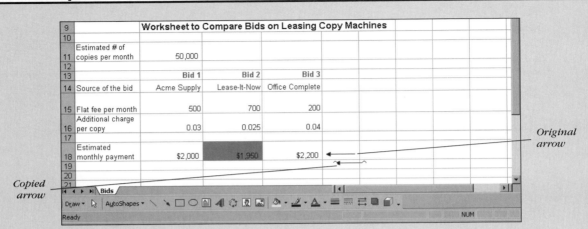

Copied arrow

Original arrow

Figure 1.12

 If you have problems...

If you can't make the arrow straight, press and hold down ⟨+Shift⟩ before releasing the mouse button. If the object is still not drawn as you want, you can select it and press ⟨Del⟩ to start over, or you can move and size it as necessary.

4 **Make sure that sizing handles display on the arrow, and click the Copy button.**

5 **Click the Paste button.**
Excel creates a copy of the original arrow (refer to Figure 1.12).

6 **Drag the copy of the arrow to cell E11, and lengthen the copied arrow by dragging its arrowhead end to cell C11 (refer to Figure 1.1).**

7 **Click the Line button on the Drawing toolbar.**

8 **Drag the line so it connects the right ends of the arrows in cells E11 and E18.**

 If you have problems...

You may find it difficult to drag an object the exact distance you need by using the mouse. You can move a selected object in very small increments by holding down ⟨Ctrl⟩ and clicking an arrow key that points to the direction you want to move the object—left, right, up, or down.

9 **Hold down ⟨+Shift⟩ and then click each of the three lines you just created.**
Sizing handles indicate that all three lines are selected.

10 **Click the down arrow to the right of the Line Color button on the Drawing toolbar, select Blue, and deselect the drawn objects.**

11 **Check your results with Figure 1.13, and make changes as necessary.**

To Add Emphasis with Lines and Arrows

9	Worksheet to Compare Bids on Leasing Copy Machines						
10							
11	Estimated # of copies per month	50,000	←				
12							
13		Bid 1	Bid 2	Bid 3			
14	Source of the bid	Acme Supply	Lease-It-Now	Office Complete			
15	Flat fee per month	500	700	200			
16	Additional charge per copy	0.03	0.025	0.04			
17							
18	Estimated monthly payment	$2,000	$1,950	$2,200	←		
19							

Figure 1.13

Three line and arrow objects show the relationship between the input variable for the model (cell B11) and the calculated results (cells B18 through D18).

⑫ Save your changes to the *LeaseOptions* workbook.
Keep the *LeaseOptions* workbook open for the next lesson, or close the workbook and exit Excel.

To extend your knowledge...

Creating Arrows and Lines

An arrow is a line with an arrowhead symbol attached to either or both ends. You can use buttons and menu items to apply styles to lines and arrows (refer to Figure 1.11).

Use the Line Style button to specify the thickness of a solid line or arrow. Use the Dash Style button to change lines and arrows from solid to different patterns of lines.

Use the Arrow Style button to add or change the style of arrowhead attached to a line or arrow. You can also specify a diamond or circular shape at one or both ends instead of an arrowhead.

Use the Lines menu on the AutoShapes menu to select advanced line drawing tools such as curved, scribble, and freeform lines. Use the Connectors menu on the AutoShapes menu to select a line style that connects two shapes and keeps them connected. After you select a connector style, blue connector sites appear on objects as you move the mouse pointer over them. The blue points indicate where you can attach a connector line.

Lesson 6: Adding Emphasis with Callouts

A ***callout*** is a text-filled object that points to other text or another object. Perhaps you have seen a callout as the balloon or cloud over a cartoon character's head showing what the character is thinking or saying.

You can select among predefined callout styles on the AutoShapes, Callouts menu (see Figure 1.14). Positioning the mouse pointer on a callout displays its name.

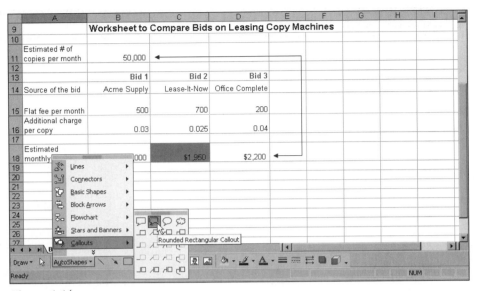

Figure 1.14

To create a callout, select the style you want to use, begin drawing the callout or click a cell on the worksheet where you want to insert the object, type the text that appears inside the callout, and size the object appropriately. Each predefined callout has an ***adjustment handle***, a yellow diamond-shaped handle used to adjust the appearance, but not the size, of most AutoShapes. To change the area pointed to by a callout, drag the yellow adjustment handle (see Figure 1.15).

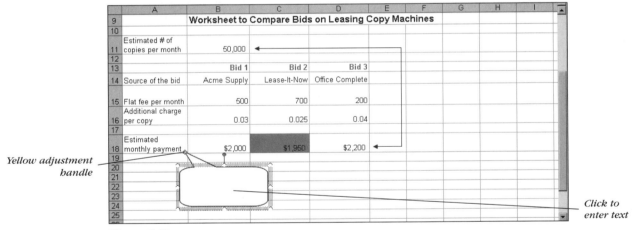

Figure 1.15

In this lesson, you create a Rounded Rectangular callout on the Bids worksheet. You select the callout style, draw it on the worksheet, type the appropriate message in the callout, and resize and position the callout.

To Add Emphasis with a Callout

❶ **Open the *LeaseOptions* workbook, if necessary.**

❷ **Select <u>C</u>allouts from the A<u>u</u>toShapes menu on the Drawing toolbar (refer to Figure 1.14).**

❸ **Choose Rounded Rectangle Callout (the second option in the first row).**

❹ **Click cell B21, and drag sizing handles to increase the size of the callout.**

To Add Emphasis with a Callout

You can resize the callout again later.

5 Click the yellow adjustment handle, and drag to point the callout toward cell A18.

6 With the callout selected, type `Lowest bid displays with a green background`.

7 Make final adjustments to the size and position of the callout similar to that shown in Figure 1.16.

	A	B	C	D	E	F	G	H	I	
9		Worksheet to Compare Bids on Leasing Copy Machines								
10										
11	Estimated # of copies per month	50,000								
12										
13		Bid 1	Bid 2	Bid 3						
14	Source of the bid	Acme Supply	Lease-It-Now	Office Complete						
15	Flat fee per month	500	700	200						
16	Additional charge per copy	0.03	0.025	0.04						
17										
18	Estimated monthly payment	$2,000	$1,950	$2,200						
19										
20		Lowest bid displays with a green background								
21										
22										
23										

Figure 1.16

8 Click outside the callout, and then save your changes to the *LeaseOptions* workbook.

Keep the *LeaseOptions* workbook open for the next lesson, or close the workbook and exit Excel.

To extend your knowledge...

Applying Shadows and 3-D Effects to Shapes

You can add a shadow or a 3-D effect to most AutoShapes, including callouts. To add a shadow effect, select the shape, click the Shadow Style button in the Drawing toolbar, and click the desired style. Follow a similar process to apply a 3-D effect, substituting the 3-D Style button in place of the Shadow Style button.

Lesson 7: Inserting Clips

When you add WordArt, a line, a callout, or another AutoShape in an Excel worksheet, you add a graphic that is available through buttons or menu selections. You can also insert a **clip**—a drawing, photograph, or other media type such as sound, animation, or movies.

The **Clip Organizer** is a Microsoft Office program you can use to find, add, and organize media clips. First-level folders include My Collections, Office Collections, and Web Collections. Subfolders are provided within each of the initial folders (see Figure 1.17). Thumbnails of clips in a selected folder display in the right side of the Clip Organizer. A **thumbnail** is a miniature representation of an image. When you position the mouse pointer on a thumbnail, a ScreenTip displays related search terms, file size in pixels, image size, and image type.

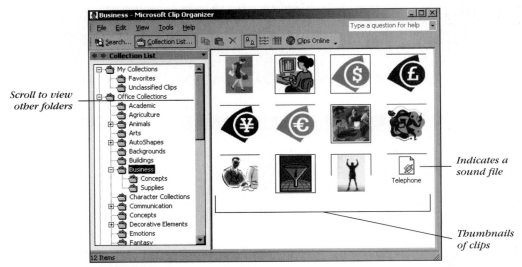

Scroll to view other folders

Indicates a sound file

Thumbnails of clips

Figure 1.17

You can copy an image from the Clip Organizer and paste it in an Excel worksheet. You can also display the Insert Clip Art task pane to search for media clips based on descriptive keywords, filename, or file format. If you have an Internet connection open, search results automatically include content from additional clips provided online by Microsoft.

In this lesson, you perform a keyword search of Microsoft Office clips, which include drawings—sometimes referred to as ***clip art***—as well as photographs and sound files. You select an image among the search results, and insert the image in the Bids worksheet of the *LeaseOptions* workbook. You also change the size and position of the inserted image.

To Insert Clip Art

① **Open the *LeaseOptions* file, if necessary, and click cell A3.**
The location for inserting clip art is specified. The upper-left corner of the current cell becomes the upper-left corner of inserted clip art.

② **Click the Insert Clip Art button on the Drawing toolbar.**

③ **If the Add Clips to Organizer dialog box displays, click the Later button to close it.**
The Insert Clip Art task pane displays at the right side of the screen.

④ **Type money in the Search text box, as shown in Figure 1.18.**

To Insert Clip Art

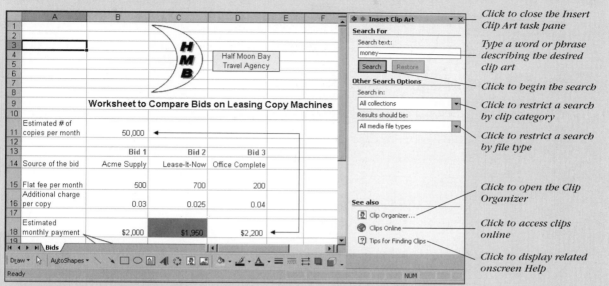

Figure 1.18

⑤ **Click the Search button in the Insert Clip Art task pane.**
Several thumbnails of money-related clips display in the Insert Clip Art task pane.

⑥ **Position the pointer in the middle of the first picture.**
A ScreenTip displays that includes related keywords, the height and width of the clip in pixels, the file size, and the file type.

⑦ **Click the down arrow at the right side of the first clip.**
A drop-down menu displays (see Figure 1.19).

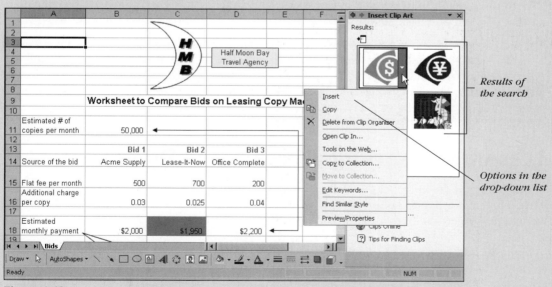

Figure 1.19

(Continues)

To Insert Clip Art (Continued)

8   **Click Insert in the drop-down list.**
Excel inserts the selected image. The upper-left corner of the image is in cell A3, and sizing handles display at the corners and midpoints. Now reduce the size of the image and reposition it.

9   **Press and hold down Ctrl and ⬆Shift, and drag the lower-right sizing handle diagonally toward the center of the image.**
The image is reduced in size, but its center does not move.

10   **Adjust the image to the approximate size and location shown in Figure 1.20, and deselect it.**

Inserted clip art

Figure 1.20

11   **Save your changes to the *LeaseOptions* workbook, and close the workbook.**

To extend your knowledge...

Graphics File Types Accepted by Excel

You are not limited to using media files provided by Microsoft. Other sources of files include clip art that you can purchase, and images scanned from hardcopy or copied from the Web.

There are several graphics file types you can insert directly into a worksheet. These file types include: Enhanced Metafile (.emf), Joint Photographic Experts Group (.jpg), Portable Network Graphics (.png), Microsoft Windows Bitmap (.bmp, .rle, .dib), Graphics Interchange Format (.gif) and Windows Metafile (.wmf). You can also install graphics filters to insert other graphics file formats. The onscreen Help topic *Graphics file types Excel can use* provides a complete list.

Lesson 8: Inserting a Predefined Diagram

A **diagram** is a drawing that generally illustrates relationships. You can use the Diagram Gallery dialog box to insert one of six predefined diagram types—Organization Chart, Cycle, Radial, Pyramid, Venn, and Target—and enter text in the diagram.

When you add or change a diagram, the diagram is outlined by a non-printing border and sizing handles. You can modify the original structure of a diagram—such as removing a layer from a pyramid diagram or adding several circles to a target diagram. You can format the entire diagram with a preset style, or you can make formatting changes to selected portions of the diagram.

In this lesson, you create an organizational chart that illustrates the positions held by the employees of the Half Moon Bay Travel Agency. You add two layers to the original chart, enter employees' names and titles, adjust font sizing as necessary, and apply a predefined style. Your efforts produce an organizational chart similar to that shown in Figure 1.21.

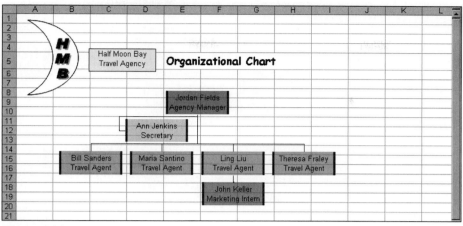

Figure 1.21

To Insert a Diagram

❶ Open the *ee2-0102* file, and save it as HMBstaff.

The workbook contains a single worksheet named *OrgChart*. The Half Moon Bay Travel Agency logo, company name, and the phrase *Organizational Chart* display at the top of the worksheet.

❷ Click the Insert Diagram or Organization Chart button on the Drawing toolbar (or choose Insert Diagram).

The Diagram Gallery dialog box displays (see Figure 1.22). To select a diagram, click its picture.

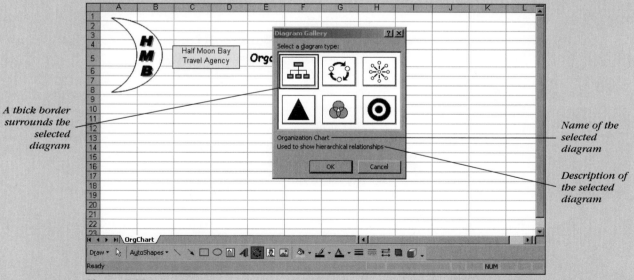

Figure 1.22

❸ Make sure that Organization Chart is the selected diagram, and click OK.

The default organizational chart displays with drawing space around it, outlined by a non-printing border and sizing handles (see Figure 1.23). The default chart includes three subordinate shapes below, and attached to, one superior shape. The Organization Chart toolbar also displays.

(Continues)

To Insert a Diagram (Continued)

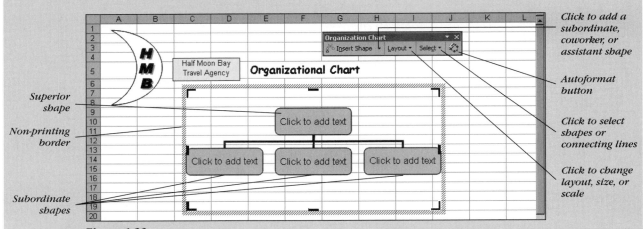

Figure 1.23

④ **If the default organizational chart overlaps existing cell contents, drag the non-printing border to reposition the chart.**

⑤ **Select the superior shape (the top shape) by clicking its border, and click the down arrow at the right end of the Insert Shape button in the Organization Chart toolbar.**

A drop-down list displays with three options (see Figure 1.24). Select Subordinate to place the new shape below the selected shape and connect it to the selected shape. Select Coworker to place the new shape next to the selected shape and connect it to the same superior. Select Assistant to place the new shape below the selected shape with an elbow connector.

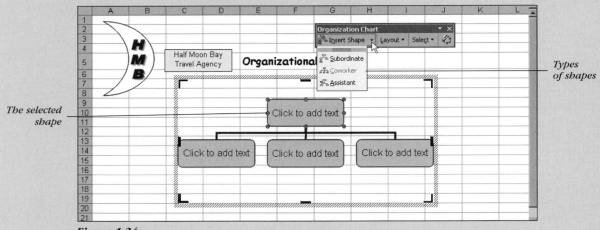

Figure 1.24

⑥ **Click Assistant.**

Excel places a new shape below the selected shape with an elbow connector.

⑦ **Click the border of the rightmost shape in a set of three shapes at the same level.**

To Insert a Diagram

8 **Display the Insert Shape drop-down list, and click Coworker.**
Excel inserts a new shape to the right of the selected shape, and connects it to the selected shape (see Figure 1.25).

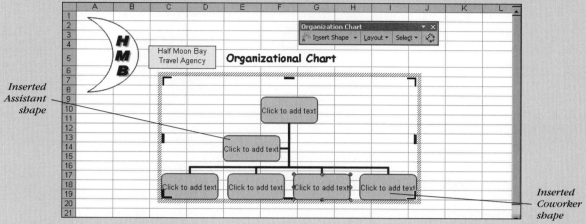

Inserted Assistant shape

Inserted Coworker shape

Figure 1.25

9 **Check that the third of four shapes on the same level is still selected, display the Insert Shape drop-down list, and click Subordinate.**
Excel inserts a new shape below the selected shape, and connects it to the selected shape. Now enter the names and positions of employees.

10 **Click within the top shape, type** Jordan Fields, **press** ⏎Enter, **and type** Agency Manager.

11 **Click within the next shape, type** Ann Jenkins, **press** ⏎Enter, **and type** Secretary.

12 **Follow the process described in the previous step, and enter the following names and positions in the four coworker shapes (refer to Figure 1.21).**

```
Bill Sanders Travel Agent

Maria Santino Travel Agent

Ling Liu Travel Agent

Theresa Fraley Travel Agent
```

13 **Click within the bottom shape, type** John Keller, **press** ⏎Enter, **and type** Marketing Intern.

14 **Adjust font sizes as necessary (font size is 10 point in the Figure 1.21 sample).**

15 **Click the Autoformat button in the Organization Chart toolbar, and select** *Bookend Fills* **in the Organization Chart Style Gallery dialog box (see Figure 1.26).**

(Continues)

To Insert a Diagram (Continued)

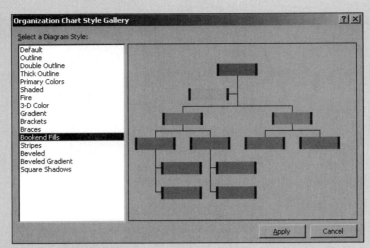

Figure 1.26

 **Click Apply. Check that your results resemble those shown in Figure 1.21, and make revisions as necessary.**

Save your changes to the *HMBstaff* workbook, and close the workbook.
This concludes Project 1. You can exit Excel, or continue with the end-of-project exercises.

 ## To extend your knowledge...

Other Types of Diagrams

Other diagram types include Cycle, Radial, Pyramid, Venn, and Target. Use a Cycle diagram to show a continuous cycle. A Radial diagram enables you to show relationships of elements to a core element. A Pyramid diagram makes it easy to show relationships that build on a foundation. A Venn diagram is used to show areas of overlap between and among elements. The Target diagram is commonly used to show the steps toward a goal.

Summary

In this project, you applied a variety of special effects to a worksheet. As an alternative to entering text in cells, you learned how to create WordArt, callouts, and text boxes. You grouped objects to be manipulated as a unit. You also focused attention on specific areas of the worksheet using lines and arrows, added a picture, and created an organizational chart.

To expand your learning, try features that you have not yet worked with, such as adding a circle or square, drawing a curve or freeform object, and attaching connector lines. Copy an image from the Web, and insert it in a worksheet. Learn how to crop an image. Onscreen Help provides guidance on how to accomplish these tasks.

Checking Concepts and Terms

Multiple Choice

Circle the letter of the correct answer for each of the following.

1. Which is not an accurate statement about AutoShapes? [L2]

   a. AutoShapes include banners, flow chart symbols, and block arrows.
   b. You cannot change an AutoShape from one style to another; instead, you must delete the one you do not want and create another.
   c. You can add fill (background) color to an AutoShape by using the Format AutoShape dialog box or the Fill Color button in the Drawing toolbar.
   d. If you select an AutoShape and click a cell on the worksheet, Excel draws the selected AutoShape for you.

2. Which of the following is true? [L1]

   a. To delete WordArt or any other object, click within the object to select it, and choose Edit, Delete.
   b. WordArt is a separate object that can be moved, sized, and edited.
   c. Both a and b
   d. Neither a nor b

3. Which of the following would best improve the readability of a text box? [L3]

   a. Use white text on a yellow background.
   b. Use green text on a red background.
   c. Use text and background with sharply contrasting colors.
   d. All of the above

4. Which is not a predefined diagram style? [L8]

   a. Target
   b. Matrix
   c. Pyramid
   d. Radial

5. Which action cannot be applied to a group containing a callout and a text box? [L4]

   a. adding fill color
   b. changing line style
   c. rotating and flipping
   d. changing line color

Discussion

1. Provide an example of how you might use each of the following diagram styles in an Excel worksheet: Cycle, Radial, Pyramid, Venn, and Target. [L8]

2. Explain why you would group objects, and what objects can be grouped. [L4]

3. Describe sources of clips. Also, discuss how copyright laws impact your use of clips that you did not create. [L7]

Skill Drill

Skill Drill exercises reinforce project skills. Each skill that is reinforced is the same, or nearly the same, as a skill presented in the project. Detailed instructions are provided in a step-by-step format.

Before beginning your first Project 1 Skill Drill exercise, complete the following steps:

1. Open the file named *ee2-0103*, and immediately save it as `ee2-p1drill`.
   The *ee2-p1drill* workbook contains seven sheets: an overview, and sheets named #1-Banner, #2-WordArt, #3-Block Arrow, #4-Callout, #5-Text Box, and #6-Arrow.
2. Click the Overview sheet to view the organization of the Project 1 Skill Drill Exercises workbook.

Each exercise is independent of the others, so you may complete the exercises in any order. Be sure to save the workbook after completing each exercise. If you need a paper copy of the completed exercise, enter your name, centered in a header, before printing. Other print options have already been set to print compressed to one page and to display the filename, sheet name, and current date in a footer.

Be sure to save your changes and close the workbook if you need more than one work session to complete the desired exercises; then continue working on *ee2-p1drill* instead of starting over again on the original *ee2-0103* file.

1. Creating a Banner

You decide to put the company name *Glenn Lakes Blue Ribbon Lawn Care* on a worksheet. To convey the name graphically, you decide to use one of the ribbons on the AutoShapes menu, type the name in the ribbon, and add a blue fill color to the ribbon. Also, you improve readability by making the text in the ribbon bold and centering it horizontally and vertically.

To add a banner to a worksheet, follow these steps:

1. Open the *ee2-p1drill* workbook, if necessary, and select the sheet named #1-Banner.
2. Display the Drawing toolbar, if necessary, and select the Curved Up Ribbon style from the AutoShapes, Stars and Banners menu.
3. Click cell A3, and drag the lower right sizing handle to cell C7.
4. Right click the ribbon object and then select Add Text.
5. Click the Bold button, and type `Glenn Lakes Blue Ribbon Lawn Care`.
6. Center the text vertically and horizontally using the Alignment tab in the Format AutoShape dialog box.
   To access the Format AutoShape dialog box containing the Alignment tab, you must first click the border around the object. A shadow border made up of dots appears when the object is correctly selected.
7. While the ribbon object is selected, turn on a sky blue fill color.
8. Resize as necessary to display text on two lines within the ribbon, and save your changes to the *ee2-p1drill* workbook.

2. Creating WordArt

You need a title on a worksheet indicating what its purpose is, and you decide to use WordArt. The worksheet's title will be *Loan Payment Analysis*, typed into one of the colorful WordArt styles and rotated slightly to give it an upward slant from left to right.

To add WordArt to a worksheet, follow these steps:

1. Open the *ee2-p1drill* workbook, if necessary, and select the sheet named #2-WordArt.
2. Select the Insert WordArt button on the Drawing toolbar.
3. Select the WordArt style in the fourth column, third row, and click OK.
4. Type `Loan Payment Analysis` in the Edit WordArt Text dialog box, and click OK.
5. Move, size, and rotate the WordArt so that it displays above the data in row 12, from column A through column D, with its right end higher than the left.

   You can drag the green circle above the WordArt object, and rotate the right end up about three rows higher than the left end.
6. Make any final adjustments to size and position, and deselect the object.
7. Save your changes to the *ee2-p1drill* workbook.

3. Adding a Block Arrow Shape

You want to call the user's attention to the monthly payments line and the fact that the cell containing the lowest monthly payment in the range B18:D18 has a green background. You decide to create a block arrow with a message.

To add a block arrow to your worksheet, follow these steps:

1. Open the *ee2-p1drill* workbook, if necessary, and select the sheet named #3-Block Arrow.
2. Select the AutoShapes button on the Drawing toolbar, and display the Block Arrows menu.
3. Select the Left Arrow style.
4. Click cell E17 to set the arrow object on the worksheet.
5. Right-click the arrow object, and select Add Text.
6. Type `Green indicates the lowest monthly payment`.
7. Resize the arrow so that the text just fits within the arrow on two lines, and reposition the arrow to point at the middle of cell E18.
8. Select the outer border of the object.
9. Using the Alignment tab on the Format AutoShapes dialog box, center the message horizontally and vertically.
10. Add the Light Yellow fill color to the object.

    You can use the Fill Color button on the Drawing toolbar or make your selections using the Colors and Lines tab on the Format AutoShapes dialog box.
11. Save your changes to the *ee2-p1drill* workbook.

4. Adding and Editing a Callout

You decide to add a note to the worksheet warning users that the lowest monthly payment may not be the best financing source. You convey this information using a callout.

To add a callout to a worksheet, follow these steps:

1. Open the *ee2-p1drill* workbook, if necessary, and select the sheet named #4-Callout.
2. Select the AutoShapes button on the Drawing toolbar, and display the Callouts menu.
3. Select the *Line Callout 2 (Border and Accent Bar)* callout, the second option in row 5.
4. Click cell E18 to set the callout on the worksheet.
5. Stretch the object right and down until it covers cell G20.
6. Click and drag one of the yellow diamond-shaped handles and extend the connector line to cell D18.
7. Click the text area of the callout, and type `Caution! The lowest monthly payment may not represent the best loan source.`
8. Make adjustments as necessary to the size and position of the callout.
9. Save your changes to the *ee2-p1drill* workbook.

5. Adding and Editing a Text Box

You decide to add a text box to the worksheet reminding users that they can only change the loan information inside the red box.

To add a text box to a worksheet, follow these steps:

1. Open the *ee2-p1drill* workbook, if necessary, and select the sheet named #5-Text Box.

2. Select the Text Box button on the Drawing toolbar.

3. Drag open the text box over cells F12 to H14.

Remember, if you click the location where you want to position the text box and then drag it open, the box appears without a border. Dragging it open immediately creates an object with a border.

4. Click the text area and type `To use the model, change data only in the range within the red border.`

5. Make final adjustments as necessary to the position and size of the text box.

6. Save your changes to the *ee2-p1drill* workbook.

6. Drawing an Arrow from a Text Box

A text box provides information about changing cells within the red border. You decide to draw two arrows from the text box toward the red-bordered cells to make sure a viewer understands the area referred to in the text box.

To add arrows to a worksheet, follow these steps:

1. Open the *ee2-p1drill* workbook, if necessary, and select the sheet named #6-Arrow.

2. Select the Arrow button on the Drawing toolbar.

3. Draw an arrow from the left border of the text box to a point on the red border between the headings Model 2 and Model 3.

4. Draw another arrow from the bottom border of the text box to a point on the red border at row 14.

5. Make final adjustments as necessary to the position and size of the arrows.

6. Save your changes to the *ee2-p1drill* workbook.

Challenge

Challenge exercises expand on or are somewhat related to skills presented in the lessons. Each exercise provides a brief narrative introduction followed by instructions in a numbered-step format that are not as detailed as those in the Skill Drill section.

Before beginning your first Project 1 Challenge exercise, complete the following steps:

1. Open the file named *ee2-0104,* and immediately save it as `ee2-p1challenge`.

The *ee2-p1challenge* workbook contains five sheets: an overview, and four exercise sheets named #1-StarText, #2-Oval, #3-Chart, and #4-Ungroup.

2. Click the Overview sheet to view the organization of the Project 1 Challenge Exercises workbook.

Each exercise is independent of the others, so that you may complete the exercises in any order. Be sure to save the workbook after completing each exercise. If you need a paper copy of the completed exercise, enter your name centered in a header before printing. Other print options have already been set to print compressed to one page and to display the filename, sheet name, and current date in a footer.

Be sure to save your changes and close the workbook if you need more than one work session to complete the desired exercises; then continue working on *ee2-p1challenge* instead of starting over again on the original *ee2-0104* file.

1. Adding Text to a Shape

You added a 16-point star to the worksheet showing budgeted revenues for the year 2003. Now you decide to enlarge the blank space in the center of the star and add text stating that the year 2003 is expected to be the best year yet.

To add text to a star shape, follow these steps:

1. Open the *ee2-p1challenge* workbook, if necessary, and select the sheet named #1-StarText.
2. Click the star until you see the yellow adjustment handle.
3. Drag the yellow handle outward to enlarge the white space in the center (the space should hold the words *Best Year Yet!*, one word to a line).
4. Center the phrase `Best Year Yet!` within the star.
5. Resize and reposition the object as desired.
6. Save your changes to the *ee2-p1challenge* workbook.

2. Circling Text Using an Oval Shape

The focus of the good news in the budget for year 2003 revenues is the Total Revenue in cell F17. You decide to emphasize this value by drawing a circle around it. The shape you draw covers the value, so you need to select the object and turn off the fill color.

To add and edit an oval shape around a cell, follow these steps:

1. Open the *ee2-p1challenge* workbook, if necessary, and select the sheet named #2-Oval.
2. Select the Oval button on the Drawing toolbar, and drag it over cell F17.
   The shape covers the value in cell F17 so you can't see it. This happens because the fill color is white.
3. Change the fill color to No Fill.
4. Change the size and position of the oval as necessary so that it surrounds the value 1,949,100 in cell F17.
5. Save your changes to the *ee2-p1challenge* workbook.

3. Drawing a Line Between a Chart and Data

You decide to create an embedded pie chart showing the expected greens fees for each quarter of the year 2003. You also want to draw a connection between the pie slice for the quarter with the highest expected revenue and the associated data cell in the worksheet. You don't want the connection to cross through the pie chart, so you decide to learn about curved lines before you start.

To create the chart and draw the connection, follow these steps:

1. Open the *ee2-p1challenge* workbook, if necessary, and select the sheet named #3-Chart.
2. Access onscreen Help; then search for and read information about your options to create curved lines.
3. Exit onscreen Help, and create the desired pie chart near the worksheet data.
   Be sure to properly label the chart. The title should clarify that the chart reflects 2003 budgeted data. Other labels should show which pie slice represents which quarter.
4. Draw a connection of your choice—a curved line or combination of straight lines—between the worksheet cell containing the highest expected greens fees for a quarter and the corresponding pie slice.
   The connection should not cross through the pie chart.

5. Apply a red color to the connection.

6. Save your changes to the *ee2-p1challenge* workbook.

4. Ungrouping, Editing, and Regrouping Objects

You created an eye-catching grouped object that includes clip art and a callout. You realize that some of the text in the callout does not display, and that an uppercase letter in the callout should be made lowercase. To make the changes, ungroup the objects, select only the callout, edit and resize as necessary, and then regroup the objects.

To ungroup, edit, and regroup objects, follow these steps:

1. Open the *ee2-p1challenge* workbook, if necessary, and select the sheet named #4-Ungroup.

2. Access onscreen Help; then search for and read information about ungrouping and regrouping objects.

3. Exit onscreen Help, and ungroup the cloud callout and clip art.

4. Increase the size of only the cloud callout, so that all text displays.

5. Change the uppercase C in *Can't* to a lowercase c.

6. Regroup the two objects.

7. Save your changes to the *ee2-p1challenge* workbook.

Discovery Zone exercises require advanced knowledge of topics presented in *essentials* lessons, application of skills from multiple lessons, or self-directed learning of new skills.

Before beginning your first Project 1 Discovery Zone exercise, complete the following steps:

1. Open the file named *ee2-0105*, and immediately save it as **ee2-p1discovery**.
The *ee2-p1discovery* workbook contains four sheets: an overview, and three exercise sheets named #1-Analyze, #2-Apply, and #3-Diagram.

2. Select the Overview worksheet to view the organization of the Project 1 Discovery Zone Exercises workbook.

Each exercise is independent of the other, so you may complete the exercises in any order. Be sure to save the workbook after completing each exercise. If you need a paper copy of the completed exercise, enter your name centered in a header before printing. Other print options have already been set to print compressed to one page and to display the filename, sheet name, and current date in a footer.

Be sure to save your changes and close the workbook if you need more than one work session to complete the desired exercises. Then, continue working on *ee2-p1discovery* instead of starting over again on the original *ee2-0105* file.

1. Determining Appropriate Use of Special Effects

An important part of the process of creating and maintaining a worksheet in Excel is applying special effects that make the worksheet more readable. To practice the process of determining what special effects to apply, select the #1-Analyze worksheet in the *ee2-p1discovery* workbook. Notice the area located just above the worksheet data. In column A is a list of numbers from 1 to 8. Next to each number is a blank cell in which you can write. Analyze the worksheet carefully; then in the space next to a number, describe a special effect you would apply to the worksheet. There is room to describe up to eight improvements. Describe as many as you think would be appropriate.

2. Applying Special Effects to a Worksheet

Assume that you decided on a number of special effects to apply to a worksheet. Open the *ee2-p1discovery* workbook, if necessary, and select the #2-Apply worksheet. Apply the special effects described in rows 4 through 8.

3. Creating a Radial Diagram

You completed a budget for Year 2003 Revenues for Glenn Lakes Golf Course. Now you want to insert a diagram showing types of revenue as the elements of total revenue. Open the *ee2-p1discovery* workbook, if necessary, and select the #3-Diagram worksheet. Create a radial diagram above row 15 and to the right of the worksheet titles. Enter **Total Revenue** in the center circle, and enter the three types of revenue—**Greens Fees**, **Golf Lessons**, and **Pro Shop Sales**—in the outer three circles. Reduce font size of the text to 8 point. Apply a different color fill to each of the outer circles, such as Light Yellow, Light Green, and Tan.

Working with Custom Formats, AutoFormats, Styles, and Templates

Objectives

In this project, you learn how to

- ✔ Insert and Delete Cells
- ✔ Replace and Rotate Text
- ✔ Create a Custom Format
- ✔ Apply an AutoFormat
- ✔ Create and Use Styles
- ✔ Copy a Worksheet
- ✔ Create a Custom Template
- ✔ Use a Built-in Template

Key terms in this project include

- ❑ AutoFormat
- ❑ built-in template
- ❑ custom format
- ❑ custom template
- ❑ default workbook template
- ❑ default worksheet template
- ❑ style
- ❑ template

Why Would I Do This?

Excel provides a variety of features to promote consistency in worksheet content and formatting with a minimum of effort. These features include defining your own formats, creating and storing a worksheet model for repeated use, and applying a predefined combination of formats to an entire worksheet.

Visual Summary

You begin this project by inserting and deleting cells, replacing and rotating cell contents, and creating your own custom format. You also define and apply your own combination of formats, and apply a predefined combination of formats, as shown in Figure 2.1. The remaining lessons focus on creating a workbook model of your own, and using a built-in worksheet model.

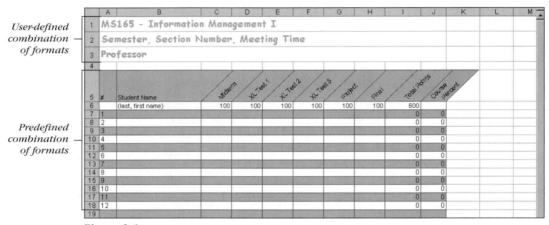

User-defined combination of formats

Predefined combination of formats

Figure 2.1

Lesson 1: Inserting and Deleting Cells

You can insert and delete worksheets, insert and delete rows and columns, and insert or delete a range of cells. The worksheet in Figure 2.2 illustrates why you might want to insert or delete cells. The worksheet calculates Total Points (column H), Course Percent (column I), and summary statistics (rows 20-22) based on scores entered in the range C7:G18.

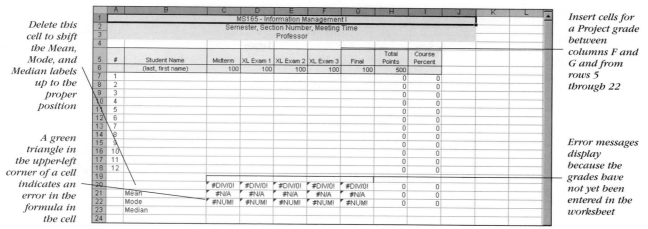

Delete this cell to shift the Mean, Mode, and Median labels up to the proper position

A green triangle in the upper-left corner of a cell indicates an error in the formula in the cell

Insert cells for a Project grade between columns F and G and from rows 5 through 22

Error messages display because the grades have not yet been entered in the worksheet

Figure 2.2

At this point in the worksheet design process, two changes are needed in the model. First, you need to make room for a Project grade between the XL Exam 3 grade and the Final grade. If you do this by inserting a column, the background shading in rows 1 through 3 will extend through column K. You would then have to remove the unwanted color from cells K1:K3. If instead you insert cells from G5 through G22, the green shading will still end in column J, and the yellow shading will align below the green.

You must also correct the problem of labels entered in the wrong rows. You could select cells in the range B21:B23 and drag the contents up one cell. Deleting cell B20 would produce the same result. You use the latter method in this lesson.

To Insert and Delete Cells

❶ Open the *ee2-0201* file, and save it as MS165grades.
The worksheet shown in Figure 2.2 displays. You can ignore the green triangles that indicate errors in formulas. The formulas in rows 20 through 22 produce correct results if grades are entered in rows 7 through 18.

❷ Select cells G5:G22.

❸ Choose Insert, Cells.
The Insert dialog box displays (see Figure 2.3).

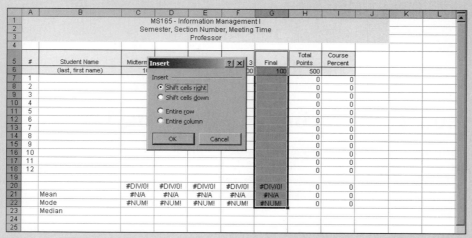

Figure 2.3

(Continues)

To Insert and Delete Cells (Continued)

4 **Make sure that *Shift cells right* is selected, and click OK.**
Excel inserts cells from row 5 through row 22 in column G. The existing cells shift right, and the yellow shading extends through column J. Inserted cells are automatically formatted the same as the corresponding cells to the left (cells F5:F22).

5 **Type** Project **in cell G5.**

6 **Type** 100 **in cell G6.**
Excel automatically adjusts the formulas in columns I and J to include the new cells. The Total Points number changes from 500 to 600. Now copy the summary formulas.

7 **Select cells F20:F22, drag the lower-right corner of cell F22 right one cell, and release the mouse button.**
The Mean, Mode, and Median formulas are copied from column F to column G.

8 **Click cell B20, and choose Edit, Delete.**
The Delete dialog box displays (see Figure 2.4).

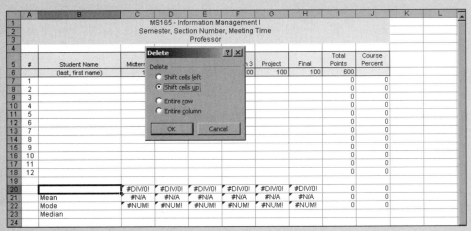

Figure 2.4

9 **Make sure that *Shift cells up* is selected, and click OK.**
The Mean, Mode, and Median labels shift up one cell.

10 **Save your changes to the *MS165grades* workbook.**
Keep the *MS165grades* workbook open for the next lesson, or close the workbook and exit Excel.

Lesson 2: Replacing and Rotating Text

Excel provides a variety of ways to manipulate both the content and appearance of text. Find and Replace are two options on the Edit menu that can substantially reduce editing time on large worksheets. Using the Find dialog box, you can search for the next occurrence of the word, number, or phrase you specify. Using the Replace dialog box, you can look for each occurrence of the word, number, or phrase you specify and replace each occurrence or all occurrences.

If the column labels in a worksheet are longer than the data they describe, you can rotate the column headings. Text can be rotated up to 90 degrees upward or downward. Changing the orientation of text in a cell can also enhance visual appeal.

In this lesson, you use Excel's Replace feature to substitute the word *Test* for each occurrence of the word *Exam*. You then rotate the column headings 45 degrees upward.

To Replace and Rotate Text

1 Open the *MS165grades* workbook, if necessary, and click cell A1.

2 Choose **E**dit, **R**eplace.
The Find and Replace dialog box opens.

3 Type Exam in the Fi**n**d what text box.

4 Type Test in the **R**eplace with text box (see Figure 2.5).

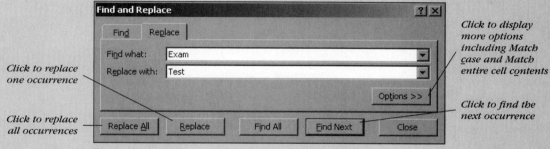

Click to display more options including Match case and Match entire cell contents

Click to replace one occurrence

Click to replace all occurrences

Click to find the next occurrence

Figure 2.5

5 Make sure that your specifications match those in Figure 2.5, and click the Replace **A**ll button in the lower-left corner of the dialog box.
A message displays that Excel has made three replacements.

6 Click OK to close the message box, and click the Close button.
The word *Exam* in cells D5, E5, and F5 is replaced with the word *Test*. Now rotate 45 degrees most of the column labels in row 5.

7 Select cells C5:J5.

8 Choose Fo**r**mat, C**e**lls; then click the Alignment tab in the Format Cells dialog box.

9 Type 45 in the **D**egrees text box (see Figure 2.6).

(Continues)

To Replace and Rotate Text (Continued)

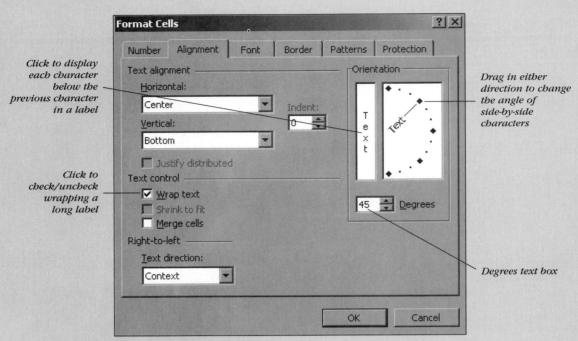

Figure 2.6

⑩ **Click OK, and click any cell to deselect the rotated range.**

Rotated text does not display well within the cells without an adjustment in row height (see Figure 2.7). Now increase the height of row 5.

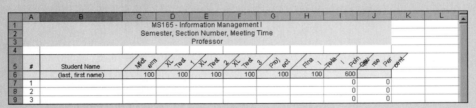

Figure 2.7

⑪ **Click any cell in row 5, and choose F<u>o</u>rmat, <u>R</u>ow, <u>H</u>eight.**

⑫ **Type 55 in the <u>R</u>ow height text box, and click OK.**

All rotated text displays after you increase the height of row 5 (see Figure 2.8).

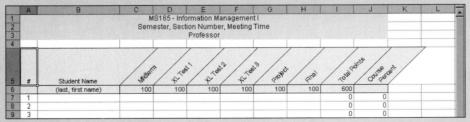

Figure 2.8

⑬ **Save your changes to the *MS165grades* workbook.**

Keep the *MS165grades* workbook open for the next lesson, or close the workbook and exit Excel.

To extend your knowledge...

Replacing Cell Formats

You can use Excel's Find and Replace feature to locate and change cell formats as well as cell contents. Click the Options button in the Find and Replace dialog box (refer to Figure 2.5) to display Format buttons and associated Preview text boxes to the right of the Find what and Replace with text boxes. Use the drop-down list for each Format button to specify the Find what and Replace with formatting.

Lesson 3: Creating a Custom Format

Formats are masks that, when applied to a cell, change the display of the content without changing the value in the cell. Excel provides a variety of formats that you can apply using the Number tab in the Format Cells dialog box.

For a unique situation in which a predefined format does not meet your needs, you can create a ***custom format***. To create a custom format, display the Number tab in the Format Cells dialog box, select the Custom category, and type the appropriate codes in the Type text box. These codes are generally separated into two groups: date and time codes, and number and text codes. Excel's onscreen Help offers a substantial coverage of custom formats and the associated codes.

You can also incorporate conditional formatting within a custom format. In this lesson, you create a custom format to display a grade in red if the value is less than 70, and to display a grade in blue if it is 70 or greater. You then apply the format to all cells in which grades are reported. Such formatting makes it easy to distinguish between grades equal to or higher than a C (blue) and those lower than a C (red). You create the custom format using the Format Cells dialog box.

To Create a Custom Format

❶ Open the *MS165grades* workbook, if necessary, and click cell C7 in the *Sectionxx* worksheet.

❷ Choose Format, Cells; then select the Number tab.

❸ Click Custom in the Category list.
Excel displays the dialog box shown in Figure 2.9.

(Continues)

To Create a Custom Format (Continued)

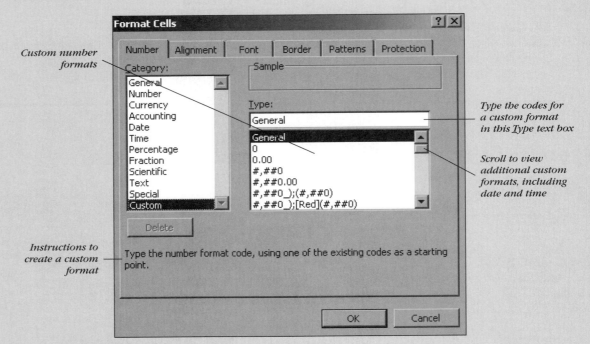

Custom number formats

Type the codes for a custom format in this Type text box

Scroll to view additional custom formats, including date and time

Instructions to create a custom format

Figure 2.9

4 **If necessary, delete the contents currently in the Type text box.**

5 **Type [red][<70];[blue][>=70] in the Type text box, and click OK.**
Your custom format has been saved, and it has also been applied to the current cell C7. The custom format enables you to quickly apply conditional formatting without specifying the criteria and font attributes required when using the Format, Conditional Formatting command. Now apply the format to all cells that will contain grades and summary statistics.

6 **Select cells in the range C7:H22.**

7 **Choose Format, Cells; select the Number tab.**

8 **Click Custom in the Category list box.**

9 **Scroll down the list of custom formats and select the new custom format, the last one in the list (see Figure 2.10).**

To Create a Custom Format

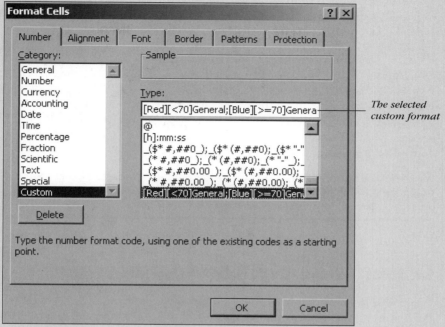

Figure 2.10

Notice that Excel appended the word *General*—indicating the General format—after each condition.

⑩ Click OK.

The new custom format has been applied to the selected cells. Now test the custom format.

⑪ Select cell C7, and enter the number 60.

If the custom format was set up properly, the number 60 displays in red in cell C7.

⑫ Select another cell in the range C7:H18, such as cell D10, and enter the number 80.

The number 80 displays in blue.

⑬ Test other numbers in the range C7:H18 as desired.

⑭ Delete the test entries, and save your changes to the *MS165grades* workbook.

Keep the *MS165grades* workbook open for the next lesson, or close the workbook and exit Excel.

To extend your knowledge...

Getting Help on Number Format Codes

You can use onscreen Help to view multiple examples of custom formats. Type the phrase *number format codes* in the Ask a Question box, and select a related topic.

Applying Special Formats

Excel provides special formats that are country-specific. For example, the choices for the location *English (United States)* include Zip Code, Zip Code + 4, Phone Number, and Social Security Number. If you apply the Phone Number format to a cell before or after you enter the number 1234567890, Excel automatically displays (123)456-7890. If you apply the Social Security Number format to a cell before or after you enter the number 123456789, Excel automatically displays 123-45-6789.

To apply a special format, select the cell(s) and then choose Format, Cells. Select the Number tab, and click Special in the Category list; then select the language in the Locale (location) drop-down list, and select a special format in the Type list.

Lesson 4: Applying an AutoFormat

The **AutoFormat** command, located on the Format menu, enables you to apply one of sixteen predefined formats to lists and cell ranges. Each predefined format combines color, line thickness, shading and/or italics to give a distinctive look to a worksheet. AutoFormats are grouped into five categories: Classic, Accounting, List, 3D Effects, and Colorful. Using the Options button, you may decide to apply or reject the AutoFormat's Number, Border, Font, Patterns, Alignment, and Width/Height formats.

In this lesson, you apply the List1 AutoFormat to your grade book. To enhance the readability of the List1 format, you deselect the Font option. After the AutoFormat has been applied, you add another enhancement—in this case, borders.

To Apply an AutoFormat

❶ Open the *MS165grades* workbook, if necessary, and select cells A5:J22 in the *Sectionxx* worksheet.

❷ Choose Format, AutoFormat; then click the Options button in the AutoFormat dialog box.
The AutoFormat dialog box shown in Figure 2.11 displays.

To Apply an AutoFormat

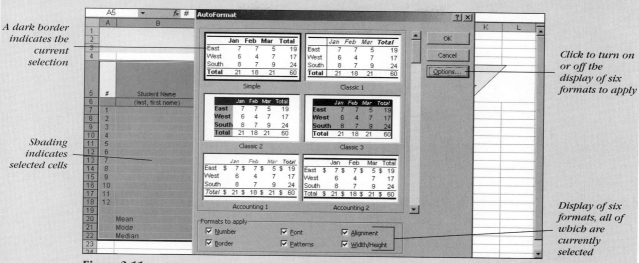

A dark border indicates the current selection

Shading indicates selected cells

Click to turn on or off the display of six formats to apply

Display of six formats, all of which are currently selected

Figure 2.11

❸ Uncheck the Font check box near the bottom of the dialog box.
Deselecting this option retains your current font formatting.

❹ Scroll down and click the List1 format when it appears (format descriptions display below the related format).
The dark border surrounding the List1 display indicates that AutoFormat has been selected.

❺ Click OK.
The List1 format is applied to the highlighted range, and the range A5:J22 remains selected. Applying the AutoFormat removed the rotation applied to the column headings in row 5.

If you have problems...

If you apply the wrong AutoFormat and want to immediately reverse this action, use the Edit, Undo command or click the Undo button on the toolbar.

❻ Choose Format, Cells and then select the Border tab.

❼ Select the Outline and Inside buttons in the Presets area.
The border colors from the applied AutoFormat are maintained (see Figure 2.12).

(Continues)

To Apply an AutoFormat (Continued)

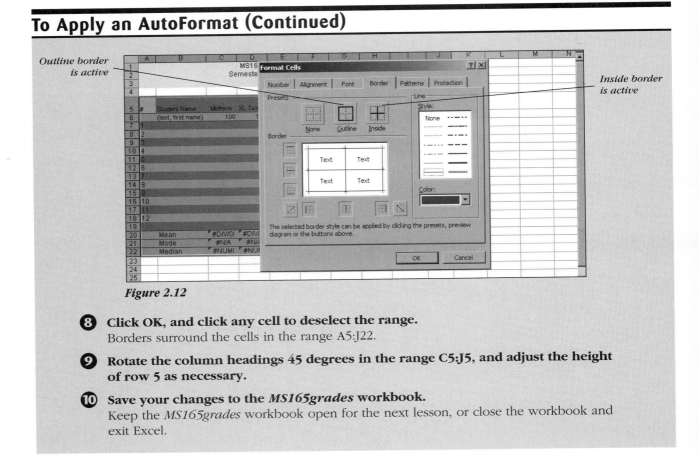

Outline border is active

Inside border is active

Figure 2.12

8 **Click OK, and click any cell to deselect the range.**
Borders surround the cells in the range A5:J22.

9 **Rotate the column headings 45 degrees in the range C5:J5, and adjust the height of row 5 as necessary.**

10 **Save your changes to the *MS165grades* workbook.**
Keep the *MS165grades* workbook open for the next lesson, or close the workbook and exit Excel.

To extend your knowledge...

Removing an AutoFormat

To remove an AutoFormat, execute the steps to apply an AutoFormat, and select the last AutoFormat named None. This action removes all formatting in the selected range unless you click the Options button and uncheck one or more of the formatting options.

Lesson 5: Creating and Using Styles

A *style* is a means of combining more than one format, such as font type, size, and color, into a single definition that can be applied to one or more cells. Use styles to maintain a consistent look to a worksheet. If you want to change that look, you can change the style once and reapply it, rather than edit individual cell attributes in multiple locations.

You may be surprised to know that you already use styles. When you create a new workbook, each cell is formatted using the Normal style containing Excel's default formats.

The easiest way to define a style is to apply all of the desired formats to a cell; select Format, Style; and give the current style a new name. You can also define a new style in the same manner as you edit a style—by selecting Format, Style; giving the current style a new name; and modifying the current formats as necessary.

Complete four steps to apply a style. First, select the cell range to receive the new style; then select Format, Style, select the appropriate style from the Style name list, and click OK. To remove the effects of applying a style, select the appropriate cell range, and apply a different style or the Normal style.

In this lesson, you define a style named *comic14gold*. The style includes settings for applying a 14-point bold Comic Sans MS font in a gold color. You create the style, apply it in another location, and remove the style from one location.

To Create and Use Styles

❶ Open the *MS165grades* workbook, if necessary, and select cell B20 in the *Sectionxx* worksheet.
You are ready to create a style by first applying several formats to cell B20.

❷ Choose Format, Cells; then select the Font tab in the Format Cells dialog box.

❸ Specify the Comic Sans MS font, Bold font style, 14-point size, and gold color settings shown in Figure 2.13.

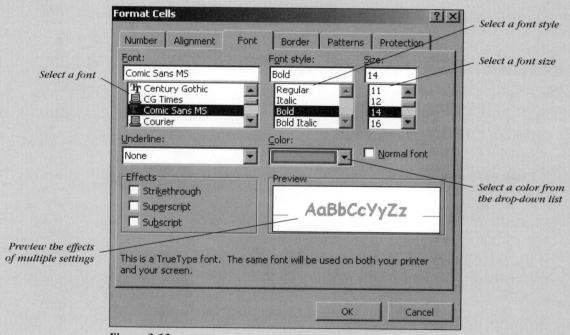

Figure 2.13

You applied to cell B20 all of the settings you want to include in this style, which specifies only font-related attributes. Now create the style.

❹ Click OK.
Excel applies the four format changes to cell B20.

❺ Make sure that cell B20 is the current cell, and choose Format, Style.
The Style dialog box opens. *Normal* displays in the Style name text box. The font assigned to the Normal style—Arial 10—is listed in the *Style includes* section.

❻ Type comic14gold to replace *Normal* in the Style name text box.
Excel automatically displays the newly-applied font settings—Comic Sans MS 14, Bold Color 44—to the right of the Font check box (see Figure 2.14).

(Continues)

To Create and Use Styles (Continued)

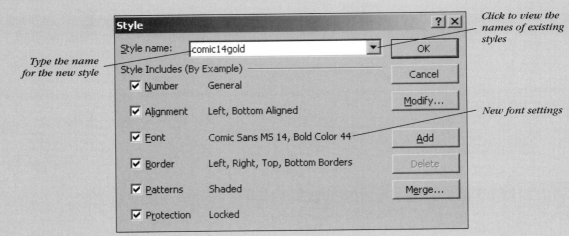

Figure 2.14

7 **Click the Add button, and click OK.**
Excel adds the comic14gold style to other defined styles. Now apply the new style.

8 **Select the range A1:A3, and choose Format, Style.**

9 **Display the Style name drop-down list, select the comic14gold style, and click OK.**
The labels in A1:A3 display left-aligned with attributes defined in the selected style—Comic Sans MS bold 14-point font in a gold color. Now remove the style applied to cell B20.

10 **Click cell B20, and choose Format, Style.**

11 **Select *Normal* from the Style name drop-down list, and click OK.**
Excel removes the elements of the comic14gold style from cell B20.

12 **Click cell A1, and save your changes to the *MS165grades* workbook.**
Keep the *MS165grades* workbook open for the next lesson, or close the workbook and exit Excel.

To extend your knowledge...

Copying Styles from Another Workbook

You can copy styles from one workbook to another. Open both workbooks. In the workbook you want to copy the styles to, complete the following steps. Choose Format, Style and then click the Merge button to display the Merge Styles dialog box.

In the *Merge styles from* list, double-click the name of the workbook that contains the styles you want to copy. If the two workbooks contain styles with the same names, you must confirm whether or not you want to replace the styles.

Lesson 6: Copying a Worksheet

You may want to create a worksheet that is very similar to an existing worksheet. If you copy and edit the existing worksheet, you can create the new one with a minimum of effort.

If you select all cells in a worksheet and copy the selection to another worksheet or workbook, Excel retains cell formats but not the column-width and row-height settings. To make an exact duplicate of a worksheet, use the Move or Copy Sheet option on the Edit menu.

In this lesson, you make an exact copy of the *Sectionxx* worksheet in the *MS165grades* workbook. You then rename the two worksheets Section01 and Section02, respectively.

To Copy a Worksheet

❶ **Open the *MS165grades* workbook, if necessary.**

❷ **Choose Edit, Move or Copy Sheet.**
The Move or Copy dialog box displays.

❸ **Click the *(move to end)* option in the Before sheet list box.**

❹ **Click the Create a copy check box.**
You have made the selections to duplicate the worksheet *Sectionxx* in the *MS165grades* workbook (see Figure 2.15).

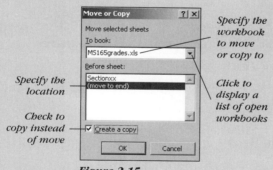

Specify the workbook to move or copy to

Specify the location

Click to display a list of open workbooks

Check to copy instead of move

Figure 2.15

❺ **Click OK.**
Excel makes a copy of the worksheet and names it *Sectionxx (2)*.

❻ **Double-click the *Sectionxx* sheet tab, type Section01, and press ↵Enter.**

❼ **Double-click the *Sectionxx (2)* sheet tab, type Section02, and press ↵Enter.**

❽ **Save your changes to the *MS165grades* workbook.**
The workbook contains two identical sheets, one named Section01 and the other named Section02.

Keep the *MS165grades* workbook open for the next lesson, or close the workbook and exit Excel.

Lesson 7: Creating a Custom Template

A *template* is a workbook (or worksheet) containing standardized content and/or formatting that you can use as the basis for other workbooks (or worksheets). A template has an .xlt extension, as compared to the .xls extension that indicates a workbook.

A *custom template* is a workbook that you create and save with your preferred content and/or formatting in one or more worksheets. For example, in the *MS165grades* workbook, only the students' names and grades change each semester. If you save the *MS165grades* workbook as a custom template, you can use it to create a new workbook each semester.

To save a workbook as a template, select the Save As option on the File menu, and select Template from the Save as type drop-down list. Excel automatically selects the Templates folder as the storage location (see Figure 2.16). You can, however, specify another location.

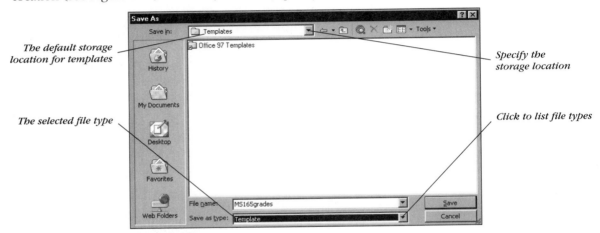

Figure 2.16

To use a template as the basis for a new workbook, choose File, New from the menu bar, find the folder containing the desired template and open it, modify labels as needed, and save the file as a workbook.

In this lesson, you save the *MS165grades* workbook as a template, and use the template to create a new workbook.

To Create and Use a Template

❶ Open the *MS165grades* workbook, if necessary.

❷ Choose File, Save As.

❸ Select Template from the Save as type drop-down list.
The settings in the Save As dialog box resemble those shown in Figure 2.16. If you are working in a lab environment, the Templates folder might be on a different drive.

❹ If you are working in a lab environment that doesn't permit saving to the Microsoft Templates folder, specify your own folder location in the Save in drop-down list.

❺ Click Save, and choose File, Close.
The *MS165grades* file now exists as both a workbook (.xls extension) and a template (.xlt extension). Now use the template to create a new workbook.

❻ Choose File, New from the menu bar.
The New Workbook task pane displays at the right side of the screen.

To Create and Use a Template

7 Click *General Templates* in the New Workbook task pane, and click the General tab in the Templates dialog box.

The *MS165grades* template displays to the right of the template for a blank workbook (see Figure 2.17).

Click to select a blank workbook

Click to select the MS165grades template

Click to access custom and built-in templates

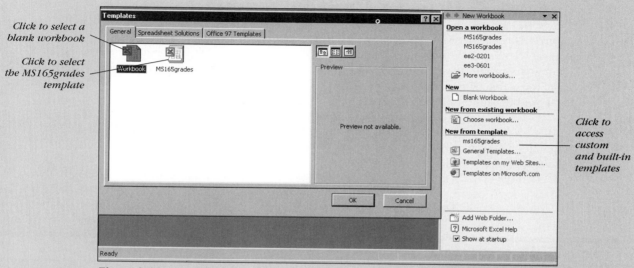

Figure 2.17

8 Click the *MS165grades* template, and click OK.

Excel opens the template as a workbook named MS165grades1.xls. Now save the file as a workbook with a name that denotes grades for Fall 2003.

9 Choose File, Save As; then specify a folder in the Save in drop-down list, and type MS165-f03 in the File name text box.

10 Make sure that *Microsoft Excel Workbook* is selected in the Save as type drop-down list, and click the Save button.

At this point you could modify the contents of cells A1:A3 and the sheet name to reflect Fall 2003, and begin to enter the names of students.

11 Close the *MS165-f03* workbook without saving any changes.

Continue with Lesson 8, or exit Excel.

To extend your knowledge...

Creating and Using Default Templates

You can also create default workbook and worksheet templates to replace the blank ones with minimal formatting provided by Excel. The **default workbook template** creates the workbook that opens when you start Excel or open a new workbook without specifying a template. Excel uses the **default worksheet template** when you insert a worksheet in a workbook.

To create your own default worksheet template, create a workbook with one worksheet that contains the formatting, column widths, text and so forth that you want to appear on all new sheets. Save the workbook as a template in the Microsoft Office XLStart folder using the name sheet. To create your own default workbook template, create a workbook that contains the worksheets, text, formulas, and so forth that you want in new workbooks. Save the workbook as a template in the Microsoft Office XLStart folder using the name book.

To restore the original default worksheet, delete sheet.xlt in the XLStart folder. To restore the original default workbook, delete book.xlt in the XLStart folder.

Lesson 8: Using a Built-in Template

A ***built-in template*** is a template provided by Excel that contains content and formatting designed to meet a common business need. Built-in templates include models for a balance sheet, expense statement, loan amortization schedule, sales invoice, and timecard. To open one of these templates as the basis for a new workbook, select the Spreadsheet Solutions tab in the Templates dialog box, and click the built-in template of choice.

In this lesson, you work with a template that generates an amortization schedule for a loan that requires equal payments at a fixed interest rate. At a minimum, an amortization schedule lists each payment across the life of the loan, shows the distribution of a payment between interest and debt reduction (principal), and displays the amount still owed at any point in time. You open the template, add user instructions, apply a fill color to emphasize the cells that a user can change, and save the file as a workbook. You also use the model by entering and changing loan terms.

To Use a Built-in Template

❶ Choose File, New from the Excel menu bar.
The New Workbook task pane displays at the right side of the screen.

❷ Click General Templates in the New Workbook task pane.
The Templates dialog box opens.

❸ Select the Spreadsheet Solutions tab, and click the Loan Amortization option (see Figure 2.18).

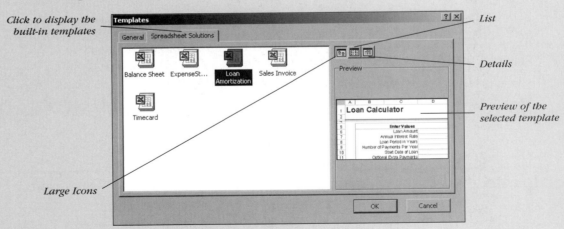

Figure 2.18

Excel displays the built-in templates and shows the selected template in the Preview area. A list may appear instead of the icons shown in Figure 2.18, depending on which view is active—Large Icons, List, or Details.

❹ Click OK.
A workbook opens that contains one worksheet named Amortization Table. Loan Amortization1—the default name assigned by Excel—displays in the title bar.

To Use a Built-in Template

5 **Reduce the zoom setting, if necessary, to display columns A through I (see Figure 2.19).**

Descriptions of values used to generate a loan amortization schedule

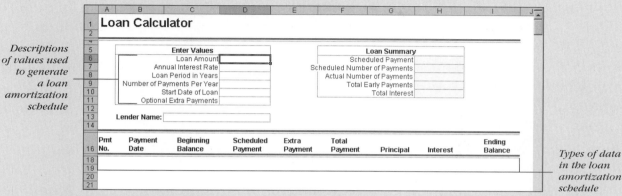

Types of data in the loan amortization schedule

Figure 2.19

The model generates an amortization schedule, beginning in row 18, after a user enters values in the range D6:D11. Worksheet protection is enabled. You can only change the contents of cell C13 and cells in the range D6:D11. Now disable worksheet protection, and add user instructions. (In-depth coverage of worksheet and workbook protection is provided in Project 3, "Documenting and Protecting Worksheets and Workbooks.")

6 **Choose Tools, point to Protection, and click Unprotect Sheet.**
Previously protected cells can now be changed.

7 **Click cell D1, and enter** `To generate the amortization schedule, enter data in the blue cells.`
User instructions are added to the worksheet. Now apply a fill color to the cells a user can change.

8 **Select the range D6:D11; then press and hold down** Ctrl**, click cell C13, and release** Ctrl**.**
Cells C13 and D6 through D11 are selected.

9 **Display the Fill Color drop-down list, select Pale Blue, and click outside the highlighted cells to deselect them.**
Color emphasizes the cells a user can change (see Figure 2.20). Now restore worksheet protection and save the workbook.

User instructions

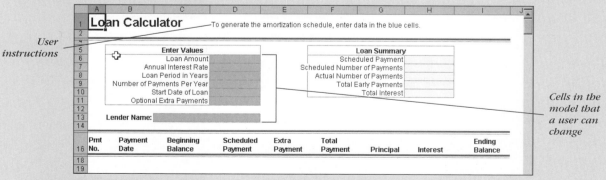

Cells in the model that a user can change

Figure 2.20

(Continues)

To Use a Built-in Template (Continued)

10 **Choose Tools, point to Protection, and click Protect Sheet; then click OK to close the Protect Sheet dialog box without specifying a password or changing the user permissions.**

Worksheet protection is restored. A user can change only the cells that have a blue background. Now save your changes to the model before using it to generate a schedule. You can save as a template if you want to modify the loan amortization template provided by Excel. In this lesson, you save as a workbook.

11 **Choose File, Save As; then specify a folder in the Save in drop-down list, and type** `loanschedule` **in the File name text box.**

12 **Make sure that *Microsoft Excel Workbook* is selected in the Save as type drop-down list, and click the Save button.**

The revised template is saved as an Excel workbook. Now enter values to generate a loan amortization schedule.

13 **Enter the following data in the cells indicated.**

In cell	Enter
D6	150000
D7	6%
D8	30
D9	12
D10	1/1/2002

Excel generates the loan amortization schedule starting with the first payment in row 18 (see Figure 2.21). Summary data displays in the range H6:H10. For a 30-year, 6%, $150,000 loan, the scheduled monthly payment is $899.33, and the total interest on the loan is $173,757.28.

Click and drag down to view the entire amortization schedule

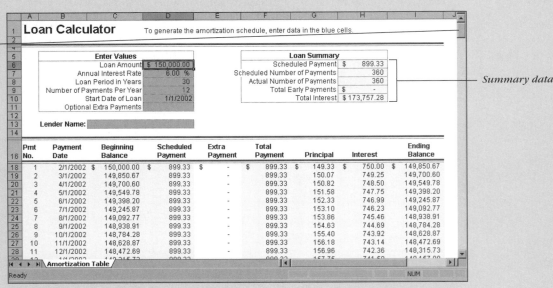

Summary data

Figure 2.21

14 **Scroll down to view row 377, the bottom of the amortization schedule.**

To Use a Built-in Template

The balance remaining in cell I377 is zero.

15 **Scroll up and click cell D8; then change the number of years to 15.**
Excel generates a new loan amortization schedule. Cutting the loan time in half raises the monthly payment to $1,265.79, an increase of $366.46 per month; however, the total interest is now only $77,841.34—$95,915.94 less than the interest on a 30-year loan.

16 **Click cell D11, and enter 100 as the optional extra payment every month.**
You can see in the Loan Summary area that paying $100 extra each month enables you to eliminate the last 20 payments—only 160 of the 180 scheduled payments are needed to pay off the loan.

17 **Generate other loan amortization schedules of your choice by varying the amount borrowed, the annual interest rate, and/or the number of years that payments are due. When you finish, close the workbook without saving your changes.**
In the *loanschedule* workbook you saved in step 12, the cells for loan terms are blank. By closing the file now without saving specific loan terms, you have a model stored on disk that you can open and use for any loan specifications.

You can exit Excel, or continue with the end-of-project exercises.

Summary

This project focused primarily on techniques to enhance worksheets with a minimum of effort for repetitive tasks. You created a custom format, applied a predefined AutoFormat, defined a style combining a number of font-related attributes, saved a workbook as a template that could serve as the starting point for creating similar workbooks, and modified a built-in template provided by Excel. You also learned to insert and delete cells, replace and rotate text, and copy a worksheet.

To expand your knowledge, explore the many Help screens on custom formats, AutoFormats, styles, and templates. Then experiment with using these features in your worksheets.

Checking Concepts and Terms

Multiple Choice

Circle the letter of the correct answer for each of the following.

1. Which of the following is a true statement about duplicating the layout and content of a worksheet? [L6]

    a. You can make a copy of a worksheet in the same workbook, but you cannot copy a worksheet to another workbook.

    b. Moving a worksheet requires the use of a different dialog box than that used to specify copying a worksheet.

    c. The two methods of reproducing a worksheet—making a copy of the worksheet, and applying a copy/paste operation to all active cells in a worksheet—produce identical results.

    d. None of the above

2. Which of the following is not an accurate statement? [L5]

    a. You can copy styles from one workbook to another.

    b. You cannot edit a style; instead, delete it and create a new style with the desired changes.

    c. To remove the effects of applying a style, select the appropriate cell range, and apply a different style or the Normal style.

    d. The easiest way to define a style is to apply all of the desired formats to a cell before you create the style.

3. A means of combining more than one format into a single definition that can be applied to one or more cells is a _____. [L5 and L7]

    a. style

    b. template

    c. Both a and b

    d. Neither a nor b

4. Which of the following is a valid statement about AutoFormat? [L4]

    a. You can apply one of sixteen AutoFormat styles to lists and cell ranges.

    b. Remove an AutoFormat by applying the AutoFormat style named "None."

    c. AutoFormats are grouped into five design groups: Classic, Accounting, List, 3D Effect, and Colorful.

    d. All of the above are valid statements.

5. Which of the following determines the workbook that opens when you start Excel? [L7 and L8]

    a. built-in template

    b. custom template

    c. default workbook template

    d. default worksheet template

Discussion

1. Excel provides special formats that are country-specific, such as the Phone Number and Social Security Number options that display when the location selected is *English (United States)*. Describe the special formats available for two non-English locations of your choice. [L3]

2. If you click the Options button in the Find and Replace dialog box, Excel displays additional options including *Match case* and *Match entire cell contents*. Provide an example of a Find operation

that produces different results depending on whether or not the *Match case* option is active. Also provide an example of a Find operation that produces different results depending on whether or not the *Match entire cell contents* option is active. [L2]

3. Open a built-in template of your choice, other than the Loan Amortization template you worked with in this project. Explain the purpose of the template. Also describe the data to be entered, and the results achieved. [L8]

Skill Drill exercises reinforce project skills. Each skill that is reinforced is the same, or nearly the same, as a skill presented in the project. Detailed instructions are provided in a step-by-step format.

Before beginning your first Project 2 Skill Drill exercise, complete the following steps:

1. Open the file named *ee2-0202*, and immediately save it as `ee2-p2drill`.
   The *ee2-p2drill* workbook contains five sheets: an overview, and sheets named #1-Replace, #2-Reapply, #3-Compare, and #4-CopyWS.
2. Click the Overview sheet to view the organization of the Project 2 Skill Drill Exercises workbook.

Each exercise is independent of the others, so you may complete the exercises in any order. Be sure to save the workbook after completing each exercise. If you need a paper copy of the completed exercise, enter your name, centered in a header, before printing. Other print options have already been set to print compressed to one page and to display the filename, sheet name, and current date in a footer.

Be sure to save your changes and close the workbook if you need more than one work session to complete the desired exercises. Then, continue working on *ee2-p2drill* instead of starting over again on the original *ee2-0202* file.

1. Replacing Multiple Occurrences of a Misspelled Word

You work for Experienced Wheels, Inc., and your responsibilities include maintaining a worksheet that lists the inventory of used cars. You realize that one of the color descriptions is misspelled.

To use Excel's Replace feature to correct all occurrences of the misspelled color in a single operation, follow these steps:

1. Open the *ee2-p2drill* workbook, if necessary, and click the sheet tab named #1-Replace.
2. Choose Edit, Replace.
3. Type `Burgandy` in the Find what text box.
4. Type `Burgundy` in the Replace with text box, choose Replace All, and click OK.
   Excel replaces all occurrences of the misspelled word *Burgandy* with the correct spelling *Burgundy*.
5. Close the Find and Replace dialog box, and save your changes to the *ee2-p2drill* workbook.

2. Applying a Different AutoFormat

The Accounting2 AutoFormat is applied to an inventory of used cars. Now you want to change that AutoFormat to one that has more color.

To apply a different AutoFormat, follow these steps:

1. Open the *ee2-p2drill* workbook, if necessary, and click the sheet tab named #2-Reapply.
2. Select the range A6:I28, and choose Format, AutoFormat.
3. Scroll down to view AutoFormats with color settings.
4. Select the AutoFormat named List 2, and click OK.
5. Click any cell to deselect the highlighted AutoFormat range.
6. Save your changes to the *ee2-p2drill* workbook.

3. Inserting Cells and Applying a Custom Format

You are constructing a worksheet to display percent, decimal, and fraction equivalents for values between zero and 1. The decimal values are already in place. Shift those values to the right so you can present percentage values in the first column. Copy the decimal values twice, creating values in the percent column the first time, and values in the fraction column the second time. Use a toolbar button to change display in the first column to percents. Apply a custom format to change display in the third column to fractions.

To make the changes, including a custom format to display fractions, follow these steps:

1. Open the *ee2-p2drill* workbook, if necessary, and click the sheet tab named #3-Compare.
2. Select the range A5:A25, and choose Insert, Cells.
3. Check that Shift cells right is selected in the Insert dialog box, and click OK.
4. Type **Percent** in cell A5.
5. Copy the contents of B6:B25 to A6:A25.
6. Copy the contents of B6:B25 to C6:C25.
7. Select A6:A25, and click the Percent Style button in the toolbar.
   Check that 5%, 10%, 15% and so forth displays in the percent column A.
8. Select C6:C25, and choose Format, Cells.
9. Select the Number tab, and click Custom at the bottom of the Category list.
10. Scroll down to view other options in the Type list; then select the custom format # ??/??, and click OK.
    Check that 1/20, 1/10, 3/20 and so forth displays in the fraction column C.
11. Right-align the labels in A5:C5; then apply a blue font to that range, and deselect the range.
12. Adjust column widths to eliminate unnecessary white space.
13. Save your changes to the *ee2-p2drill* workbook.

4. Copying a Worksheet to a New Workbook

You developed a worksheet to track revenues for Glenn Lakes Golf Course. While you have the worksheet open, you decide to make a copy of the worksheet in a new workbook for use at another golf course.

To copy a worksheet to a new workbook, complete the following steps:

1. Open the *ee2-p2drill* workbook, if necessary, and click the sheet tab named #4-CopyWS.
2. Choose Edit, Move or Copy Sheet.
   The Move or Copy dialog box displays.
3. Display the drop-down list for the To book text box, and click the *(new book)* option.
4. Click the Create a copy check box, and click OK.
   Excel makes a copy of the worksheet in a new workbook. Now rename the worksheet, change its title for use at another golf course, and save and close the file.
5. Double-click the worksheet tab #4-CopyWS in the new workbook, type **West Glenn**, and press ⏎Enter.
6. Change the contents of cell A4 to **West Glenn Golf Course**.
7. Save the new workbook as **WGGCrev**, and close the file.

Challenge

Challenge exercises expand on or are somewhat related to skills that are presented in the lessons. Each exercise provides a brief narrative introduction, followed by instructions in a numbered-step format that are not as detailed as those in the Skill Drill section.

Before beginning your first Project 2 Challenge exercise, complete the following steps:

1. Open the file named *ee2-0203,* and immediately save it as `ee2-p2challenge.`
   The *ee2-p2challenge* workbook contains four sheets: an overview, and three exercise sheets named #1-RotateAlign, #2-Remove2, and #3-Find.
2. Click the Overview sheet to view the organization of the Project 2 Challenge Exercises workbook.

Each exercise is independent of the others, so you may complete the exercises in any order. Be sure to save the workbook after completing each exercise. If you need a paper copy of the completed exercise, enter your name centered in a header before printing. Other print options have already been set to print compressed to one page and to display the filename, sheet name, and current date in a footer.

If you need more than one work session to complete the desired exercises, continue working on *ee2-p2challenge* instead of starting over again on the original *ee2-0203* file.

1. Changing Rotation and Alignment

You work for Experienced Wheels, Inc., and currently you are trying out various enhancements in a worksheet that lists the inventory of used cars. You want to see if the column headings in row 9 would look better if they were centered vertically within the row, but not rotated.

To change rotation and alignment, follow these steps:

1. Open the *ee2-p2drill* workbook, if necessary, and select the worksheet named #1-RotateAlign.
2. Set rotation in cells A9:I9 to zero degrees.
3. Set both vertical and horizontal alignment in cells A9:I9 to Center.
4. Apply bold and the color Blue to the column headings in row 9.
5. Narrow the height of row 9 as desired, and save your changes to the *ee2-p2challenge* workbook.

2. Removing a Style and an AutoFormat

You are concerned that too many enhancements have been applied to a worksheet listing the inventory of used cars. You want to compare ways to remove enhancements. You decide to restore the Normal style to data in columns F through I, and to remove the AutoFormat effects that remain in other columns.

To remove a style and an AutoFormat, follow these steps:

1. Open the *ee2-p2challenge* workbook, if necessary, and select the worksheet named #2-Remove2.
2. Select the range F9:I31, and apply the Normal style.
   Applying the Normal style removes the AutoFormat effects from columns F through I. Previously set number styles no longer apply. Prices do not display a comma separator. Each APR—annual percentage rate—displays as a decimal instead of as a percent.

3. Select the range A9:E31, access the AutoFormat option, and select None.

Excel automatically applies the Normal style to the selected range. Now apply predefined number styles to three columns.

4. Apply the Comma, zero decimal places format to the values in Column F.
5. Apply the Percent, one decimal place format to the values in Column G.
6. Apply the Currency, two decimal places format to the values in Column I.
7. Save your changes to the *ee2-p2challenge* workbook.

3. Using the Find Command

You operate a lawn mowing service, and you use an Excel worksheet to list the locations you are currently servicing. You want to change the mowing day from Tues to Weds for a customer named Sandy Bell.

To use Excel's Find command to locate the customer's record, and make the change, follow these steps:

1. Open the *ee2-p2challenge* workbook, if necessary, and select the worksheet named #3-Find.
2. Choose Edit, Find.

The Find and Replace dialog box opens. The Find tab is active.

3. Enter **Bell** in the Find what text box, and click Find All.

The Find and Replace dialog box expands to include the locations of four cells that contain the letters *Bell*. Three occurrences are the last names *Bellwood*, *Bellingham*, and *Bell*; the other is an address on *Bellflower Circle*.

4. Click the *Match entire cell contents* check box, and click Find Next.

The first cell containing only the letters *Bell* becomes the active cell. You can achieve the same result by clicking *$B$18* in the Cell column or *Bell* in the Value column at the bottom of the dialog box.

5. Close the Find and Replace dialog box, and change the day to mow from *Tues* to **Weds** for customer Sandy Bell.
6. Save your changes to the *ee2-p2challenge* workbook.

4. Creating a Custom Template from a Built-in Template

You discover that the built-in templates provided by Excel include a sales invoice. The only change needed to meet your needs is the addition of your company's name at the top of the invoice.

To modify the Sales Invoice template, and save it as a custom template, follow these steps:

1. Display the New Workbook task pane, and choose General Templates.
2. Select the Spreadsheet Solutions tab, and select the Sales Invoice template.

The built-in Sales Invoice template opens. Excel assigns the name Sales Invoice1 in the title bar.

3. Double-click the italicized phrase *Insert Company Information Here* at the top of the Sales Invoice.
4. Type **Your Name & Associates** (substitute your own full name in place of *Your Name*).
5. Press [Alt]+[↵Enter] to enter a second line of text in the same cell.
6. Type **1234 Village Way**, and press [Alt]+[↵Enter].
7. Enter two more lines of text in the same cell—a city, state, and zip code of your choice on the third line, and (800)999-9999 on the fourth line.
8. Save the file as a template named **myinvoice** (save to the folder in which you are saving the files you create in this book).

Make sure that you select Template in the Save as type drop-down list at the bottom of the Save As dialog box.

9. Experiment with adding data to the invoice as desired, and close the custom template without saving the data entered.

Discovery Zone exercises require advanced knowledge of topics presented in *essentials* lessons, application of skills from multiple lessons, or self-directed learning of new skills.

Before beginning your first Project 2 Discovery Zone exercise, complete the following steps:

1. Open the file named *ee2-0204*, and immediately save it as `ee2-p2discovery`.
   The *ee2-p2discovery* workbook contains three sheets: an overview, and two exercise sheets named #1-Style and #2-Weekly Pay.
2. Select the Overview worksheet to view the organization of the Project 2 Discovery Zone Exercises workbook.

Each exercise is independent of the other, so you may complete the exercises in any order. Be sure to save the workbook after completing each exercise. If you need a paper copy of the completed exercise, enter your name centered in a header before printing. Other print options have already been set to print compressed to one page and to display the filename, sheet name, and current date in a footer.

Be sure to save your changes and close the workbook if you need more than one work session to complete the desired exercises. Then, continue working on *ee2-p2discovery* instead of starting over again on the original *ee2-0204* file.

1. Creating and Applying a Style

Open the *ee2-p2discovery* workbook, if necessary, and create a style in the worksheet named #1-Style. The style should apply a thick blue outline border, a light yellow fill, wrap text, right-alignment, and Arial Bold Italic 12 point font to selected cells. Name the style `combo1`. Apply the style to the labels in B10:D10. Adjust the height of row 10 as desired, and save your changes.

2. Moving a Workbook and Creating a Template

Move the #2-Weekly Pay worksheet in the *ee2-p2discovery* workbook to a blank workbook. Prepare the moved worksheet for repeated use by making the following changes. Apply a Classic 2 AutoFormat to the range A10:D20, delete the Hours Worked data in C11:C20, and delete the date in cell B8. Widen columns B through D and then decrease the height of row 10. Save the worksheet as a template named `Weekly Pay` in the same location as your other student solution files.

Documenting and Protecting Worksheets and Workbooks

Objectives

In this project, you learn how to

✔ Create and Use Range Names
✔ Attach Comments to a Cell
✔ Get Help on Protection Features in Excel
✔ Protect Cell Contents and Objects
✔ Unlock Cells and Objects
✔ View and Set File Properties
✔ Set a Password for a Worksheet Range
✔ Set a Password for a Workbook

Key terms in this project include

❑ comment
❑ comment indicator
❑ file property
❑ password
❑ range name
❑ read-only
❑ unlock
❑ write access

Why Would I Do This?

Excel provides a variety of features that you can use to document and protect your work. For example, you can assign a name to a cell or range of cells and then use that name instead of a cell reference in a formula. User-specified comments can be added to any cell. You can unlock only the cells for which content might change, and prevent editing or deleting the contents of any other cells. You can also require a password to view a worksheet range or open a workbook.

Visual Summary

In this project, you first work with creating and using English-like names for one or more cells. You enter a formula that includes the name num_of_copies instead of a reference to cell B6 (see Figure 3.1). You continue documenting a worksheet by attaching comments to cells.

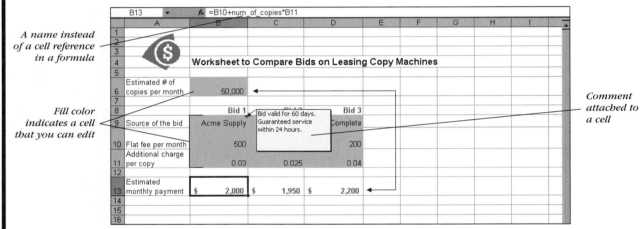

A name instead of a cell reference in a formula

Fill color indicates a cell that you can edit

Comment attached to a cell

Figure 3.1

In the next two lessons you learn to apply cell protection appropriately. You specify the cells that a user can edit (refer to the cells with color fill in Figure 3.1), and prevent changes to other cells. Remaining topics include specifying workbook properties and setting passwords.

Lesson 1: Creating and Using Range Names

A ***range name*** is an English-like name applied to a cell or range of cells. The most common use for a range name is to make a formula easier to read and understand. You can also move the cell pointer to another section of a large worksheet by specifying the name assigned to that section instead of a cell reference.

A name must start with a letter or an underscore. The rest of the name can include numbers and letters up to a maximum of 255 characters. Spaces are not allowed, but you can use underscore characters and periods to separate words.

In this lesson, you specify two range names: one to use in a formula and the other to identify a section of the worksheet. You then include one defined name in a formula and use the other to go to the named location in the worksheet.

To Create and Use Range Names

1 **Open the *ee2-0301* file, and save it as** protection**.**
The file contains a single worksheet named *Copy Bids.*

2 **Click cell B6, and click the Name box at the left end of the formula bar.**

3 **Type** num_of_copies **in the Name box, and press** ⏎Enter**.**
The name *num_of_copies* is assigned to cell B6 (see Figure 3.2).

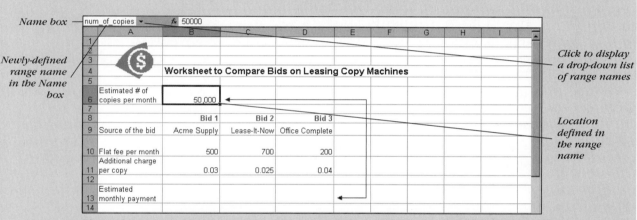

Figure 3.2

4 **Select the range A20:A34, and click the Name box at the left end of the formula bar.**

5 **Type** ContactVendor **in the Name box, and press** ⏎Enter**.**
The name *ContactVendor* is assigned to the range A20:A34. Now enter a formula to calculate the first bid.

6 **In cell B13, use the type-and-point method to enter the formula** =B10+B6*B11**, and make cell B13 the active cell.**
When you click a cell reference instead of typing it as you create a formula, Excel displays its associated range name instead of the row-and-column reference (see the range name *num_of_copies* representing cell B6 in Figure 3.3).

(Continues)

To Create and Use Range Names (Continued)

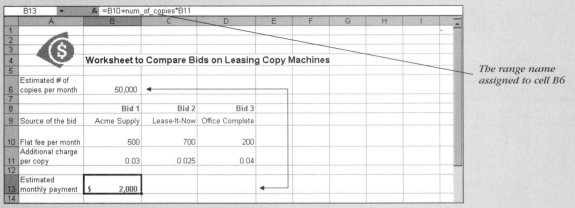

Figure 3.3

If you have problems...

If B6 displays in the formula instead of *num_of_copies*, you typed the reference to cell B6 instead of clicking cell B6.

❼ Copy the formula in cell B13 to the range C13:D13.

The monthly payments for Bid 2 and Bid 3 are $1,950 and $2,200, respectively. The formula copies correctly because a range name uses absolute cell references.

❽ Choose Edit, Go To (or press F5).

The Go To dialog box opens (see Figure 3.4).

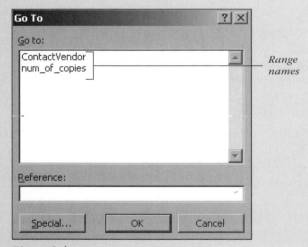

Figure 3.4

❾ Click ContactVendor, and click OK.

The worksheet display shifts to the range containing vendor contact information.

❿ Click any cell to deselect the highlighted range A20:A34, and save your changes to the *protection* workbook.

Keep the *protection* workbook open for the next lesson, or close the workbook and exit Excel.

To extend your knowledge...

Deleting a Range Name

You can delete a range name using a three-step process. Select the command sequence Insert, Name, Define, select the name to delete from the list that appears in the Define Name dialog box, and then click the Delete button.

Documenting Range Names

If you want to find out what a name refers to without moving the cell pointer to the defined location, select the command sequence Insert, Name, Define, and select the name. Its associated range displays in the Refers to text box in the Define Name dialog box.

You can also create a two-column list of range names and associated ranges in the worksheet. Select a cell to be the upper-left cell in a blank area large enough to hold the list; then select the command sequence Insert, Name, Paste. Complete the process by clicking the Paste List button in the lower-left corner of the Paste Name dialog box.

Lesson 2: Attaching Comments to a Cell

You can easily attach a comment to any cell in an Excel worksheet. A **comment** is an annotation attached to a cell that displays within a box whenever the mouse pointer rests on the cell. If a comment has been attached, you see the **comment indicator**—a small red triangle—in the cell's upper-right corner. Use the comment feature when you want supplementary information available, but not visible all the time.

You can alter the size of the comment box by dragging the handles on its sides and corners. You can also move a comment, change its text font or color, and hide or display comments and their indicators. The Page Setup dialog box includes options to print comments below the worksheet or where they are displayed on the worksheet.

In this lesson, you set a View option to display only comment indicators. You then create and view three comments, one for each vendor providing a bid for leasing copy machines.

To Attach Comments to a Cell

❶ Open the *protection* workbook, if necessary, and choose Tools, Options.
The Options dialog box opens.

❷ Select the View tab.
The View tab includes four sections: Show, Comments, Objects, and Window options.

❸ Make sure that *Comment indicator only* is selected in the Comments section, and click OK.

❹ Click cell B9.
The cell containing *Acme Supply* is selected. Acme is the provider of the first bid.

❺ Select Insert, Comment.
Excel displays a comment box. An arrow extends from the upper-left corner of the box to the comment indicator in cell B9.

❻ Delete existing text in the box, if any, and type the following comment:
Bid valid for 60 days. Guaranteed service within 24 hours.

❼ Click outside the box to deselect it.

(Continues)

To Attach Comments to a Cell (Continued)

8 **Position the mouse pointer on cell B9.**
The newly created comment displays (see Figure 3.5).

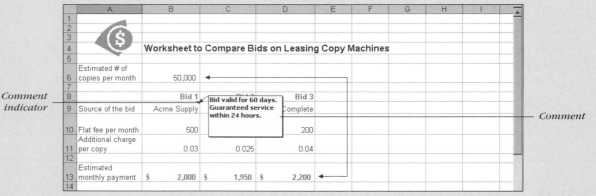

Comment indicator

Comment

Figure 3.5

9 **Click cell C9, and repeat the previous steps to create the following comment:**
`Started business 6 months ago. Bid valid for 30 days. Same-day ser-`
`vice if call before noon.`

10 **Click cell D9, and repeat the previous steps to create the following comment (also drag a sizing handle to enlarge the box as necessary):**
`Bid valid for 30 days. Promises service within 4 hours but has not`
`been reliable in the past.`

11 **Select View, Comments.**
The three comments and the Reviewing toolbar display. You can click Next Comment or Previous Comment on the Reviewing toolbar to scroll through the comments.

12 **Select View, Comments again to remove display of the comments.**

13 **Close the Reviewing toolbar, and save your changes to the *protection* workbook.**
Keep the *protection* workbook open for the next lesson, or close the workbook and exit Excel.

To extend your knowledge…

Editing and Deleting Comments

Right-clicking a cell with an attached comment displays a shortcut menu. Select Edit Comment to revise the text in a comment. Select Delete Comment to remove the comment entirely.

If you want to remove all comments, select Go To on the Edit menu, click the Special button, click Comments, and click OK. This highlights all cells with attached comments; then select Edit, Clear, Comments.

Printing Comments

You can print comments by selecting File, Page Setup and accessing the Sheet tab. Select the Comments drop-down list, and select *At end of sheet* or *As displayed on sheet*. Click OK.

Lesson 3: Getting Help on Protection Features in Excel

Excel provides a wide variety of protection features that enable you to control accessing or editing worksheets and workbooks. Use onscreen Help to get an overview of the protection features.

To Get Help on Protection Features in Excel

1 **Open the *protection* workbook, if necessary; then type** protection **in the Ask a Question box, and press** ⏎Enter**).**
Help topics associated with the phrase *protection* display in the Ask a Question drop-down list (see Figure 3.6).

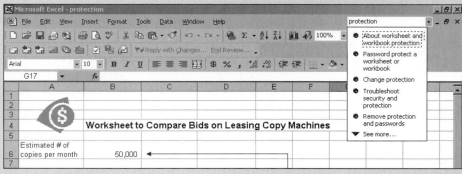

Figure 3.6

2 **Select *About Worksheet and Workbook Protection*.**
A window titled Microsoft Excel Help opens.

3 **Read the short introductory paragraphs about *Worksheet Protection* and *Workbook-level Protection*.**

4 **Click the blue link titled *Protecting worksheet elements*, and scroll to view the related information.**

5 **Click the blue link titled *Protecting workbook elements and files*, and scroll to view the related information.**

6 **Display the Contents tab, if necessary; then click and read other topics listed in the *Workbook and Worksheet Protection* subtopic under *Security* on the Contents tab.**

7 **When you finish, close the Help window.**
Keep the *protection* workbook open for the next lesson, or close the workbook and exit Excel.

Lesson 4: Protecting Cell Contents and Objects

If you protect the contents of a worksheet, you cannot make changes to cell contents or objects unless you unlock them before activating protection. Excel also prevents viewing hidden rows or columns and making changes to items on chart sheets. You cannot add or edit comments, move or size objects, or make any changes in formatting.

Protection is an option on the <u>T</u>ools menu. In this lesson, you protect an entire worksheet and then attempt to modify the worksheet—changing cell contents, moving an object, applying a different color, and selecting another font style—all without success. You then remove the worksheet protection. In the next lesson, you learn how to unlock selected cells and objects, and protect remaining elements.

To Protect Cell Contents and Objects

1 **Open the *protection* workbook, if necessary, and select <u>T</u>ools, <u>P</u>rotection, <u>P</u>rotect Sheet.**
The Protect Sheet dialog box displays (see Figure 3.7).

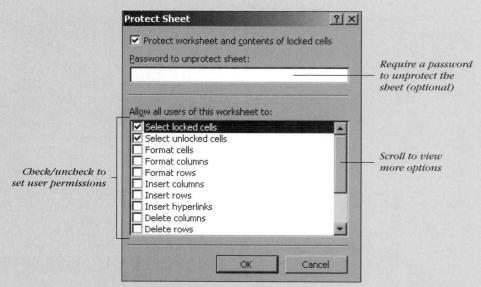

Require a password to unprotect the sheet (optional)

Check/uncheck to set user permissions

Scroll to view more options

Figure 3.7

2 **Click OK.**
All worksheet elements are protected. Now try to change the contents of cell B6.

3 **Click cell B6, and start to type 40000.**
As soon as you type the 4, a message states that the cell is protected. Now try moving an object.

4 **Click OK to close the message, and click within the $ sign image at the upper-left corner of the worksheet.**
Sizing handles do not appear. You cannot select the object because it is protected.

5 **Select the range B8:D8, and display the Font Color drop-down list in the toolbar.**
A grid of sample squares displays without any colors, indicating that you cannot apply a color change.

6 **Display the Font drop-down list and then select Times New Roman.**
You are able to make the selection, but the new font style is not applied because the selected cells are protected.

7 **Deselect any selected items, and save your changes to the *protection* workbook.**
Keep the *protection* workbook open for the next lesson, or close the workbook and exit Excel.

Lesson 5: Unlocking Cells and Objects

In the previous lesson, you protected every worksheet element. In some situations, however, you may need to unlock cells or objects that you are likely to change. As a general guideline, all formulas, and most labels and objects, should remain locked. Cells containing numbers are generally unlocked.

When you **unlock** a cell or object, you remove the default locked setting that prevents change when worksheet protection is active. Unlocking a cell requires a four-step process—select the cell(s), open the Format Cells dialog box, select the Protection tab, and clear the <u>L</u>ocked check box. The steps to unlock an object are similar; only the dialog box varies.

In this lesson, you disable worksheet protection, unlock several cells and an object, and restore worksheet protection.

To Unlock Cells and Objects

1 **Open the** *protection* **workbook, if necessary, and select <u>T</u>ools, <u>P</u>rotection, <u>U</u>nprotect Sheet.**
Worksheet protection is disabled. Now unlock the cells you want to be able to change—estimated # of copies in cell B6, and vendor data in the range B9:D11.

2 **Click cell B6, press and hold down** Ctrl**, select the range B9:D11, and release** Ctrl**.**

3 **Select F<u>o</u>rmat, C<u>e</u>lls; then select the Protection tab (see Figure 3.8).**

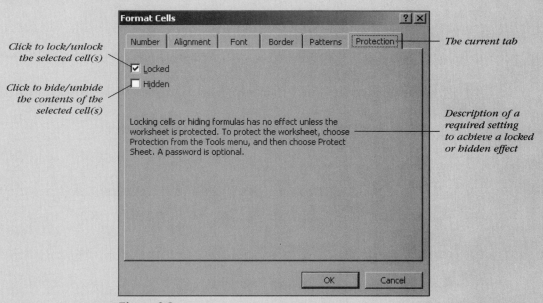

Figure 3.8

4 **Click the box in front of <u>L</u>ocked to clear the check mark, and click OK.**
Cells B6 and B9 through D11 are unlocked; they remain selected.

5 **Apply a Tan fill color to the selected cells.**
Shading unlocked cells before protecting a worksheet provides a visual means to identify cells that users can change. Now unlock the $ sign object just below cell A1.

6 **Right-click the $ sign object, select Format P<u>i</u>cture from the shortcut menu, and select the Protection tab in the Format Picture dialog box (see Figure 3.9).**

(Continues)

To Unlock Cells and Objects (Continued)

The selected object

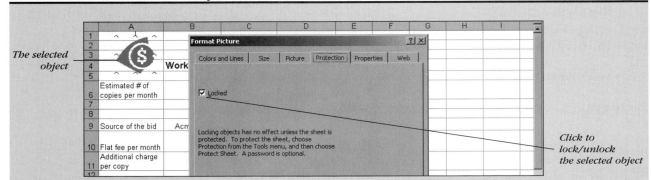

Click to lock/unlock the selected object

Figure 3.9

⑦ Click the box in front of <u>L</u>ocked to clear the check mark; then click OK, and click outside the object to deselect it.
The $ sign object is unlocked. Now activate worksheet protection, and try again to make changes.

⑧ Select <u>T</u>ools, <u>P</u>rotection, <u>P</u>rotect Sheet; then leave the Password text box blank, and click OK.
Worksheet protection is active for all locked cells. Now make sure that you can access unlocked cells as well as the unlocked object.

⑨ Enter 40000 in cell B6.
Excel accepts the change because you unlocked cell B6 before enabling worksheet protection. The revised values for estimated monthly payments display in row 13—*$1,700* for bids 1 and 2, and *$1,800* for bid 3.

⑩ Press Tab↹ repeatedly.
You can press Tab↹ to move the cell pointer from one unlocked cell to the next in a protected worksheet.

⑪ Click the $ sign object.
Sizing handles indicate the object is selected. You can work with the object because you unlocked it before activating worksheet protection.

⑫ Deselect the object, and save your changes to the *protection* workbook.
Keep the *protection* workbook open for the next lesson, or close the workbook and exit Excel.

To extend your knowledge...

Protecting a Workbook

Excel enables you to protect workbooks as well as worksheets within workbooks. After selecting the two-command sequence <u>T</u>ools, <u>P</u>rotection, select Protect <u>W</u>orkbook instead of <u>P</u>rotect Sheet.

Protection at this level applies to structure and windows. If you protect structure, users cannot view hidden worksheets. They also cannot insert, delete, move, hide, or rename worksheets. If you protect a workbook's windows, users cannot move, resize, hide, unhide, or close windows.

Lesson 6: Viewing and Setting File Properties

The term *file property* describes a characteristic of a file such as file type, file size, storage location, author's name, and date last revised. You can view the properties of the active workbook by selecting File, Properties and choosing one of five tabs in the Properties dialog box: General, Summary, Statistics, Contents, and Custom. You can also view the properties of any Microsoft Excel or Office file through the Open dialog box.

In this lesson, you display the Properties dialog box, view assorted information, and specify your name as the author of the current workbook.

To View and Set File Properties

1 **Open the *protection* workbook, if necessary, and then select File, Properties.**
The Properties dialog box opens.

2 **Select the General tab.**
Excel displays information about the current workbook's name, type, location, and size. You also see the equivalent MS-DOS name (restricted to eight characters) and the dates created, modified, and accessed.

3 **Select the Summary tab, and delete any existing text (see Figure 3.10).**

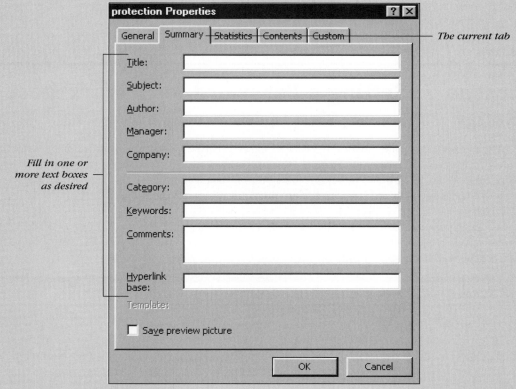

Figure 3.10

4 **Click within the Author text box, and type your name.**

(Continues)

To View and Set File Properties (Continued)

5 **Click the Statistics tab.**
Excel displays information about key dates and editing time.

6 **Click the Contents tab.**
Excel lists the worksheets and named ranges in the workbook.

7 **Click the Custom tab.**
You can use the Custom tab to set up one or more information items in the Name list.

8 **Click OK.**
The Properties dialog box closes, and revised settings are in effect. If you click the Cancel button or the dialog box's Close button instead of OK, any revisions to settings are not saved.

9 **Save and close the *protection* workbook.**
You can continue with the next lesson or exit Excel.

To extend your knowledge…

Viewing the Properties of Any Workbook

In this lesson, you viewed the properties of the active workbook. You can also view the properties of any workbook from the Open dialog box. Select Open from the File menu, display the folder containing the file you want to review, and click the filename to select it (but do not click the Open button yet). Click the Tools button in the Open dialog box menu bar and select Properties.

Lesson 7: Setting a Password for a Worksheet Range

A ***password*** is a collection of up to 255 case-sensitive characters that must be known to use a password-protected range, worksheet, or workbook. It can contain any combination of letters, numbers, spaces, and symbols. Make sure that you choose a password you can remember, because you cannot access a password-protected element without specifying it.

You can require a password to open or edit a workbook, access a worksheet, or make changes to a range within a worksheet. In this lesson, you password-protect a range—the vendor-specific data in a worksheet that compares bids on providing copier service.

To Set a Password for a Worksheet Range

1 **Open the *ee2-0302* file, and save it as** rangecode.
The *rangecode* file consists of a single worksheet named Copy Bids. The worksheet reflects the content and settings developed in Lessons 1 through 6 with one exception. In this worksheet, the cells containing vendor data in the range B9:D11 are locked. Cell B6 is the only unlocked cell, and worksheet protection is turned on.

2 **Select Tools, Protection, Unprotect Sheet.**
Worksheet protection is disabled. Now select the range of locked cells that you want to be accessible if a password is supplied.

3 **Select the range B9:D11.**
The range containing vendor-specific data is selected.

To Set a Password for a Worksheet Range

4 **Select Tools, Protection, Allow Users to Edit Ranges.**
The Allow Users to Edit Ranges dialog box opens.

5 **Click the New button in the dialog box.**
The New Range dialog box opens.

6 **Type Bids in the Title text box, and type 123change in the Range password text box.**
Excel displays an asterisk for each character in the password you specify (see Figure 3.11).

Enter a name for the password-protected range

Enter the range to password-protect

Specify a password

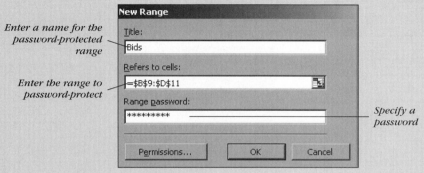

Figure 3.11

7 **Make sure that your specifications match those in Figure 3.11, and click OK.**
The Confirm Password dialog box opens.

8 **Type 123change in the Reenter password to proceed text box, and click OK.**
The Allow Users to Edit Ranges dialog box displays the newly-defined range (see Figure 3.12). Now restore worksheet protection from within the current dialog box.

Defined range

Click to modify a selected range

Click to delete a selected range

Click to enable worksheet protection

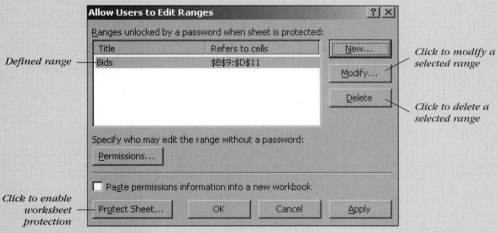

Figure 3.12

(Continues)

To Set a Password for a Worksheet Range (Continued)

9 **Click the Protect Sheet button in the lower-left corner of the dialog box.**
The Protect Sheet dialog box opens.

10 **Click OK to restore protection without setting a password at the worksheet level.**
Worksheet protection is enabled. Now try making a change to vendor data.

11 **Click cell B10, and start to type 600.**
The Unlock Range dialog box displays (see Figure 3.13). You must enter a password or you cannot continue with the edit.

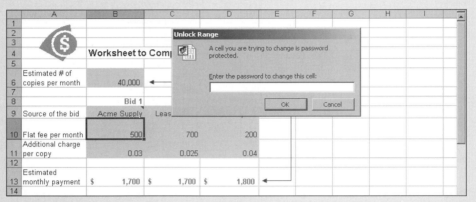

Figure 3.13

12 **Type 123change in the *Enter the password to change this cell* text box, and click OK.**

13 **Type 600 in cell B10, and press ⏎Enter.**
Excel accepts the change because you supplied the correct password. The revised value for the Bid 1 estimated monthly payment is *$1,800*.

14 **Save and close the *rangecode* workbook.**
Continue with the last lesson, or exit Excel.

To extend your knowledge...

Giving Specific Users Access to Protected Cells

If you are using the Windows 2000 (or later) operating system, you can enable specific users to edit locked cells in a protected worksheet without specifying a password. Use the Permissions button in the Allow Users to Edit Ranges dialog box to identify the users (refer to Figure 3.12).

Lesson 8: Setting a Password for a Workbook

Excel supports password protection of a workbook at two levels: opening a workbook, and editing a workbook (see Figure 3.14). Each is independent of the other; you can set either one or both. Password protection is set up during execution of a Save As command.

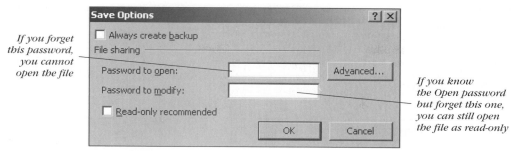

If you forget this password, you cannot open the file

If you know the Open password but forget this one, you can still open the file as read-only

Figure 3.14

If a password is required to open a workbook but you don't know the password, you cannot access the file. If you can access a password-protected workbook but a password is required to modify it, you can at least open the file as read-only if you don't know the modify password. A ***read-only*** file can be viewed but not changed if you save it under the same name. You can, however, modify it if you save it under a different name or save it to a different location.

In this lesson, you set up one password to open a workbook and another to modify that workbook. Because you are just learning this feature, you use a different file from the ones you used in previous lessons. That way, if you inadvertently set up a password to open a file that doesn't match the one in the instructions, and you can't remember what you typed, you can start the lesson over at step 1.

To Set a Password for a Workbook

❶ Open the *ee2-0303* file, and immediately save it as bookcode**.**
The *bookcode* file consists of a single worksheet named Copy Bids. The worksheet reflects the content and settings developed in Lessons 1 through 6. Cell B6 and cells in the range B9:D11 are unlocked. Worksheet protection is turned on.

❷ Choose <u>F</u>ile, Save As, and click the small arrow to the right of Too<u>l</u>s near the upper-right corner of the dialog box.
The Too<u>l</u>s drop-down list displays.

❸ Select <u>G</u>eneral Options.
The Save Options dialog box opens (refer to Figure 3.14).

❹ Type abc123 **in the Password to <u>o</u>pen text box.**
Be sure to type in the first text box, and type the letters in the password in lowercase.

❺ Type xyz999 **in the Password to <u>m</u>odify text box.**
Be sure to type in the second text box, and type the letters in the password in lowercase.

❻ Click OK.
The Confirm Password dialog box opens, with a message to reenter the password to proceed (which is the same as the password to open).

❼ Type abc123 **in the text box, and click OK.**
The Confirm Password dialog box displays again, with a message to reenter the password to modify.

❽ Type xyz999 **in the text box, and click OK.**

❾ Save the file again, and close the workbook.
The workbook is saved with password protection at two levels. Now verify that the passwords work as intended.

❿ Open the *bookcode* workbook.
The Password dialog box opens with a message that the file is protected.

(Continues)

To Set a Password for a Workbook (Continued)

⑪ Type abc123 in the Password text box, and click OK.
The Password dialog box displays again with a message to enter the password for write access or open as read-only. *Write access* means you can modify a file.

If you have problems…
If you do not enter the correct password to open the file, which should be abc123, Excel displays a message that the password supplied is not correct. Repeat the process to open the password-protected file and supply the correct password (be sure to use the same capitalization as when you set up the password). If you still have problems, start the lesson over.

⑫ Type xyz999 as the password for write access, and click OK.
The Copy Bids worksheet in the *bookcode* file displays onscreen.

If you have problems…
If you enter text other than xyz999, Excel displays a message that the password supplied is not correct. If you cannot remember the modify password, you can open the file as read-only and make changes as long as you save it under another name.

⑬ Close the *bookcode* workbook.
This concludes Project 3. You can continue with end-of-project exercises, or exit Excel.

To extend your knowledge…

Changing or Removing a Password

To change or remove a password, start the process to set up a password—that is, select Save As from the File menu, display the Tools drop-down list, and select General Options. This displays current passwords in the Save Options dialog box. To change a password, select (highlight) the existing password and type a new one. To remove a password, select the existing password and press Del.

Summary

In this project, you worked with a variety of ways to document and protect worksheets and workbooks. To document your work, you assigned names to one or more cells, attached comments to cells, and entered summary information as part of the file's properties. You used two approaches to protect your work—one at the cell level and the other at the workbook level. At the cell level, you unlocked cells you wanted to be able to change, and then enabled protection for all other cells in the worksheet. You also set up password protection for a range of cells. At the file level, you set up different passwords to open and to modify the workbook.

To expand your learning, try variations of the documentation and protection techniques. Set up an entire formula using range names instead of cell references. Experiment with screen display of comments depending on which of three options you pick in the Comments section of the Options dialog box (Tools, Options, View tab). Include in a file's properties one or two keywords to describe the work-book, and then learn how to search for the file based on keywords. Change or modify an existing password. Don't forget to use the extensive onscreen Help feature to support your efforts.

Checking Concepts and Terms

Multiple Choice

Circle the letter of the correct answer for each of the following.

1. A range name [L1]

   a. displays when you position the mouse pointer on a cell

   b. must start with a letter or underscore

   c. cannot include numbers

   d. none of the above

2. Which of the following is not a valid statement relating to comments? [L2]

   a. Right-clicking a cell with an attached comment displays a shortcut menu through which you can edit or delete the comment.

   b. A small red triangle in a cell's upper-right corner indicates that a comment is attached to the cell.

   c. You can alter the size of a comment box.

   d. You can view comments attached to cells, but you cannot print them.

3. To permit changing the contents of some cells, but prevent changing the contents of other cells, _____. [L5]

   a. enable worksheet protection, and unlock the cells subject to change

   b. set a worksheet password

   c. unlock the cells subject to change, and enable worksheet protection

   d. Either A or B

4. A password protecting an Excel range, worksheet, or workbook _____. [L7]

   a. is case-sensitive

   b. can contain any combination of letters, numbers, spaces, and symbols up to 255 characters

   c. Both A and B

   d. Neither A nor B

5. Which of the following describes a file that can be viewed but not changed if you save it under the same name? [L8]

   a. read-only

   b. write access

   c. locked

   d. none of the above

Discussion

1. You can use the *Allow all users of this worksheet to* section in the Protect Sheet dialog box to turn on or off each listed modification in a protected worksheet. List at least ten settings that you can turn on or off. [L4]

2. Use onscreen Help to learn about protecting charts. Describe how to protect an embedded chart versus a chart sheet. Explain the changes, if any, to a protected chart if you change the data on which the chart is based.

3. Review the worksheet shown in Figure 3.15. The worksheet is a planning tool for a party. The amounts for number of attendees, and costs of food per person, site rental, invitations, decorations, film, gift, and cake are all estimates and still subject to change. You feel confident, however, that you have set up the calculations correctly and that you have not forgotten any cost category. You want to protect the worksheet cells but still have the flexibility to change estimated costs. Which cells would you unlock and why? [L5]

B16		=	=B3*B4+B5*B6								
	A	B	C	D	E	F	G	H	I	J	
1	**Aunt Marie's 90th Birthday Celebration**										
2											
3	# of children	33									
4	Food cost per child	4.50									
5	# of adults	68									
6	Food cost per adult	8.00									
7											
8	Target Budget	1,200									
9											
10	Site rental	150									
11	Invitations/stamps	15									
12	Decorations/paper products	120									
13	Film/Developing	75									
14	Gift	100									
15	Decorated cake	35									
16	Food (includes beverages)	693									
17	Total expected costs	1,188									
18											
19											

Figure 3.15

Skill Drill

Skill Drill exercises reinforce project skills. Each skill that is reinforced is the same, or nearly the same, as a skill presented in the project. Detailed instructions are provided in a step-by-step format.

Before beginning your first Project 3 Skill Drill exercise, complete the following steps:

  1. Open the file named *ee2-0304*, and immediately save it as **ee2-p3drill**.
    The workbook contains an overview sheet and four exercise sheets labeled #1-Name, #2-Protect, #3-AutoShape, and #4-Comment.
  2. Click the Overview sheet to view the organization and content of the Project 3 Skill Drill Exercises workbook.

There are six exercises, four of which use worksheets in the *ee2-p3drill* workbook. The #5 and #6 Skill Drill exercises are not based on worksheet data. Each exercise is independent of the others, so you may complete the exercises in any order. However, once you complete Exercise #6 that sets a password to open the workbook, you must supply that password whenever you open the workbook again. The password is **drill3**.

Be sure to save the workbook after completing each exercise. If you need a paper copy of the completed exercise, enter your name centered in a header before printing. Other print options have already been set to print compressed and to display the filename, sheet name, and current date in a footer.

Be sure to save your changes and close the workbook if you need more than one work session to complete the desired exercises; then, continue working on *ee2-p3drill* instead of starting over again on the original *ee2-0304* file.

1. Creating a Range Name and Using It in a Formula

One formula must still be entered in a worksheet that budgets quarterly revenue for the year 2003. The formula calculates the average quarterly revenue expected in a "best case" scenario. You decide to assign a name to the range of cells to average, and use the range name in the formula.

To create a range name and use it in a formula, follow these steps:

1. If necessary, open the *ee2-p3drill* workbook. If prompted for a password, enter **drill3**.
2. Select the worksheet named #1-Name.
3. Select the range B14:E14, and click the Name box at the left end of the formula bar.
4. Type **QtrRev** and then press **↵Enter**.
   The name *QtrRev* is assigned to the range B14:E14.
5. Enter **=average(QtrRev)** in cell A16, and make cell A16 the current cell.
   The amount *487275* displays in cell A16, and *=AVERAGE(QtrRev)* displays in the formula bar.
6. Format cell A16 to Comma, zero decimal places.
7. Save your changes to the *ee2-p3drill* workbook.

2. Protecting Formulas and Labels

You completed a worksheet that budgets quarterly revenue for the year 2003. Now you want to apply worksheet protection appropriately. You decide that you want to be able to change only the numbers used as revenue projections.

To unlock the cells subject to change, and protect the rest of the worksheet—the labels, the formulas, and the AutoShape describing the scenario—follow these steps:

1. If necessary, open the *ee2-p3drill* workbook. If prompted for a password, enter **drill3**.
2. Select the #2-Protect worksheet.
3. Select the range B10:E12, and choose Format, Cells.
4. Select the Protection tab in the Format Cells dialog box.
5. Click the Locked check box to remove the check mark.
6. Click OK, apply a Light Yellow fill to the range B10:E12, and deselect the range.
   Applying a fill color is not required, but it does help to show a user which cells are unlocked.
7. Select Tools, Protection, Protect Sheet; then click OK without specifying a password.
8. Make sure that you can change any estimated quarterly revenue in the range B10:E12, and undo each change.
9. Make sure that you cannot select the AutoShape, change a label, or change a formula.
10. Save your changes to the *ee2-p3drill* workbook.

3. Unlocking an AutoShape

You unlocked cells containing numbers in a budget worksheet, and protected the rest of the worksheet. Now you decide that the AutoShape needs to be unlocked as well, so that you can edit its description (such as changing it from "Best Case" Scenario to "Worst Case" Scenario).

To turn protection off, unlock the AutoShape, and then turn protection back on, follow these steps:

1. If necessary, open the *ee2-p3drill* workbook. If prompted for a password, enter **drill3**.
2. Select the worksheet named #3-AutoShape.
3. Select Tools, Protection, Unprotect Sheet.
4. Click within the star-shaped AutoShape, and right-click the border that appears around the star-shaped AutoShape.
   The sizing handles display. You can select the object because protection is turned off.

5. Select Format Aut<u>o</u>Shape from the shortcut menu.

6. Select the Protection tab in the Format AutoShape dialog box, and click the <u>L</u>ocked check box to remove the check mark.

7. Click the Lock <u>t</u>ext check box to remove the check mark, click OK, and deselect the AutoShape.

8. Select <u>T</u>ools, <u>P</u>rotection, <u>P</u>rotect Sheet; then click OK without specifying a password.

9. Make sure that you can select the AutoShape and change its text, even though protection is turned on again.

10. Save your changes to the *ee2-p3drill* workbook.

4. Adding, Editing, and Deleting a Comment

You decide to modify documentation for a budget worksheet by adding, editing, and deleting comments. Follow these steps:

1. If necessary, open the *ee2-p3drill* workbook. If prompted for a password, enter `drill3`.

2. Select the worksheet named #4-Comment.

3. Click cell B10, and select <u>I</u>nsert, Co<u>m</u>ment.

4. Delete any existing text in the comment box, type `Net of seasonal discounts`, and click outside the comment box.

5. Right-click cell E12, and select <u>E</u>dit Comment from the shortcut menu.

6. Change *Christmas sales* to `Holiday sales` in the comment box, and click outside the box.

7. Right-click cell A16, and select Delete Co<u>m</u>ment from the shortcut menu.

8. Save your changes to the *ee2-p3drill* workbook.

5. Viewing the Properties of an Unopened Excel Workbook

You decide to view the properties of an unopened workbook while working in Excel. Follow these steps:

1. Choose <u>F</u>ile, <u>O</u>pen.

2. Display the folder containing the student files for this project.

3. Click *ee2-0301* (but do not click the Open button).

4. Select Too<u>l</u>s in the Open dialog box menu bar, and select <u>P</u>roperties from the drop-down list.

5. View the information on the General, Summary, Statistics, and Contents tabs.

6. Close the Properties dialog box.

7. Click *ee2-0302* (but do not click the Open button).

8. Select Too<u>l</u>s in the Open dialog box menu bar, and select <u>P</u>roperties from the drop-down list.

9. View the information on the General, Summary, Statistics, and Contents tabs.

10. Close the Properties dialog box.

11. View the properties for any other unopened file as desired, and close the Open dialog box.

6. Setting a Password to Open a Workbook

You want to set a password to open the *ee2-p3drill* workbook. Follow these steps:

1. Open the *ee2-p3drill* workbook, if necessary.

2. Choose <u>F</u>ile, Save <u>A</u>s, and click the small arrow to the right of Too<u>l</u>s near the upper-right corner of the dialog box.
   The Too<u>l</u>s drop-down list displays.

3. Select <u>G</u>eneral Options to display the Save Options dialog box.

4. Type `drill3` in the Password to <u>o</u>pen text box.
   Be sure to type in the first text box, and type the letters in the password in lowercase.

5. Click OK.
   The Confirm Password dialog box opens with a message to reenter the password to proceed (which is the same as the password to open).

6. Type `drill3` and then click OK.

7. Click <u>S</u>ave in the Save As dialog box.

8. If the message displays that *ee2-p3drill* already exists, click <u>Y</u>es to replace the file.

Challenge

Challenge exercises expand on or are somewhat related to skills that are presented in the lessons. Each exercise provides a brief narrative introduction, followed by instructions in a numbered-step format that are not as detailed as those in the Skill Drill section.

Before beginning your first Project 3 Challenge exercise, complete the following steps:

1. Open the file named *ee2-0305*, and immediately save it as `ee2-p3challenge`.

The *ee2-p3challenge* workbook contains five sheets: an overview, and four exercise sheets named #1-DelComments, #2-EditComments, #3-DisplayNames, and #4-DelChart.

2. Click the Overview sheet to view the organization of the Project 3 Challenge Exercises workbook.

Each exercise is independent of the others, so you may complete the exercises in any order. Be sure to save the workbook after completing each exercise. If you need a paper copy of the completed exercise, enter your name centered in a header before printing. Other print options have already been set to print compressed to one page and to display the filename, sheet name, and current date in a footer.

If you need more than one work session to complete the desired exercises, continue working on *ee2-p3challenge* instead of starting over again on the original *ee2-0305* file.

1. Deleting Comments

You decide to delete the comments attached to cells in a worksheet. Follow these steps:

1. Open the *ee2-p3challenge* workbook, if necessary, and select the worksheet named #1-Del-Comments.

2. Right-click cell A15, and select Delete Co<u>m</u>ment from the shortcut menu.

This technique is useful to delete a comment attached to one cell. Now you want to find out how to delete all comments.

3. Enter `delete comments` in the Ask a Question box, and select the topic *Delete comments*.

4. Read the information on removing all comments from a worksheet, and use the technique on the current worksheet.

5. Close the Help window, and save your changes to the *ee2-p3challenge* workbook.

2. Finding and Editing a Comment

You remember attaching a comment that includes the phrase "Expected loss." You decide this is not a comment you want users of the worksheet to see. To find and remove a comment, follow these steps:

1. Open the *ee2-p3challenge* workbook, if necessary, and select the worksheet named #2-Edit-Comments.

2. Change a View setting so that you can see all comments and indicators instead of only the comment indicators.

3. Select the cell that includes the phrase *Expected loss* in its attached comment.

4. Edit that comment to remove the phrase *Expected loss*.

5. Restore the original display so that only the comment indicators appear (that is, a comment should not display unless you position the mouse pointer on a cell with an attached comment). Close the Reviewing toolbar.

6. Save your changes to the *ee2-p3challenge* workbook.

3. Displaying a List of Range Names

You would like to create a list of range names and their definitions in the current worksheet. Follow these steps:

1. Open the *ee2-p3challenge* workbook, if necessary, and select the worksheet named #3-DisplayNames.

2. Position the cell pointer on the upper-left cell of a two-column blank area on the worksheet. The blank area needs to be large enough to display all range names in one column and the associated cell references in the next column.

3. Start the process to insert a range name, and select Paste.

4. Make the remaining selection(s) to create the list.
The worksheet contains five named ranges.

5. Save your changes to the *ee2-p3challenge* workbook.

4. Deleting an Embedded Chart in a Protected Worksheet

You decide to delete an embedded chart, but it is part of a protected worksheet. Follow these steps:

1. Open the *ee2-p3challenge* workbook, if necessary, and select the worksheet named #4-DelChart.

2. Disable worksheet protection.

3. Select the column chart below the monthly data, and delete it.

4. Restore worksheet protection.

5. Save your changes to the *ee2-p3challenge* workbook.

iscovery Zone

Discovery Zone exercises require advanced knowledge of topics presented in *essentials* lessons, application of skills from multiple lessons, or self-directed learning of new skills.

Before beginning your first Project 3 Discovery Zone exercise, complete the following steps:

1. Open the file named *ee2-0306*, and immediately save it as `ee2-p3discovery`.
The *ee2-p3discovery* workbook contains four sheets: an overview, and three exercise sheets named #1-Protect, #2-Chart, and #3-Password.

2. Select the Overview worksheet to view the organization of the Project 3 Discovery Zone Exercises workbook.

Each exercise is independent of the others, so you may complete the exercises in any order. Be sure to save the workbook after completing each exercise. If you need a paper copy of the completed exercise, enter your name centered in a header before printing. Other print options have already been set to print compressed to one page and to display the filename, sheet name, and current date in a footer.

Be sure to save your changes and close the workbook if you need more than one work session to complete the desired exercises. Then, continue working on *ee2-p3discovery* instead of starting over again on the original *ee2-0306* file.

1. Deciding Which Cells to Unlock and Protecting the Rest

You completed a worksheet showing monthly and annual revenues, expenses, net income, and gross profit percentages. Now you want to apply protection to the worksheet. Select the #1-Protect worksheet in the *ee2-p3discovery* workbook, and set up worksheet protection so that you can change only raw numbers, date last revised, and the name of the person who revised it. Apply a light fill color to the unprotected cells.

2. Unlocking an Embedded Chart

You know how to unlock worksheet cells and objects before applying worksheet protection. Now you want to unlock a chart. Unlock the column chart in the #2-Chart sheet in the *ee2-p3discovery* workbook, and apply protection to the rest of the worksheet. (Hint: Select the chart before you select Format on the menu bar.)

3. Password-Protecting a Worksheet

You own and manage a small firm. You created a list of employees that includes a column for last name, a column for first name, and a hidden column with the related wage per hour data. You unlocked cells in the name columns so that your assistant can enter the full name of a new employee. Now you want to enable worksheet protection in the #3-Password worksheet of the *ee2-p3discovery* workbook, but restrict turning that protection off unless a password is provided. Use the password FWFwages.

Integrating Applications

Objectives

In this project, you learn how to

- ✔ Link Excel Data to a Word Document
- ✔ Embed Excel Data in a Word Document
- ✔ Link Excel Data to a PowerPoint Slide
- ✔ Link an Excel Chart to a PowerPoint Slide
- ✔ Import Data from a Text File
- ✔ Import Data from an Access Database

Key terms in this project include

- ❏ destination file
- ❏ embedded object
- ❏ linked object
- ❏ object
- ❏ Object Linking and Embedding (OLE)
- ❏ source file

Why Would I Do This?

One of the advantages of using Office as an integrated set of programs is that any of the programs can refer to data generated by another program. For example, you can insert data from an Excel workbook in a Word document, and continue to use Excel to edit and update the workbook. You can copy an Excel chart to a PowerPoint slide, and import data from an Access database to an Excel file.

Integrating applications is not limited to Microsoft Office programs. You can, for example, import data from a text file or another spreadsheet program.

Visual Summary

In this project, you sample the powerful integrating opportunities available when using Excel. The lessons focus primarily on integrating Excel data with Word, PowerPoint, and Access data. The procedures, however, are basically the same no matter what objects or programs you use.

You begin the project by copying an Excel worksheet to a Word document. You also copy Excel data to a PowerPoint slide (see Figure 4.1), import data from an Access database, and work in Excel with data from a text file.

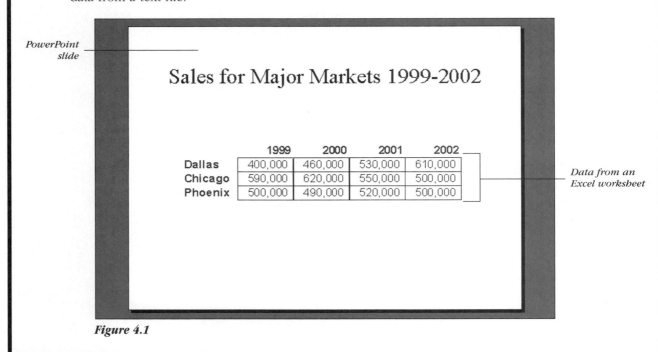

PowerPoint slide

Data from an Excel worksheet

Figure 4.1

Lesson 1: Linking Excel Data to a Word Document

Object Linking and Embedding (OLE) is a method of sharing data that is supported by many different programs, including all Office XP applications. An *object* in this context has properties, and can be referenced and used by another program. In Excel, an object can be as large as an entire workbook, or as small as a worksheet cell. Charts, clip art, and WordArt in an Excel worksheet are also examples of objects.

You can link or embed an object from a source file to a destination file. The file that contains linked or embedded data is called the ***destination file***. The file providing the data to link or embed is the ***source file***. For example, if you copy a section of an Excel worksheet to a Word document, the source file is the Excel workbook and the destination file is the Word document.

A ***linked object*** is an object in a destination file that updates whenever the data in the source file changes. If files are linked, a change in the source file results in the same change in the destination file.

An ***embedded object*** is an object in a destination file that does not update when the data in the source file changes. Changing data in the source file does not change the same data in the destination file.

In this lesson, you link a range of cells containing annual sales data to a sales report in Word. After creating the link you test it by changing data in the worksheet.

To Link Excel Data to a Word Document

1 **Open the Excel workbook *ee2-0401*, and save it as** `SalesData01`.
The file contains worksheet data and a chart. Now copy a range of data to a Word document.

2 **Select cells A3:E6 and then choose** **Edit**, **Copy** **or click the Copy button.**

3 **Start Microsoft Word, open the Word document *ee2-0402*, and save it as**
`SalesReport01`.
The document consists of a title and the opening sentence in a sales report.

4 **Place the insertion point below the single sentence in the document, and choose** **Edit**, **Paste** **Special.**
The Paste Special dialog box opens.

5 **Click the Paste** **link** **option and then click Microsoft Excel Worksheet Object in the** **As** **list box (see Figure 4.2).**

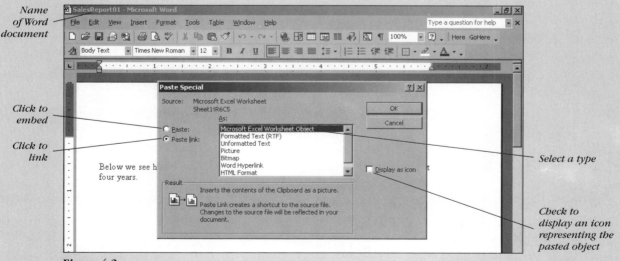

Figure 4.2

6 **Leave the** **Display as icon** **option unchecked, and click OK.**
The results of the Paste Special operation display in the sales report (see Figure 4.3). Now center the object.

(Continues)

To Link Excel Data to a Word Document (Continued)

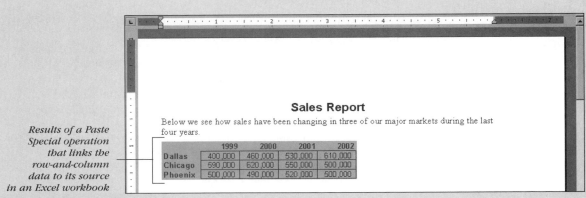

*Results of a Paste
Special operation
that links the
row-and-column
data to its source
in an Excel workbook*

Figure 4.3

7 **Right-click within the worksheet data and then select Format Object from the shortcut menu.**
The Format Object dialog box opens.

8 **Select the Layout tab and then select Square as the Wrapping style.**

9 **Click the Center option in the Horizontal alignment area, and click OK.**
The inserted cells are centered horizontally. Now, test the link by changing data in the original worksheet.

10 **Make sure the worksheet object is selected in the Word document (sizing handles display), and choose Edit, Linked Worksheet Object, Edit Link. (If the object is not already selected, you can double-click it to produce the same results.)**
The original source file *SalesData01* displays in Excel.

11 **Press Esc to clear the marquee from the previous copy operation and then change the contents of cell B4 to 600,000 instead of *400,000*.**

12 **Display the Word document *SalesReport01*. Make sure that the change to 600,000 is also reflected in the Word document and then deselect the worksheet data (see Figure 4.4).**

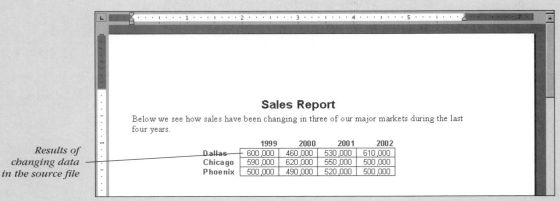

*Results of
changing data
in the source file*

Figure 4.4

13 **Save and close both the Word document and the Excel workbook.**
This concludes Lesson 1. Continue with the next lesson, or exit Excel.

To extend your knowledge...

Comparing File Size: Embedded and Linked Objects

A destination file containing an embedded object is much larger than a destination file in which the same object is linked to its source. Embedding inserts a copy of the object. Think of linking as inserting a picture of the object with a shortcut (that is, link) between the destination file and the source of the data. There are size-of-file benefits to this approach. The destination file is only a few bytes larger than it would have been without the link to data in another application. The primary disadvantage of this approach is that the link is broken if the destination file is not stored in the same location as the source file.

Lesson 2: Embedding Excel Data in a Word Document

Embedded data actually becomes a part of the destination file. Initially the results of an embed operation appear to be the same as if a link operation was executed. One major difference, however, is that if the source data in the worksheet changes, the change is not reflected in the destination file. Because embedded data does not have links, you do not have to be concerned about breaking links if a source file gets moved or renamed. This is especially important if you send the file(s) to someone else.

In this lesson, you execute the same copy operation as you did in Lesson 1, except that you embed—rather than link—the annual sales data from a worksheet into the sales report. You then access Excel features from within Word, change a value, and verify that the change is not reflected in the source worksheet.

To Embed Excel Data in a Word Document

1 Open the Excel file named *ee2-0401,* and save it as SalesData02.

2 Select cells A3:E6 and then choose **E**dit, **C**opy.

3 In Microsoft Word, open the *ee2-0402* file, and save it as SalesReport02.

4 Place the insertion point below the single sentence, and choose **E**dit, Paste **S**pecial.

5 In the Paste Special dialog box, click the **P**aste option (not the Paste **l**ink option).

6 Click Microsoft Excel Worksheet Object in the **A**s list.

7 Leave the **D**isplay as icon option unchecked, and click OK.
    The results look the same as those achieved by linking, rather than embedding (refer to Figure 4.3 in Lesson 1). Now center the embedded object.

8 Right-click within the worksheet data, select **F**ormat Object from the shortcut menu, select the Layout tab in the Format Object dialog box, and select Square as the Wrapping style.

9 Click the **C**enter option in the Horizontal alignment area and then click OK.
    The inserted cells are centered horizontally. Now make sure that links do not exist between the source file and the destination file. Start by accessing Excel features from within the Word document.

(Continues)

To Embed Excel Data in a Word Document (Continued)

⑩ Right-click within the embedded worksheet in the *SalesReport02* document, select Worksheet Object from the shortcut menu, and select Edit.

A miniature Excel worksheet displays, and Word's horizontal menu and toolbars are temporarily replaced with Excel's horizontal menu and toolbars (see Figure 4.5).

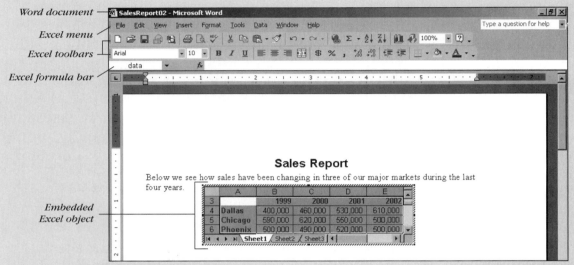

Figure 4.5

⑪ In the Excel window, change the contents of cell B4 to 500,000 instead of *400,000*.

⑫ Click an area in the Word document that is outside the Excel window.

The object is deselected, and Word's menu and toolbars reappear.

⑬ Save your changes to *SalesReport02* and then switch to the *SalesData02* workbook.

Making a change to an embedded worksheet in a Word document does not change the corresponding data in the Excel source file. The original value of *400,000* still displays in cell B4 of the *SalesData02* workbook. Now make a change in the source file.

⑭ Change the contents of cell B4 in *SalesData02* to 600,000 instead of *400,000*, and check the associated cell in the Word document.

The edited value of *500,000* in *SalesReport02* does not change. The two files are not linked in either direction.

⑮ Save and close both the Word document *SalesReport02* and the Excel workbook *SalesData02*.

This concludes Lesson 2. Continue with the next lesson, or exit Excel.

Lesson 3: Linking Excel Data to a PowerPoint Slide

When creating a PowerPoint presentation, you may want to include row-and-column data or a chart that already exists in an Excel worksheet. The two options you worked with in previous lessons—linking in Lesson 1, and embedding in Lesson 2—are available when integrating between Excel and any Microsoft Office application. The procedures are quite similar.

In this lesson you copy a section of an Excel worksheet to the first of two slides in a PowerPoint presentation. You paste the copied data as a link.

To Link Excel Data to a PowerPoint Slide

1 Open the Excel file *ee2-0401,* and save it as SalesData03.

2 Select cells A3:E6 and then choose **E**dit, **C**opy.

3 Start Microsoft PowerPoint, open the PowerPoint presentation named *ee2-0403,* and save it as SalesReport03.
This file contains two slides that are the start of a sales report presentation.

4 Select the first slide and then choose **E**dit, Paste **S**pecial.

5 Click Paste **l**ink, specify Microsoft Excel Worksheet Object in the **A**s list box, and click OK.
The copied cells display on Slide 1, but the cells are too small to read easily. Now enlarge the worksheet display.

6 Resize and move the object similar to the size and position shown in Figure 4.6. Hold the ⬆Shift key while dragging a corner sizing handle to maintain the object's proportions while resizing.

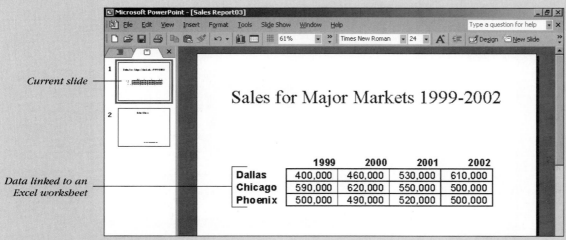

Figure 4.6

7 Save your changes to the *SalesReport03.ppt* presentation.
This concludes Lesson 3. Keep both the PowerPoint file *SalesReport03* and the Excel workbook *SalesData03* open for the next lesson, in which you link an Excel chart to the second slide.

Lesson 4: Linking an Excel Chart to a PowerPoint Slide

Charts and graphics can greatly enhance a presentation. Although you can create charts within Power-Point, you may already have a chart within an existing Excel workbook. If you link an Excel chart to a PowerPoint slide, the chart on the slide can be updated for any changes in the Excel source file containing the chart.

In this lesson, you link an Excel chart of annual sales to the second slide in a PowerPoint presentation. You also test the links by varying the data in the Excel source file.

To Link an Excel Chart to a PowerPoint Slide

1   **Open the Excel workbook named *SalesData03*, if necessary.**

2   **Click within a blank area of the chart to select it, and choose _E_dit, _C_opy.**

3   **Open the PowerPoint file named *SalesReport03*, if necessary (when prompted that the file contains links, select Update Links to update the links).**
This file contains the two slides that are the start of a Sales Report presentation. Slide 1 already contains data linked to an Excel worksheet.

4   **Press [PgDn] to display Slide 2 and then choose _E_dit, Paste _S_pecial.**

5   **Click Paste _l_ink, select Microsoft Excel Chart Object in the _A_s list box, and click OK.**
The copied chart displays on Slide 2. Now enlarge the chart.

6   **Resize and move the chart similar to the size and position shown in Figure 4.7.**

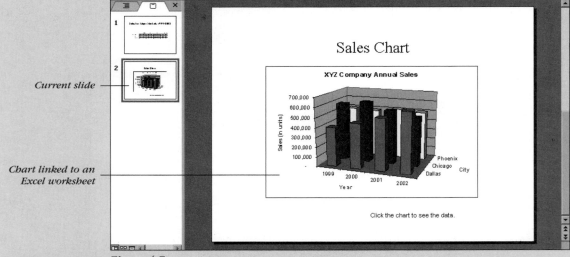

Current slide ———

Chart linked to an Excel worksheet ———

Figure 4.7

7   **Save your changes to PowerPoint file *SalesReport03*, and close the file.**

8   **Test the links, as desired, by changing one or more values within the range of charted data in the Excel file *SalesData03*.**

9   **Open the PowerPoint file *SalesReport03* to verify that changes in the Excel source file are reflected on both Slides 1 and 2. (Click Update Links when you see a prompt asking if you want to update the links).**

To Link an Excel Chart to a PowerPoint Slide

🔟 **Close the PowerPoint file *SalesReport03* and the Excel file *SalesData03* without saving changes made to verify the links.**
This concludes Lesson 4. Continue with the next lesson, or exit Excel.

Lesson 5: Importing Data from a Text File

Data can be stored as a text file. This sometimes happens because the data is in the process of being converted between two products that cannot exchange data directly. Data in text form appears as a string of characters. Spaces or commas separate (delimit) fields, although other characters are sometimes used to delimit fields in a string. Excel's Text Import Wizard is available to guide you through the process of importing text data into the columns and rows of a worksheet.

In this lesson, you use the Text Import Wizard to import data in a text file concerning donations to the Save the Manatee fund.

To Import Data from a Text File

❶ **Open a new workbook in Excel.**

❷ **Choose File, Open. Select Text Files in the Files of type drop-down list and then open the text file named *ee2-0404*.**
The first Text Import Wizard dialog box is displayed (see Figure 4.8). Records display in the Preview area across the bottom of the dialog box. Data fields in each record are separated by commas (name, address, city, and so on).

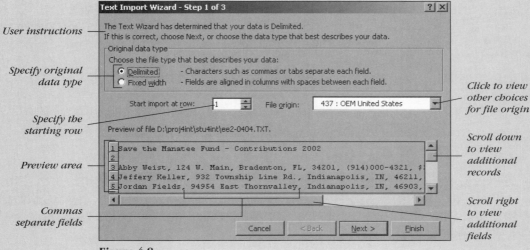

Figure 4.8

❸ **Select Delimited as the original data type and then click Next.**
The Text Import Wizard – Step 2 of 3 dialog box is displayed. An explanation of the screen is provided at the top of the dialog box.

❹ **In the Delimiters area, uncheck Tab and then check Comma (see Figure 4.9).**

(Continues)

To Import Data from a Text File (Continued)

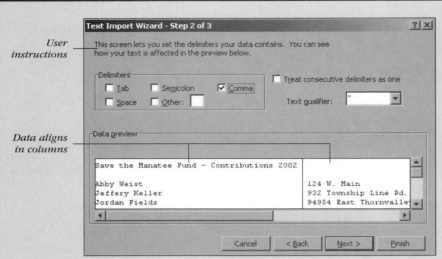

User instructions — This screen lets you set the delimiters your data contains. You can see how your text is affected in the preview below.

Data aligns in columns

Figure 4.9

5 **Click Next.**

The Text Import Wizard – Step 3 of 3 dialog box is displayed (see Figure 4.10).

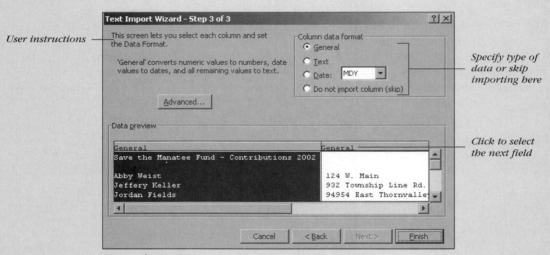

User instructions

Specify type of data or skip importing here

Click to select the next field

Figure 4.10

6 **Click Finish to accept the current settings.**

Excel imports the data and arranges it in rows (records) and columns (fields) as shown in Figure 4.11. Now make adjustments to the layout and content of the imported data.

To Import Data from a Text File

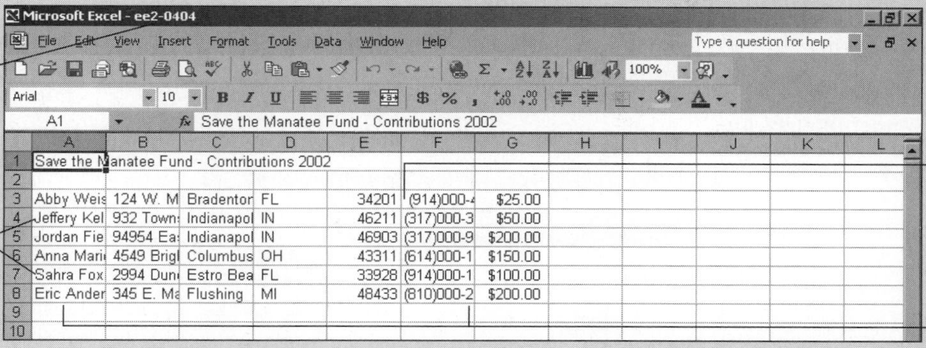

Excel assigns the original filename

Correct spelling of first names

Remove the extra space

Change column widths as needed

Figure 4.11

7 **Widen or narrow columns as needed.**

8 **Change *Jeffery* to** Jeffrey **in cell A4; then change *Sahra* to** Sarah **in cell A7, and remove the extra space at the beginning of the phone number in cell F3.**

9 **Choose File, Save As, and select *Microsoft Excel Workbook* from the Save as type drop-down list.**

10 **Change the filename to** Save the Manatee; **then click Save, and close the workbook.**

This concludes Lesson 5. Continue with the next lesson, or exit Excel.

Lesson 6: Importing Data from an Access Database

When data becomes too voluminous and complex, it is stored in a relational database program such as Microsoft Access rather than as a list in Excel. Yet for some information needs—such as producing a chart—Excel may be the better program to use. Excel's Import External Data feature enables you to reach from Excel into an Access database and create or edit a query using data in the Access database.

In this lesson, you work with an Access database that lists properties for sale. You use Excel's Import External Data feature to produce a list in an Excel worksheet of the properties for sale in the Glenn Lakes subdivision.

The lesson is intended to focus only on the mechanics of getting data from an Access database into an Excel worksheet, and does not include using the results. The sample Access database has only one table—most databases have multiple tables—which is sufficient to illustrate the process of creating a query prior to extracting data to an Excel worksheet.

To Import External Data from Access

1 **Open the Excel workbook named *ee2-0405*, and save it as** Clients.

2 **Choose Data, Import External Data, and select New Database Query. If a message displays that Microsoft Query is not installed, click Yes to begin the installation.**

(Continues)

To Import External Data from Access (Continued)

The Choose Data Source dialog box is displayed (see Figure 4.12). If the Office Assistant asks whether you want help, click *No, don't provide help now.*

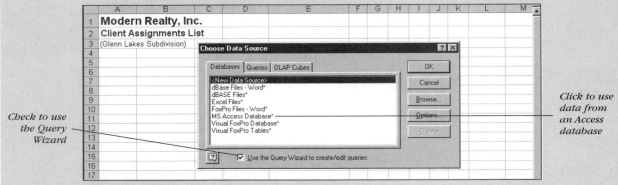

Figure 4.12

3 **On the Databases tab, select MS Access Database, make sure a check mark displays in the *Use the Query Wizard to create/edit queries* check box, and click OK.**

The Select Database dialog box is displayed. Use this dialog box to select the Access file that contains the data you want to import into Excel (see Figure 4.13).

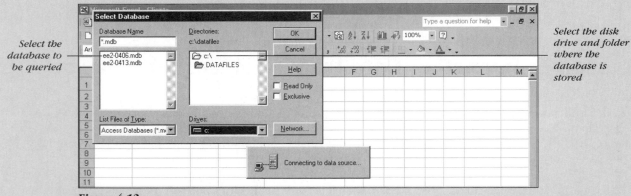

Figure 4.13

4 **Select the folder containing the student data files; then select the Access *ee2-0406.mdb* database, and click OK.**

The Query Wizard – Choose Columns dialog box is displayed (see Figure 4.14). A single table named Client Assignments appears in the *Available tables and columns* list.

To Import External Data from Access

Click to display the field names in the Client Assignments table

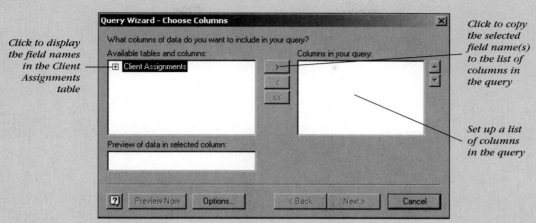

Click to copy the selected field name(s) to the list of columns in the query

Set up a list of columns in the query

Figure 4.14

5 Click the + indicator next to the Client Assignments table name in the *Available tables and columns* list box.

6 Select the Client Assignments table name and then click the > button.
When you highlight a table name and click the > button, all fields in the table are transferred to the *Columns in your query* list box (see Figure 4.15). To specify fewer fields, select individual field names instead of selecting the table name. The order in which the fields are selected is the order in which they will appear in your worksheet.

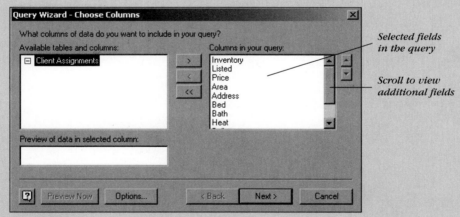

Selected fields in the query

Scroll to view additional fields

Figure 4.15

7 Click **Next**.
The Query Wizard – Filter Data dialog box displays.

8 Select Area in the *Column to filter* list box.

9 Select *equals* from the drop-down list in the first of two active text boxes in the *Only include rows where* section for Area (see Figure 4.16).

(Continues)

To Import External Data from Access (Continued)

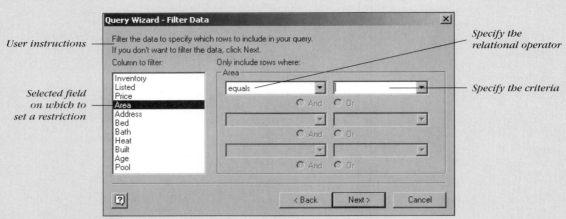

Figure 4.16

⑩ **Click the drop-down list in the blank text box to the right of the one in which you specified a relational operator, and select *Glenn Lakes*.**
You have set a filter to select only those records from the Access database in which the entry in the Area field equals Glenn Lakes.

⑪ **Click Next.**
The Query Wizard – Sort Order dialog box is displayed.

⑫ **Click the Sort by drop-down list; then select Inventory, and click Ascending.**
Check that your settings match those shown in Figure 4.17.

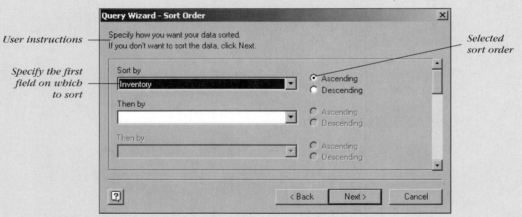

Figure 4.17

⑬ **Click Next.**
The Query Wizard – Finish dialog box is displayed.

⑭ **Select *Return Data to Microsoft Excel* and then click Finish.**
The Import Data dialog box displays, asking where you want to put the data.

⑮ **Specify *Existing worksheet* and then click cell A5 in the worksheet.**

To Import External Data from Access

Check that the settings in your Import Data dialog box match those shown in Figure 4.18.

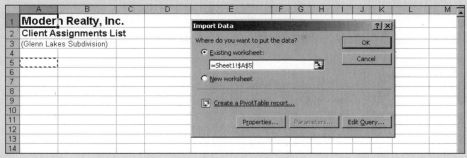

Figure 4.18

16 Click OK.

This completes your Import External Data operation. The records shown in Figure 4.19 are copied from the Access database and placed in Excel's list format beginning in cell A5.

*Field names
and eight
records from
an Access
database*

	A	B	C	D	E	F	G	H	I	J	K	L	M
1	**Modern Realty, Inc.**												
2	**Client Assignments List**												
3	(Glenn Lakes Subdivision)												
4													
5	Inventory	Listed	Price	Area	Address	Bed	Bath	Heat	Built	Age	Pool		
6	LC004	1/23/2002 0:00	172300	Glenn Lakes	3452 Cortez Street	3	2	Elec	1996	4	Y		
7	LC009	1/5/2002 0:00	170000	Glenn Lakes	1025 Wellington Circle	3	2	Elec	1998	2	Y		
8	LF005	1/15/2002 0:00	121500	Glenn Lakes	5562 Kensington Drive	4	2.5	Elec	1998	2	N		
9	LF006	2/5/2002 0:00	174600	Glenn Lakes	4874 Manatee Avenue	3	2	Elec	1995	5	Y		
10	MF003	3/6/2002 0:00	123800	Glenn Lakes	3492 54th Avenue W.	2	2	Elec	1996	4	Y		
11	MF008	3/3/2002 0:00	167200	Glenn Lakes	5778 Wellington Drive	3	2	Elec	1997	3	Y		
12	MF009	1/3/2002 0:00	180500	Glenn Lakes	6873 Wellington Drive	4	2	Elec	1997	3	Y		
13	MF014	3/3/2002 0:00	169700	Glenn Lakes	2984 44th Street West	3	2	Elec	1997	3	Y		
14													

*The query
limited record
selection to
listings in the
Glenn Lakes
area*

Figure 4.19

17 Save and close the *Clients* workbook.

This concludes Project 4. You can exit Excel, or continue with the end-of-project exercises.

To extend your knowledge...

Getting Data from Excel into Access

Excel's list capability enables you to perform sorts and filters based on data in a single worksheet that is the equivalent of one table in an Access database. By using Access, however, you can create many related tables within a database, perform queries based on multiple tables, and generate complex reports.

To import Excel data to an Access database, first make sure that the Excel data is in a list format—each column has a label in the first row and holds similar data, each row contains related data items, and there are no blank rows or columns within the list. Also make sure that the Excel workbook is closed. To create a new Access database, simply open the Excel workbook in Access, and follow the directions in the Link Spreadsheet Wizard. To add Excel data to an existing Access database, open the Access database where you want to copy the Excel data; on the Access File menu, select Get External Data and click Import; locate and select the workbook you want to import, click Import, and follow directions in the Import Spreadsheet Wizard. Refer to onscreen Help in Access for more information.

Summary

The first four lessons in this project focused on linking or embedding data from one Microsoft application to another. The result is an object in the destination file that you can move and size. If the result is a linked object, a change in the source data is reflected also in the destination file. If the result is an embedded object, changing the source data does not change data in the destination file. In the remaining lessons, you imported data from two sources—the entire contents of a text file, and selected records from an Access database.

To expand your knowledge, try variations of integrating other applications according to your interests, such as embedding—instead of linking—an Excel chart in a PowerPoint presentation or getting data from Excel into Access.

Checking Concepts and Terms

Multiple Choice

Circle the letter of the correct answer for each of the following.

1. What is the term that describes sharing data among Microsoft Office applications? [L1]

   a. Object Linking and Embedding (OLE)
   b. Object Sharing and Round-tripping (OSR)
   c. Object Data Sharing (ODS)
   d. None of the above

2. Which of the following can become an Excel linked or embedded object? [L1]

   a. a single cell
   b. a chart
   c. both a and b
   d. neither a nor b

3. What is the term for a file that contains a link or embedded data? [L1]

   a. source file
   b. destination file
   c. application file
   d. object file

4. Which is a true statement about a file containing an embedded object? [L1]

   a. The file is only a few bytes larger than it would have been without the data from another application.
   b. There is no connection between the file containing the embedded object and its source file.
   c. You can edit the connection between the file containing the embedded object and the source file.
   d. both a and b

5. Which of the following is a step in the process to link an Excel chart to a PowerPoint slide? [L4]

   a. In Excel, select the chart and copy it.
   b. In PowerPoint, select the target slide and click the Paste button.
   c. both a and b
   d. neither a nor b

Discussion

1. You completed an Excel worksheet summarizing the results of last week's swim meet. Now you are about to copy the data to a report you are preparing in Word. Should you embed or link the swim meet data? Why? [L1-L2]

2. You learned to create links in this project. Use onscreen Help to learn how to break links, and briefly explain the process.

3. You can display a linked or embedded object as it appears in the source program or as an icon. Provide a common reason for displaying a linked or embedded object as an icon, and summarize the process to create such an icon. Onscreen Help provides the information you need to answer this question.

Skill Drill

Skill Drill exercises reinforce project skills. Each skill that is reinforced is the same, or nearly the same, as a skill presented in the project. Detailed instructions are provided in a step-by-step format.

Before beginning your first Project 4 Skill Drill exercise, complete the following steps:

1. Open the Excel file named *ee2-0407* and immediately save it as `ee2-p4drill.`
   The workbook contains an overview sheet and three exercise sheets labeled #1-Client List, #2-Expenses, and #3-Mileage.
2. Click the Overview sheet to view the organization and content of the Project 4 Skill Drill Exercises workbook.

There are four exercises. The first three exercises use data stored in the *ee2-p4drill* workbook. To complete the fourth exercise, you access onscreen Help. Each exercise is independent of the others, so you may complete the exercises in any order.

Be sure to save the workbook after completing each exercise. If you need a paper copy of the completed exercise, enter your name centered in a header before printing. Other print options have already been set to print compressed and to display the filename, sheet name, and current date in a footer.

Be sure to save your changes and then close the workbook if you need more than one work session to complete the desired exercises. Continue working on *ee2-p4drill* instead of starting over again on the original *ee2-0407* file.

1. Creating a Link and Viewing Information about Links

You maintain data in an Excel worksheet on homes available for sale. You created a memo in Word to convey information about properties available in the Glenn Lakes subdivision. Now you want to link the data in the worksheet to the Word memo so that each time the Word document is opened, the linked data can be updated. You also want to view information about links in the memo.

To create a link, and view information about links:

1. Open the *ee2-p4drill* workbook in Excel, if necessary, and select the worksheet named #1-Client List.
2. Open the *ee2-0408* document in Word, and save it as `Glenn Lakes`.
3. Switch to the #1-Client List worksheet; then select the list range A8:I16, and click the Copy button.
4. Switch to the *Glenn Lakes* document, and position the insertion point below the last sentence.
5. Choose <u>E</u>dit, Paste <u>S</u>pecial.

6. Select Paste link, specify pasting as a Microsoft Excel Worksheet Object, and click OK.

   The range of data from an Excel worksheet is linked within the Word document. Now view information about the links in the document.

7. Deselect the linked object, and choose Edit, Links.

   The Links dialog box displays and lists one link. The description of Item #1 near the bottom of the dialog box indicates that the link is a Microsoft Excel Worksheet containing data from an Access query.

8. Click OK to close the dialog box.

9. Save your changes to the *Glenn Lakes* document, and exit Word.

10. Deselect the list range in the #1-Client List worksheet, and press [Esc] to remove the marquee from the copy operation.

2. Importing Data to an Existing Worksheet from a Text File

You are keeping a record of the business miles you drive using Notepad, which creates a text file. Now you want to import that text file into Excel as the starting point for a worksheet that computes business expenses.

To import data to an existing worksheet from a text file:

1. Open the *ee2-p4drill* workbook, if necessary, and select the worksheet named #2-Expenses.

2. Click cell A4.

3. Choose Data, Import External Data, and select Import Data.

   The Select Data Source dialog box opens.

4. Display the Look in drop-down list, and select the folder containing the student data files.

5. Select the *ee2-0409* text file and then click Open.

6. Check that Delimited is selected in the Text Import Wizard – Step 1 of 3 dialog box, and click Next.

7. Make sure that a check mark displays in the Tab check box in the Text Import Wizard – Step 2 of 3 dialog box, and click Finish.

8. Make sure that *Existing worksheet* and =$A$4 are the settings for the location of imported data, and click OK.

   Excel imports the text data, starting in cell A4.

9. Save your changes to the *ee2-p4drill* workbook.

3. Linking a Pivot Table and Chart to a PowerPoint Slide

A vital part of a PowerPoint presentation is the capability to display current data and charts. Often this information is maintained in Excel and linked to a slide presentation. In this exercise, you link an Excel pivot table and associated chart to a PowerPoint slide. A pivot table summarizes data, as explained in Project 7, titled "Creating PivotTable and PivotChart Reports."

To create the links, follow these steps:

1. Open the *ee2-p4drill* Excel workbook, if necessary, and select the worksheet named #3-Mileage.

2. Open the *ee2-0410* PowerPoint file, and save it as `Mileage`.

3. Page down to display Slide 2.

4. Switch to the #3-Mileage worksheet and then copy the range E8:F13.

5. Switch to Slide 2 in the PowerPoint file *Mileage* and then click the text box on the left.

6. Choose Edit, Paste Special; then click Paste link, specify pasting as a Microsoft Excel Worksheet Object, and click OK.

   The text box on the left and the graphics placeholder on the right disappear. The copied data displays in a small worksheet; sizing handles indicate the object is selected. For now, do not change the size or location of the copied pivot table data.

7. Switch to the #3-Mileage worksheet; then click within the pie chart, and click the Copy button.

8. Switch to PowerPoint and then choose <u>E</u>dit, Paste <u>S</u>pecial. Click Paste <u>l</u>ink, specify pasting as a Microsoft Excel Chart Object, and click OK.

9. Rearrange and resize the three objects—the title is an object—as desired to improve display. (For example, you can reduce the size of the title text box and position it top-right on the slide, reduce the size of the pivot table data and display it to the left of the slide title, and enlarge the chart and center it below both of the other objects.)

10. Save your changes to *Mileage*, and exit PowerPoint.

11. Deselect ranges as necessary in the #3-Mileage worksheet.

4. Getting Help on Linking and Embedding

You know how to embed and link objects, but you want to know more about when each method should be selected. Onscreen Help can provide the information you desire.

To access related onscreen Help, follow these steps:

1. Display a blank Excel workbook and then enter `about linking` in the Ask a Question box.

2. Select the topic *About linking to another workbook or program*.

3. Click the topic *The difference between linking and embedding other programs in Excel* in the right pane.

4. Study the diagram showing an embedded object, a linked object, and a source file.

5. Read the next two sections titled *When to use linked objects* and *When to use embedded objects*.

6. Read other topics of your choice listed in the <u>C</u>ontents tab, such as *Edit a linked or embedded object*.

7. Close onscreen Help, and close the blank workbook without saving.

Challenge

Challenge exercises expand on or are somewhat related to skills that are presented in the lessons. Each exercise provides a brief narrative introduction, followed by instructions in a numbered-step format that are not as detailed as those in the Skill Drill section.

Before beginning your first Project 4 Challenge exercise, complete the following steps:

1. Open the Excel file named *ee2-0411,* and immediately save it as **ee2-p4challenge.**
The *ee2-p4challenge* workbook contains three sheets: an overview, and two exercise sheets named #1-Embed and #2-FromAccess.

2. Click the Overview sheet to view the organization of the Project 4 Challenge Exercises workbook.

There are four challenge exercises. The first two exercises use data stored in the *ee2-p4challenge* workbook. In the third exercise, you break a link in a PowerPoint slide to an Excel worksheet. For the fourth exercise, you use Windows Explorer to compare file sizes. Each exercise is independent of the others, so you may complete the exercises in any order. Be sure to save the workbook after completing each exercise. If you need a paper copy of the completed exercise, enter your name centered in a header before printing. Other print options have already been set to print compressed to one page and to display the filename, sheet name, and current date in a footer.

If you need more than one work session to complete the desired exercises, continue working on *ee2-p4challenge* instead of starting over again on the original *ee2-0411* file.

1. Embedding Excel Data in a Word Document

You prepared a memo to the Accounting department, asking for a review of your monthly expenses. Embed in the memo a copy of those expenses, which are available in an Excel worksheet.

To embed Excel data in a Word document, follow these steps:

1. Open the Word document *ee2-0412*, and save it as a document named `review`.
2. Open the *ee2-p4challenge* workbook, if necessary, and select the #1-Embed worksheet.
3. Turn off display of gridlines and row and column headings on printed output.
4. Copy the range A7:E21 and then switch to the *review* document.
5. Paste the copied Excel data after the last sentence, making sure that you embed (not link) the data as a Microsoft Excel Worksheet Object.
6. Use an option on the Edit menu to verify that there is no link to the #1-Embed worksheet in the document.
7. Save your changes to the *review* document; then close the document and exit Word.
8. Deselect ranges as necessary in the #1-Embed worksheet.

2. Importing Access Data into an Excel Worksheet

Expense data is currently stored in an Access database, and you want to import selected data into an Excel worksheet. If you wanted to import all records with fields in the same order as stored in the Access database, you would choose Data, Import External Data, and select Import Data. You want, however, to extract only the Office and Other category expenses (category 1 or 4 expenses), and you want the columns in a slightly different order. Use Excel's Import External Data feature, and select New Database Query instead of Import Data, to produce the desired result.

To import Access data into an Excel worksheet, follow these steps:

1. Open the *ee2-p4challenge* workbook, if necessary, and select the #2-FromAccess worksheet; then click cell A9.
2. Choose Data, Import External Data, and select New Database Query.
3. Choose MS Access Database as the data source, and specify that you want to use the Query Wizard.
4. In the Select Database dialog box, find and open the *ee2-0413* Access database.
5. Click the + sign to display fields (columns) in the Expense List table; then choose columns ID, Category, Expense, Date, Amount, and Client (select them in the order given).
6. Filter the data so only category 1 or 4 records are imported.
   To do this, you must use two filter lines and specify the OR button between the two specifications.
7. Sort the data by the Expense field in Ascending order.
8. Select Return Data to Microsoft Excel and then click Finish. Make sure that cell A9 in the existing worksheet is the location for imported data, and click OK.
   Imported data displays starting in cell A9 of the #2-FromAccess worksheet. The Client column is blank because Category 1 and 4 type expenses do not have clients.
9. Reformat as needed, including changes in column widths and formatting entries in the Date column to show the date only. Save your changes to the *ee2-p4challenge* workbook.

3. Breaking a Link

You want to break the links in a PowerPoint slide to data and a chart in an Excel worksheet. You know that when you break a link to a source, the action cannot be undone.

To break links, follow these steps:

1. Open the PowerPoint file *ee2-0414*, click Cancel to bypass updating links, and save the file as `nolinks`.
   The data and chart on Slide 2 are linked to an Excel worksheet.

   2. Choose <u>E</u>dit, Lin<u>k</u>s.

   The Links dialog box is displayed.

   3. Select both of the links listed, click <u>B</u>reak Link, and close the Links dialog box.

   4. Choose <u>E</u>dit.

   The Links option on the <u>E</u>dit menu is dim, indicating that there are no links in the file.

   5. Close the <u>E</u>dit menu, save your changes to *nolinks*, and exit PowerPoint.

4. Comparing Sizes of Linked Versus Embedded Files

In Lesson 1, you created *SalesReport01.doc*, in which you linked a worksheet range. In Lesson 2, you created *SalesReport02.doc*, in which you embedded the same range. You want to compare the sizes of the two files.

To compare file sizes by using Windows Explorer:

   1. Open Windows Explorer, and display the contents of the folder in which you stored the solutions to this project.

   2. Note that the file size of *SalesReport01.doc* (containing only a link to data in an Excel worksheet) is smaller than the file size of *SalesReport02.doc* (containing embedded Excel data).

   3. Close Windows Explorer.

Discovery Zone exercises require advanced knowledge of topics presented in *essentials* lessons, application of skills from multiple lessons, or self-directed learning of new skills.

Each exercise is independent of the other, so you may complete the exercises in any order.

1. Display a Linked Object as an Icon

You created a PowerPoint slide that contains links to Excel data and an Excel chart. You want the entire chart to display, but you want the associated data to display as an icon to minimize the amount of space that the data occupies. As you present the slide show, you can double-click the icon if a viewer wants to see the actual data from which the chart is drawn.

Use onscreen Help to learn how to display an object as an icon. Open the PowerPoint file *ee2-0415*, click Cancel to bypass updating links, and save it as `icondemo`. Display Slide 2 and then convert the data object in the upper-left corner to a Microsoft Excel Worksheet displayed as an icon. Deselect the icon, save your changes to *icondemo*, and exit PowerPoint.

2. Inserting a Non-Microsoft Office Object

Expand your knowledge of how Excel can integrate with other programs. Create a new Excel workbook, and choose <u>I</u>nsert, <u>O</u>bject. Scroll through the object types, and experiment with inserting objects other than those associated with Microsoft Word, PowerPoint, and Access. For example, you might insert a Paintbrush picture or a Netscape hypertext document. Near each object you insert, enter a label describing the object's source.

Using Functions to Create Data

Objectives

In this project, you learn how to

- ✔ Use VLOOKUP to Create Data
- ✔ Use VLOOKUP with Multiple Values
- ✔ Summarize Data with FREQUENCY
- ✔ Chart the Results of a Frequency Distribution
- ✔ Interpret Data with COUNTIF
- ✔ Interpret Data with SUMIF
- ✔ Create an IF Function within an IF Function

Key terms in this project include

- ❏ array constant
- ❏ array formula
- ❏ array range
- ❏ bin
- ❏ COUNTIF function
- ❏ frequency distribution
- ❏ FREQUENCY function
- ❏ nested IF
- ❏ SUMIF function
- ❏ VLOOKUP function

Why Would I Do This?

Excel provides hundreds of functions—predefined formulas—to help you with tasks such as adding a list of values and determining loan payments. Functions are presented in nine categories: Financial, Date & Time, Math & Trig, Statistical, Lookup & Reference, Database, Text, Logical, and Information. In this project, you expand your knowledge of functions by working with one or more functions from three categories: Lookup & Reference, Statistical, and Math & Trig.

Visual Summary

Functions can be simple or complex, depending on the calculations required. Examples of simple calculations using functions include adding the contents of a range of cells (SUM function) or finding the maximum value in a range of cells (MAX function). In this project, you work with functions involving more complex calculations, including VLOOKUP and FREQUENCY.

Use the **VLOOKUP function** to search for a value in the leftmost column of a table. If found, the function displays the contents of a cell in that same row for the column you specify. In this project, you use the VLOOKUP function to convert numeric data to text (see Figure 5.1).

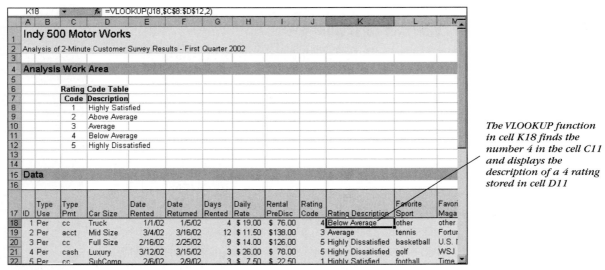

The VLOOKUP function in cell K18 finds the number 4 in the cell C11 and displays the description of a 4 rating stored in cell D11

Figure 5.1

The **FREQUENCY function** calculates how many times values occur within a range. In this project, you use FREQUENCY to create summary data about the favorite magazine of survey respondents (see Figure 5.2).

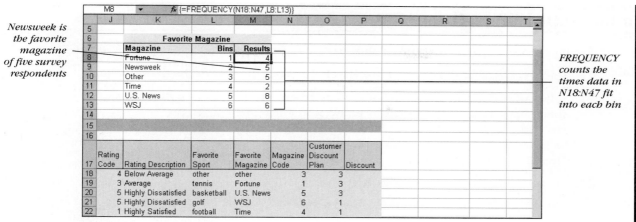

Newsweek is the favorite magazine of five survey respondents

FREQUENCY counts the times data in N18:N47 fit into each bin

Figure 5.2

You also chart the frequency distribution results, and analyze them using SUMIF and COUNTIF. You end the project by nesting an IF function within an IF function.

Lesson 1: Using VLOOKUP to Create Data

You are analyzing survey data completed by customers who recently rented vehicles from Indy 500 Motor Works. When you print a report showing satisfaction ratings, you want descriptions to appear instead of the numeric codes 1 through 5.

Excel provides several functions that you can use to create data by converting numbers to text and text to numbers. You can also use these functions to expand coded data, such as displaying the term *Accounting* each time the code *AC* is found. If the data you want to look up is stored vertically in a table—that is, in columns—then use the VLOOKUP function. If the data is stored horizontally—that is, in rows—use the HLOOKUP function. Figure 5.3 illustrates the important components of the VLOOKUP function you create in this lesson.

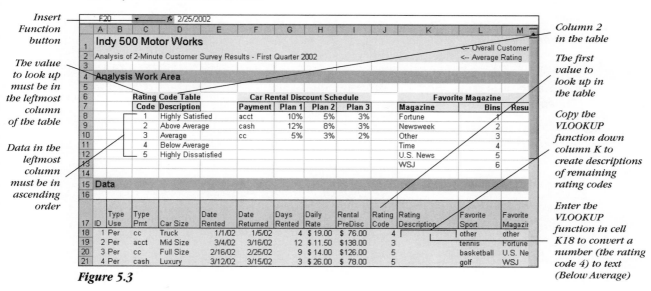

Insert Function button

The value to look up must be in the leftmost column of the table

Data in the leftmost column must be in ascending order

Column 2 in the table

The first value to look up in the table

Copy the VLOOKUP function down column K to create descriptions of remaining rating codes

Enter the VLOOKUP function in cell K18 to convert a number (the rating code 4) to text (Below Average)

Figure 5.3

To Use VLOOKUP to Create Data

① Open the *ee2-0501* workbook, and save it as Indy500functions.

② Select cell K18 and then click the Insert Function button in the formula bar.

③ Select the Lookup & Reference category in the Insert Function dialog box, select VLOOKUP as the function name, and click OK.

The Function Arguments dialog box for the VLOOKUP function displays. If you prefer to select ranges with a mouse instead of typing them, you can drag the dialog box away from the cells you need to select.

④ Enter J18 in the Lookup_value text box.

⑤ Enter $C$8:$D$12 in the Table_array text box.

In this case, the range C8:D12 is an **_array constant_**, which means a group of constants arranged in a special way and used as an argument in a formula. Specifying dollar signs makes the reference to the table absolute. This is necessary because you are going to copy the VLOOKUP function.

⑥ Enter 2 in the Col_index_num text box (see Figure 5.4).

Data to find in the table

Look in column 2 for the description to enter in K18

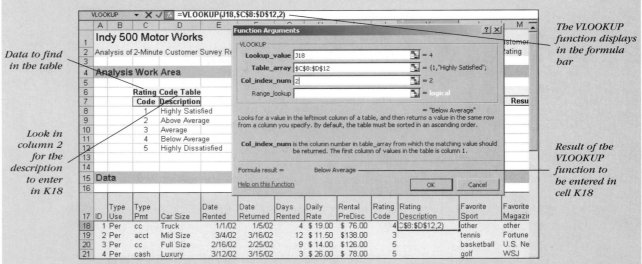

The VLOOKUP function displays in the formula bar

Result of the VLOOKUP function to be entered in cell K18

Figure 5.4

Col_index_num tells the VLOOKUP function that when it finds the appropriate value in the table, it should select the corresponding value from the second column in the Table_array.

⑦ Click OK to close the dialog box.

Below Average displays in cell K18 as the description for rating code 4.

If you have problems...

When cell K18 is selected, =VLOOKUP(J18,$C$8:$D$12,2) should display in the formula bar. Edit the formula as needed. Be sure to include the dollar signs that make the reference to the range C8:D12 absolute before you copy the function in the next step.

To Use VLOOKUP to Create Data

8 Copy the function in cell K18 to the range K19:K47.

9 Widen column K as needed, and save your changes to the *Indy500functions* workbook.

You can close the *Indy500functions* workbook now, or leave it open and continue to the next lesson.

To extend your knowledge...

Finding an Exact Match with the VLOOKUP Function

There is an optional fourth component to the VLOOKUP function named Range_lookup. If you specify the logical value TRUE for this component, or omit it—as in the previous illustration—the function uses the largest value that is less than or equal to the lookup_value. For example, if the rating code being looked up is 2.5—which is not one of the whole number choices in the leftmost column of the table—the function selects the description for rating code 2. If you specify FALSE as the Range_lookup, however, only exact matches satisfy the lookup.

Lesson 2: Using VLOOKUP with Multiple Values

Indy 500 Motor Works offers three discount plans to its customers. The discount under each plan varies with the type of payment—credit card (cc), corporate account (acct), and cash. Now you want to use VLOOKUP to enter the applicable discount for the first rental record (see Figure 5.5), and copy the formula to create the discount data for the remaining records. You can use VLOOKUP to create data based on two conditions—in this case, looking up the discount percent for a combination of payment type and discount plan.

	A	B	C	D	E	F	G	H	I	O	P	Q	R	
4	**Analysis Work Area**													
5														
6			**Rating Code Table**			**Car Rental Discount Schedule**				<-- Total Number of Surveys				
7			**Code**	**Description**		**Payment**	**Plan 1**	**Plan 2**	**Plan 3**					
8			1	Highly Satisfied		acct	10%	5%	3%	<-- Enter Plan Number (1, 2, or 3)				
9			2	Above Average		cash	12%	8%	3%	**For this plan:**				
10			3	Average		cc	5%	3%	2%	Number of respondents				
11			4	Below Average						Percent of respondents				
12			5	Highly Dissatisfied						Sum of rentals (prediscount)				
13										Average rental (prediscount)				
14														
15	**Data**													
16														
17	ID	Type Use	Type Pmt	Car Size	Date Rented	Date Returned	Days Rented	Daily Rate	Rental PreDisc	Customer Discount Plan	Discount			
18	1 Per	cc		Truck	1/1/02	1/5/02	4	$ 19.00	$ 76.00	3				
19	2 Per	acct		Mid Size	3/4/02	3/16/02	12	$ 11.50	$138.00	3				
20	3 Per	cc		Full Size	2/16/02	2/25/02	9	$ 14.00	$126.00	3				
21	4 Per	cash		Luxury	3/12/02	3/15/02	3	$ 26.00	$ 78.00	1				

Figure 5.5

Discounts for Plan 3 are located in the fourth column of the table

Plan 3 provides a 2% discount if a credit card (cc) is the type of payment

Use VLOOKUP in cell P18 to enter the appropriate discount from the table of values in the range F8:I10

To Use **VLOOKUP** with Multiple Values

1 If necessary, open the *Indy500functions* workbook.

2 Scroll to display cell A4 in the upper-left corner of the worksheet window, select cell J14, and choose <u>W</u>indow, <u>F</u>reeze Panes.

This allows you to continue displaying data in columns A through I as you scroll to view remaining columns.

3 Scroll to display data in columns O and P (refer to Figure 5.5).

4 Select cell P18 and then click the Insert Function button in the formula bar.

5 Select Lookup & Reference as the function category, select VLOOKUP as the function name, and click OK.

The Function Arguments dialog box for the VLOOKUP function displays.

6 Enter C18 in the Lookup_value text box.

7 Enter $F$8:$I$10 in the Table_array text box.

8 Enter O18+1 in the Col_index_num text box.

9 Enter FALSE in the Range_lookup text box (see Figure 5.6).

Copy the formula in cell P18 to create the discount percent data in P19:P47

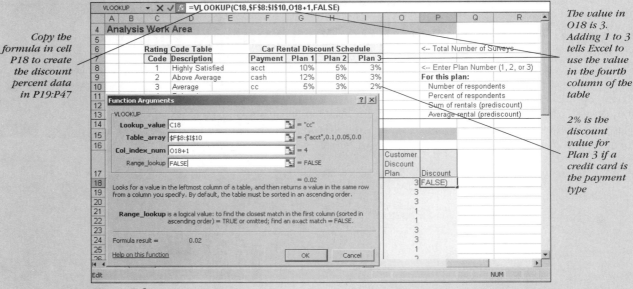

The value in O18 is 3. Adding 1 to 3 tells Excel to use the value in the fourth column of the table

2% is the discount value for Plan 3 if a credit card is the payment type

Figure 5.6

10 Click OK to close the dialog box.

The value *0.02* displays in cell P18.

 ## If you have problems...

The function =VLOOKUP(C18,$F$8:$I$10,O18+1,FALSE) should display in the formula bar when you select cell P18. Edit the formula as needed. Be sure to type the letter "O" and not the number zero in the reference to cell O18. Also include the dollar signs that make the reference to the range F8:I10 absolute before you copy the function in the next step.

To Use VLOOKUP with Multiple Values

⑪ Format cell P18 to Percent, zero decimal places.

The value *2%* displays in cell P18.

⑫ Copy the function in cell P18 to the range P19:P47 and then click cell P21 (see Figure 5.7).

VLOOKUP adds 1 to the value in cell O21

The discount for Plan 1 and method of payment cash

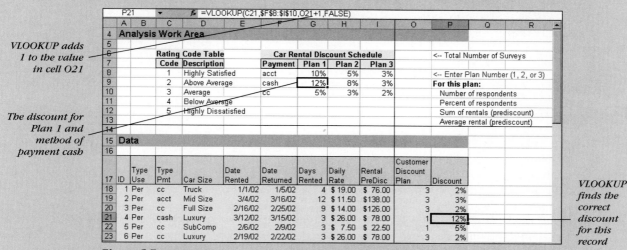

VLOOKUP finds the correct discount for this record

Figure 5.7

⑬ Choose Window, Unfreeze Panes.

⑭ Save your changes to the *Indy500functions* workbook.

You can close the *Indy500functions* workbook now, or leave it open and continue to the next lesson.

Lesson 3: Summarizing Data with FREQUENCY

You have likely seen surveys or other forms that request information on age, gender, highest year of formal education completed, annual or hourly income, and so forth. Those who analyze such data are generally interested in counting occurrences in selected categories, such as the number of respondents in each predetermined age range (20-29, 30-39, and so forth). A category is sometimes referred to as a **bin**. The counts for how often specific values occur within a set of values comprise a **frequency distribution**.

One of your responsibilities at Indy 500 Motor Works involves placing ads to attract customers. You decide to analyze survey results by counting customers who read various magazines. You intend to place ads in the magazines mentioned most frequently.

The FREQUENCY function counts the occurrences of values in a range of cells and creates an array range to display results. An **array range** is a rectangular area of cells that share a common formula. Figure 5.8 illustrates how the FREQUENCY function works.

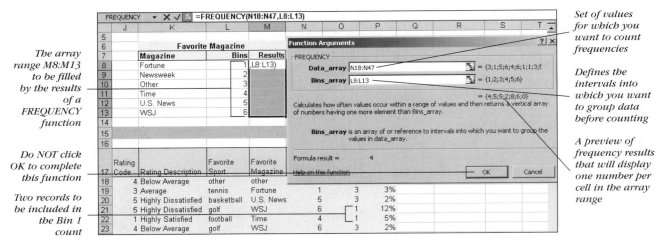

The array range M8:M13 to be filled by the results of a FREQUENCY function

Do NOT click OK to complete this function

Two records to be included in the Bin 1 count

Set of values for which you want to count frequencies

Defines the intervals into which you want to group data before counting

A preview of frequency results that will display one number per cell in the array range

Figure 5.8

The FREQUENCY function generates an array; therefore, you must enter it as an ***array formula***, which means you must press the three-key combination Ctrl+⬆Shift+⏎Enter instead of clicking OK in the Insert Function dialog box or pressing ⏎Enter. You cannot edit or delete the contents of individual cells in an array. To remove the array, select all cells in the array and press Del.

In this lesson you use FREQUENCY to tally the number of survey respondents who indicated a favorite magazine. The bins are already set up as the magazine codes, arranged in ascending numeric order (see the range L8:L13 in Figure 5.8). The magazine names in the range K8:K13 are used for documentation of the bins and are not required for the function to work; however, the magazine titles make it easier to understand the frequency distribution, and they can be used as labels if you want to chart the results.

To Summarize Data with FREQUENCY

❶ If necessary, open the *Indy500functions* workbook.

❷ Select (highlight) the range M8:M13.

❸ Click the Insert Function button on the formula bar and then select Statistical as the function category.

❹ Select FREQUENCY as the function name and then click OK.
The Function Arguments dialog box for the FREQUENCY function displays.

❺ Enter N18:N47 in the Data_array text box.

❻ Enter L8:L13 in the Bins_array text box, but DO NOT click OK or press ⏎Enter.

❼ Check that your specifications match those shown in Figure 5.8, press the three-key combination Ctrl+⬆Shift+⏎Enter, and click any cell within M8:M13 to deselect the range.
Excel creates the frequency distribution in the range M8:M13 (see Figure 5.9). If the FREQUENCY function operates as intended, the numbers 4 (Fortune), 5 (Newsweek), 5 (Other), 2 (Time), 8 (U.S. News), and 6 (WSJ) display in the range M8:M13.

To Summarize Data with FREQUENCY

The FREQUENCY function displays in the formula bar if you select any cell in the range M8:M13

	J	K	L	M	N	O	P	Q	R	S	T
M13 ▼ *fx* =FREQUENCY(N18:N47,L8:L13)

	K	L	M		P
5					
6	Favorite Magazine				<-- Total Number of Surveys
7	Magazine	Bins	Results		
8	Fortune	1	4		<-- Enter Plan Number (1, 2, or 3)
9	Newsweek	2	5		For this plan:
10	Other	3	5		Number of respondents
11	Time	4	2		Percent of respondents
12	U.S. News	5	8		Sum of rentals (prediscount)
13	WSJ	6	6		Average rental (prediscount)
14					

A set of {} brackets encase an array formula

FREQUENCY results display in the range M8:M13

Figure 5.9

If you have problems...

If you only have results in the first cell of the range—the number 4 in cell M8—there are three possible explanations. You may have selected only the first cell of the result range (M8) instead of selecting M8:M13. You may have completed the FREQUENCY function by pressing ⏎Enter instead of pressing Ctrl+⬆Shift+⏎Enter. To repeat the process, delete the contents of cells M8:M13, and repeat steps 2 through 7.

If you continue to have problems, abandon the use of the Insert Function feature. Delete the contents of cells M8:M13, select the range M8:M13, type =FREQUENCY(N18:N47,L8:L13), and press the three-key combination Ctrl+⬆Shift+⏎Enter.

8 Enter =COUNT(N18:N47) in cell O6.
There are 30 records in the list.

9 Enter =SUM(M8:M13) in cell M14.
The counts in the frequency distribution should also sum to 30.

If you have problems...

The results of the count and sum functions should be the same. If either result is not 30, check that you used the appropriate ranges in your calculations.

10 Delete the contents of cell M14.
After you check the frequency counts against the total records in the list, you no longer need the value in cell M14.

11 Save your changes to the *Indy500functions* workbook.
You can close the *Indy500functions* workbook now, or leave it open and continue to the next lesson.

To extend your knowledge...

Entering the FREQUENCY Function

FREQUENCY is an array function because it returns an array of results. Array functions work differently from other functions and are entered on the worksheet differently.

Be sure you select the entire output range before attempting to enter the FREQUENCY function. You cannot enter the function in the first cell and then copy the results to other cells as you do regular functions. The output range does not have to be adjacent to the bins, but it is easier to understand the results if they are adjacent.

FREQUENCY ignores blank cells and text. If all the occurrences of numeric data to be counted exactly match bin specifications—for example, one code number representing each magazine—the bin range and output range are the same size. However, if bins represent ranges of data and not exact matches, you should include one more cell for frequency results than there are bins. The extra cell displays the count for any data items that are greater than the highest interval value stated. For example, if you want to do a frequency distribution on age, you might set bin values of 19, 34, 49, and 64. You should then specify five cells, not four, in the range for frequency results. The five cells in the output range would display counts for five age groups: 19 and under, 20 to 34, 35 to 49, 50 to 64, and 65 or older.

Lesson 4: Charting the Results of a Frequency Distribution

When analyzing data using Excel, visualizing the data is critical to understanding what information the data conveys. You may find it hard to make comparisons or draw conclusions just looking at numbers. Generally, a chart can help you to analyze or interpret the data.

In this lesson, you chart the results of a frequency distribution. On a separate sheet, you create a pie chart that converts number data to percentages. Each pie slice represents a favorite source for news, such as the Wall Street Journal (WSJ) or Newsweek.

To Chart the Results of a Frequency Distribution

1 If necessary, open the *Indy500functions* workbook.

2 Select the range K8:K13.

3 Press and hold down Ctrl, and select the range M8:M13.

4 Click the **Chart Wizard** button on the toolbar and then select the default Pie chart.

5 Advance to Step 3 of 4 – Chart Options, select the Titles tab, and enter `Favorite Magazine (Sample Size 30)` as the chart title.

6 Select the Data Labels tab. Click Category name and then click <u>P</u>ercentage.

7 Select the Legend tab, and uncheck <u>S</u>how legend.

8 Advance to Step 4 of 4 – Chart Location, select As new <u>s</u>heet, and click <u>F</u>inish.
Excel creates the specified chart on a sheet named Chart1 (see Figure 5.10). Each pie slice represents the contents of one cell in the frequency distribution in relation to the sum of all cell contents in the frequency distribution.

To Chart the Results of a Frequency Distribution

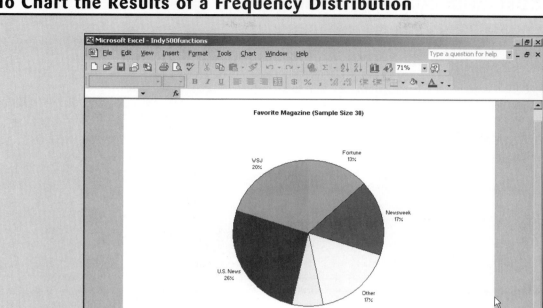

Figure 5.10

9 **Save your changes to the *Indy500functions* workbook.**

You can close the *Indy500functions* workbook now, or leave it open and continue to the next lesson.

Lesson 5: Interpreting Data with COUNTIF

You finally have time to do some analysis related to offering customers one of three discount plans for rentals they make through Indy 500 Motor Works. For example, you would like a count of those eligible for each plan.

Excel provides a ***COUNTIF function*** that you can use to count the number of cells within a range that meet your specified criteria. The function requires two arguments—the range of cells from which the counts will be tallied, and the criteria that limit which cells in that range are counted. You can use this tool now to limit analysis to one plan at a time, starting with Plan 1.

To Interpret Data with COUNTIF

1 **If necessary, open the *Indy500functions* workbook.**

2 **Select cell O8 in Sheet1, and enter 1 as the plan number.**

3 **Select cell O10, click the Insert Function button on the formula bar, and select Statistical as the function category.**

4 **Select COUNTIF as the function name and then click OK.**

The Function Arguments dialog box for the COUNTIF function displays.

(Continues)

To Interpret Data with COUNTIF (Continued)

5 Enter O18:O47 in the Range text box.

6 Enter O8 in the Criteria text box.

7 Check that your specifications match those shown in Figure 5.11, and make corrections as necessary.

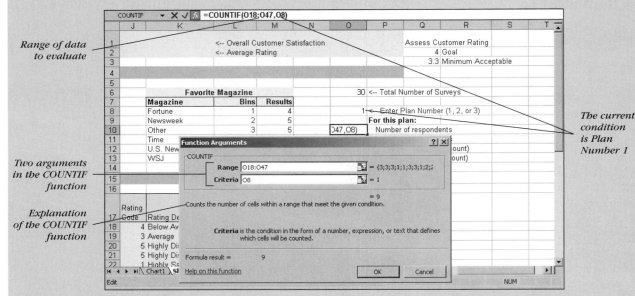

Figure 5.11

8 Click OK.
The number 9 displays in cell O10 as the count for Plan 1.

9 Select cell O11 and then enter =O10/O6.

10 Apply a percent format with zero decimal places to cell O11.
Plan 1 applies to 30% of survey respondents.

11 Save your changes to the *Indy500functions* workbook.
You can close the *Indy500functions* workbook now, or leave it open and continue to the next lesson.

Lesson 6: Interpreting Data with SUMIF

Excel provides a **SUMIF function** that you can use to add the contents of cells within a range that meet your specified criteria. The function requires three arguments: the range of cells you want to evaluate, the criteria, and the actual cells to sum.

You are continuing your analysis related to offering customers one of three discount plans for rentals they make through Indy 500 Motor Works. Now you want to sum the pre-discount rental charges, limited to one plan at a time. You can use the SUMIF function to produce the desired results.

To Interpret Data with SUMIF

① **If necessary, open the *Indy500functions* workbook.**

② **Select cell O12, click the Insert Function button on the formula bar, and select Math & Trig as the function category.**

③ **Select SUMIF as the function name and then click OK.**
The Functions Arguments dialog box for the SUMIF function displays.

④ **Enter O18:O47 in the Range text box.**

⑤ **Enter O8 in the Criteria text box.**

⑥ **Enter I18:I47 in the Sum_range text box.**

⑦ **Check that your specifications match those shown in Figure 5.12, and make corrections as necessary.**

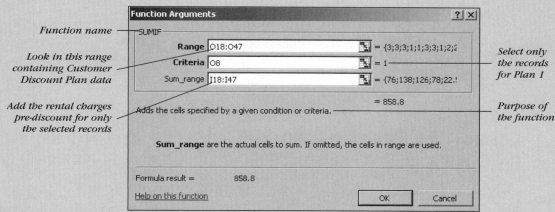

Figure 5.12

⑧ **Click OK.**
The value *858.8* displays in cell O12 as the sum for Plan 1 (see Figure 5.13).

Figure 5.13

If you have problems...

If your result is different from *858.8*, check that the ranges used in your function are correct and that the criteria in cell O8 is the number 1.

⑨ **Select cell O13 and then enter =O12/O10.**

(Continues)

To Interpret Data with SUMIF (Continued)

⑩ Apply a Currency format with two decimal places to cells O12 and O13.

⑪ Enter 3 in cell O8.
Excel recalculates the values in the range O10:O13 to reflect Plan 3 instead of Plan 1 (see Figure 5.14). You can perform analysis on Plan 1, 2, or 3 by changing the number in cell O8.

Analysis for Plan 3 in the range O10:O13

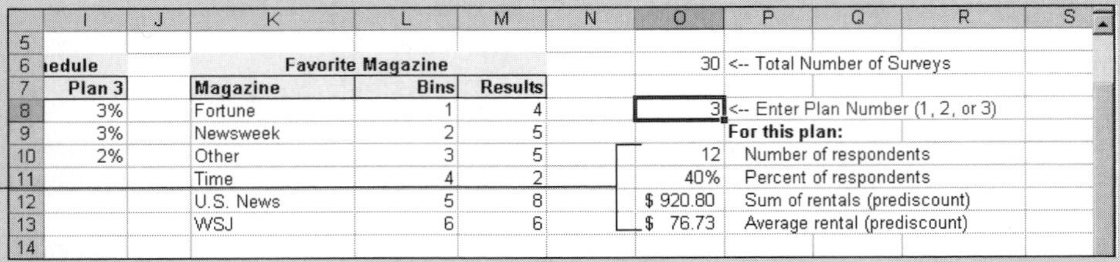

	I	J	K	L	M	N	O	P	Q	R	S
5											
6	edule		Favorite Magazine				30	<-- Total Number of Surveys			
7	Plan 3		Magazine	Bins	Results						
8	3%		Fortune	1	4		3	<-- Enter Plan Number (1, 2, or 3)			
9	3%		Newsweek	2	5			For this plan:			
10	2%		Other	3	5		12	Number of respondents			
11			Time	4	2		40%	Percent of respondents			
12			U.S. News	5	8		$ 920.80	Sum of rentals (prediscount)			
13			WSJ	6	6		$ 76.73	Average rental (prediscount)			
14											

Figure 5.14

⑫ Save your changes to the *Indy500functions* workbook.
You can close the *Indy500functions* workbook now, or leave it open and continue to the last lesson in this project.

Lesson 7: Creating an IF Function Within an IF Function

You are interested in analyzing the level of customer satisfaction. You have set a goal of a 4.0 average customer rating, and you have set a 3.3 average as the minimum acceptable. Now you want to compute the average customer rating. You plan to display one of three messages, depending on how the actual average compares to the goal and the minimum acceptable rating.

You can create an IF function within an IF function—sometimes referred to as a ***nested IF***—to automatically display the appropriate message out of three messages. Create this complex function now using the Insert Function button on the formula bar.

To Create an IF Function Within an IF Function

❶ If necessary, open the *Indy500functions* workbook.

❷ Select cell K2, enter =AVERAGE(J18:J47), and apply a Comma format with two decimal places to the cell.
The average rating of *3.37* displays in cell K2.

❸ Select cell K1 and then click the Insert Function button on the formula bar. Select the IF function from the Logical category, and click OK.

❹ Enter K2>=Q2 in the Logical_test text box.

❺ Enter Met Goal in the Value_if_true text box.

❻ Click the Value_if_false text box.
Check that your settings match those in the IF dialog box shown in Figure 5.15. Excel automatically inserts the quotation marks that must encase text entered in a Value_if_true or Value_if_false text box. Now embed another IF function as the Value_if_false.

To Create an IF Function Within an IF Function

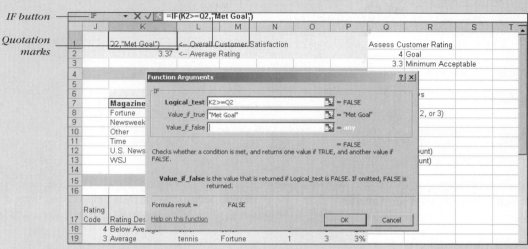

IF button

Quotation marks

Figure 5.15

7 **Click the IF button at the left end of the formula bar (refer to Figure 5.15).**
The existing Function Arguments dialog box for an IF function is replaced by a new Function Arguments dialog box for another IF function.

8 **Enter K2>=Q3 in the Logical_test text box.**

9 **Enter Close to Goal in the Value_if_true text box.**

10 **Enter Below Minimum in the Value_if_false text box.**
Check that your settings match those shown in Figure 5.16, and make changes as necessary.

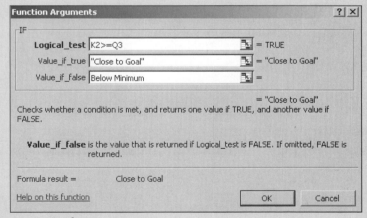

Figure 5.16

11 **Click OK.**
The message *Close to Goal* displays in cell K1 (see Figure 5.17).

(Continues)

To Create an IF Function Within an IF Function (Continued)

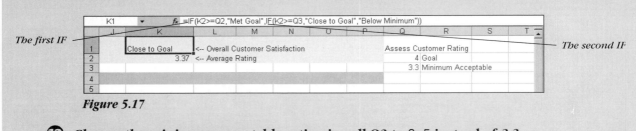

Figure 5.17

⓬ **Change the minimum acceptable rating in cell Q3 to 3.5 instead of *3.3*.**
The message *Below Minimum* displays in cell K1. The 3.37 average rating in cell K2 does not meet the minimum acceptable rating of 3.5.

⓭ **Save your changes to the *Indy500functions* workbook, and close the workbook.**
This concludes Project 5. You can exit Excel or continue with end-of-project exercises.

Summary

In this project, you used functions to create, convert, and interpret data. You used the VLOOKUP function to convert numeric data to text. You used the FREQUENCY function to count how often specified data occurred within a range, and you charted the frequency distribution results. SUMIF and COUNTIF functions provided the tools to restrict analysis to data meeting specified conditions. At the end of the project, you found that you could specify multiple test conditions in an IF statement by nesting an IF function within another IF function.

You can expand your learning by experimenting with a variety of other functions. For example, you worked with the SUMIF function from the Math & Trig category. Use onscreen Help to learn about other functions in that category, such as ABS, ROUND, ROUNDUP, and ROUNDDOWN.

Checking Concepts and Terms

Multiple Choice

Circle the letter of the correct answer for each of the following.

1. Which of the following is the key combination used to generate a frequency distribution? [L3]

   a. Ctrl + Alt + Del

   b. Ctrl + Shift + Enter

   c. Ctrl + Enter

   d. Shift + Alt + Enter

2. Which function would you use to calculate the occurrences of values in a range of cells and return a vertical array of cells containing the distribution of these occurrences? [L3]

   a. VLOOKUP

   b. HLOOKUP

   c. FREQUENCY

   d. SUMIF

3. Which of the following is/are true? [L1,L3]

   a. When using the VLOOKUP function, the search values in column one of the Table_array must be in ascending order.

   b. You can use the FREQUENCY function to convert text data to numbers so the data can be summarized.

   c. both a and b

   d. neither a nor b

4. Which of the following could you use to display one of three results in a cell, depending on conditions you specify? [L7]

   a. COUNTIF

   b. nested IF

   c. conditional IF

   d. SUMIF

5. Assume you are setting up bins for use in creating a frequency distribution. The first value in the bin range is $1,000, and the second value in the bin range is $2,000. Which of the following is a true statement? [L3]

   a. Any occurrence of $1,000 is counted in the first bin.

   b. Any occurrence of a number greater than $2,000 is counted in the second bin.

   c. both a and b

   d. neither a nor b

Discussion

	A	B	C	D	E	F	G	H	I	J	K
1	Residential Real Estate Listings - Year 2002 Real Estate, Inc.										
2											
3	Listed	Price	Area	Address	Bed	Bath	Heat	Built	Age	FinType	
4	6-Feb	85,622	Cape Cod Village	7421 Crook Drive	2	2	Solar	1988	13	FHA	
5	22-Feb	180,000	Hunter's Run	4191 Glenn Avenue	4	2.5	Oil	1995	6	VA	
6	9-Jan	125,200	Hocking Hills	11250 Spruce Street	4	2.5	Elec	1992	9	FHA	
7	23-Jan	172,159	Glenn Lakes	3452 Cortez Street	3	2	Elec	1996	5	Other	
8	12-Feb	133,900	Whispering Pines	7235 42nd Street	3	2	Gas	1970	31	FHA	
9	25-Feb	225,000	Hunter's Run	3360 Glade Avenue	5	3	Elec	1995	6	Other	
10	23-Jan	98,200	Autumn Woods	6370 Elm Street	3	1.5	Oil	1994	7	VA	
11	6-Jan	120,736	Champions Village	8882 Derby Lane	3	1.5	Elec	1990	11	VA	
12	5-Jan	170,000	Glenn Lakes	1025 Wellington Circle	3	2	Elec	1998	3	FHA	
13	26-Mar	115,539	Champions Village	3654 Silk Lane	3	1.5	Gas	1991	10	FHA	
14	13-Mar	127,502	Champions Village	3456 Silk Lane	3	1.5	Elec	1991	10	VA	
15	6-Feb	91,684	Cape Cod Village	8247 Cape Cod Drive	3	2	Oil	1988	13	FHA	
16	7-Mar	123,745	Glenn Lakes	3492 54th Avenue W.	2	2	Elec	1996	5	VA	
17	23-Feb	109,900	Rolling Hills	9981 Cortez Lane	3	2	Solar	1985	16	FHA	
18	6-Feb	87,301	Cape Cod Village	2394 Gerking Court	2	2	Solar	1988	13	FHA	
19	18-Feb	325,000	Sago Estates	12990 Augusta Lane	6	3.5	Elec	1994	7	Other	
20	15-Jan	155,900	West Glenn	6571 Keystone Avenue	3	2	Elec	1996	5	VA	
21	4-Mar	167,242	Glenn Lakes	5778 Wellington Drive	3	2	Oil	1997	4	FHA	
22	3-Jan	180,541	Glenn Lakes	6873 Wellington Drive	4	2	Elec	1997	4	VA	
23	13-Mar	240,000	Sago Estates	12983 Augustine Court	4	3	Elec	1993	8	Other	
24	13-Mar	290,000	Sago Estates	12543 Augusta Lane	4	3	Solar	1993	8	Other	

Figure 5.18

1. Refer to Figure 5.18. Describe two ways that you can use the FREQUENCY function to analyze the real estate listings data.

2. Refer to Figure 5.18. Describe two ways that you can use the VLOOKUP function to analyze the real estate listings data.

3. Refer to Figure 5.18. Describe one way that you can use the SUMIF function to analyze the real estate listings data, and one way that you can use the COUNTIF function to analyze the real estate listings data.

Skill Drill exercises reinforce project skills. Each skill that is reinforced is the same, or nearly the same, as a skill presented in the project. Detailed instructions are provided in a step-by-step format.

Before beginning your first Project 5 Skill Drill exercise, complete the following steps:

1. Open the file named *ee2-0502,* and immediately save it as `ee2-p5drill`.
   The workbook contains an overview sheet and six exercise sheets named #1-VLOOKUP, #2-FREQ1, #3-FREQ2, #4-Chart, #5-COUNTIF, and #6-Nested IF.
2. Click the Overview sheet to view the organization and content of the Project 5 Skill Drill Exercises workbook.

There are six exercises. Each exercise is independent of the others, so you may complete the exercises in any order. Be sure to save the workbook after completing each exercise. If you need a paper copy of the completed exercise, enter your name centered in a header before printing. Other print options have already been set to print compressed and to display the filename, sheet name, and current date in a footer.

Be sure to save your changes and close the workbook if you need more than one work session to complete the desired exercises; then continue working on *ee2-p5drill* instead of starting over again on the original *ee2-0502* file.

1. Using a VLOOKUP Function to Convert Data

You decide to create a frequency distribution on type of heat for homes in your residential real estate list. To create the distribution, you must first convert the data in the Heat column to numeric values in a new column. You can do this using the VLOOKUP function. To use a VLOOKUP function to convert data, follow these steps:

1. Open the *ee2-p5drill* workbook, if necessary, and select the #1-VLOOKUP worksheet.
   The VLOOKUP table data is already entered in the range G4:H7. For example, for every occurrence of Solar in the Heat column G, you want the number 1 assigned in the Hcode (heat code) column H. Before continuing, however, the data in the leftmost column of a VLOOKUP table must be in ascending order.
2. Click any cell within the range G4:G7, and click the Sort Ascending button in the toolbar.
3. Enter `VLOOKUP Table - Heat` in cell G3.
4. Click cell H14 and then click the Insert Function button on the formula bar.
5. Select the Lookup & Reference category, select the VLOOKUP function, and click OK.
6. Enter `G14` in the Lookup_value text box.
7. Enter `$G$4:$H$7` in the Table_array text box.
   Make sure that you include the dollar signs making cell references absolute, as you are going to copy the VLOOKUP function to remaining cells in the Hcode column.
8. Enter `2` in the Col_index_num box and then click OK to execute the function.
   Make sure that VLOOKUP returns the number 1 in cell H14. Compare that result to your Table_array to see that the number 1 is the number used to represent Solar heat.
9. Copy the contents of cell H14 to the range H15:H48 and then deselect the range.
   Visually scan your results. If you see errors, make sure that your cell references are correct and that the reference to the Table_array is absolute. If necessary, rework the exercise steps to generate accurate results.
10. Save your changes to the *ee2-p5drill* workbook.

2. Creating a Frequency Distribution (Exact Matches)

Your residential real estate list includes a field named Hcode, which contains numbers that correspond to the heat type entered in the Heat column—1 for Solar, 2 for Oil, 3 for Elec (electric), and 4 for Gas. You can use the FREQUENCY function to summarize the number of homes in the list that are heated by each type of energy source. Set up bins and then enter the function. To create a frequency distribution on data that match entries in the VLOOKUP table, follow these steps:

1. Open the *ee2-p5drill* workbook, if necessary, and select the #2-FREQ1 worksheet.
2. Enter the following bin values (1 through 4) and descriptive labels in the cells indicated:

In Cell	Enter
D4	Solar
E4	1
D5	Oil
E5	2
D6	Elec
E6	3
D7	Gas
E7	4

3. Select cells F4:F7.
   Be sure all four cells in the range F4:F7 display highlighted.
4. Type =FREQUENCY(H14:H48,E4:E7), but DO NOT press ⏎Enter.
5. Press the three-key combination Ctrl+⬆Shift+⏎Enter, and deselect the highlighted range.
   The frequency function returns 6 (Solar), 5 (Oil), 17 (Elec), and 7 (Gas). If you only have results in the first cell of the range—the number 6 in cell F4—you may have selected only the first cell of the result range (F4) instead of selecting F4:F7, or you may have pressed ⏎Enter after setting up the FREQUENCY function instead of the required three-key combination. Delete the contents of cells F4:F7 and repeat steps 3 through 5.
6. Make sure that your results are accurate, and save your changes to the *ee2-p5drill* workbook.

3. Creating a Frequency Distribution (Data Ranges)

Your residential real estate list includes a field named Price. You can use the FREQUENCY function to summarize the number of homes in the list that sell within the ranges you specify. Set up bins and then enter the function. To create a frequency distribution on data that fit within specified ranges, follow these steps:

1. Open the *ee2-p5drill* workbook, if necessary, and select the #3-FREQ2 worksheet.
2. Enter the following bin values in the cells indicated:

In Cell	Enter
A4	100000
A5	150000
A6	200000
A7	250000

3. Select cells B4:B8.
   Make sure that all five cells in the range B4:B8 display highlighted. While there are only four bin values, you must specify a fifth cell to display the counts for data that exceed the maximum bin value.
4. Type =FREQUENCY(B14:B48,A4:A7), but DO NOT press ⏎Enter.
5. Press the three-key combination Ctrl+⬆Shift+⏎Enter.
   The frequency function returns 9 ($100,000 or less), 11 ($100,001-$150,000), 10 ($150,001-$200,000), 2 ($200,001-$250,000), and 3 (more than $250,000). If you only have results in the

first cell of the range—the number 9 in cell B4—you may have selected only the first cell of the result range (B4) instead of selecting B4:B8, or you may have pressed ↵Enter after setting up the FREQUENCY function instead of the required three-key combination. Select cells B4:B8, press Del, and repeat steps 3 through 5.

6. Make sure that your results are accurate, and save your changes to the *ee2-p5drill* workbook.

4. Charting the Results of a FREQUENCY Distribution

You are confident reading and understanding frequency results; however, you feel that other users of the data will have a better understanding of availability by number of bedrooms if they can view a chart based on frequency results. To chart the results of a frequency distribution, follow these steps:

1. Open the *ee2-p5drill* workbook, if necessary, and select the #4-Chart worksheet.

2. Select cells D4:D7 and F4:F7.

Remember that to select non-adjacent cell ranges, select the first range; then press and hold down Ctrl while you select the next range(s).

3. Click the Chart Wizard button on the toolbar, and select the default Column Chart.

4. Advance to the Step 3 of 4 dialog box, select the Titles tab, and enter `Count of Homes by # of Bedrooms` for the chart's title.

5. Select the Legend tab, and uncheck <u>S</u>how legend.

6. Advance to the Step 4 of 4 dialog box, select As new <u>s</u>heet, and click <u>F</u>inish.

Excel creates the column chart on the sheet named Chart1.

7. Make sure that your results are accurate, and save your changes to the *ee2-p5drill* workbook.

5. Using COUNTIF to Analyze Data

As you use your listings database, you want answers to clients' questions concerning availability of homes based on a specific condition, such as solar heat. You can use COUNTIF to get the information you need. To use COUNTIF to analyze data, follow these steps:

1. Open the *ee2-p5drill* workbook, if necessary, and select the #5-COUNTIF worksheet.

2. Select cell E4, and click the Insert Function button on the formula bar.

3. Select the Statistical category, select the COUNTIF function, and click OK.

4. Enter `G14:G48` in the Range text box.

5. Enter `Solar` in the Criteria text box and then click OK.

Excel counts the occurrences of Solar in the Heat column and displays the number 6 in cell E4.

6. Select cell E5 and then click the Insert Function button on the formula bar.

7. Select the Statistical category, select the COUNTIF function, and click OK.

8. Enter `I14:I48` in the Range text box.

9. Enter `<1990` in the Criteria text box, and click OK.

Excel counts the occurrences of data less than 1990 in the Built column and displays the number 9 in cell E5.

10. Select cell E6 and enter a COUNTIF function to count the number of homes with five or more bedrooms.

The number 3 displays in cell E6.

11. Make sure that your results are accurate, and save your changes to the *ee2-p5drill* workbook.

6. Creating New Data Using a Nested IF Function

Selling a product requires that you complete a "package" of paperwork. You decide to label each home in the Paperwork field with the paperwork package name so that an assistant starting the paperwork knows which package to use. FHA and VA use the Fed FHA or Fed VA package, and all other financing arrangements require the Conventional package. You can create the new data by nesting one IF function within another. To create new data using a nested IF function, follow these steps:

1. Open the *ee2-p5drill* workbook, if necessary, and select the #6-Nested IF worksheet.
2. Select cell L14, and click the Insert Function button on the formula bar. Select the IF function from the Logical category and then click OK.
3. Enter K14="FHA" in the Logical_test text box.
4. Enter "Fed FHA" in the Value_if_true text box.
5. Select the Value_if_false text box, and click the IF button at the left end of the formula bar. Excel temporarily hides the original IF dialog box and displays a new, blank IF dialog box.
6. Enter K14="VA" in the Logical_test text box.
7. Enter "Fed VA" in the Value_if_true text box.
8. Enter "Conventional" in the Value_if_false text box, and click OK.
   Excel displays *Fed FHA* in cell L14.
9. Copy the nested IF function in cell L14 to the range L15:L48 and then deselect the highlighted range.
   Check that the entries in the Paperwork column L are correct, given the FinType entry in column K. For example, Conventional should display in cell L17.
10. Save your changes to the *ee2-p5drill* workbook.

Challenge

Challenge exercises expand on or are somewhat related to skills that are presented in the lessons. Each exercise provides a brief narrative introduction, followed by instructions in a numbered-step format that are not as detailed as those in the Skill Drill section.

Before beginning your first Project 5 Challenge exercise, complete the following steps:

1. Open the file named *ee2-0503,* and immediately save it as ee2-p5challenge.
   The *ee2-p5challenge* workbook contains five sheets: an overview, and four exercise sheets named #1-HLOOKUP, #2-FREQUENCY, #3-Double IF, and #4-IFcalcs.
2. Click the Overview sheet to view the organization of the Project 5 Challenge Exercises workbook.

Each exercise is independent of the others, so you may complete the exercises in any order. Be sure to save the workbook after completing each exercise. If you need a paper copy of the completed exercise, enter your name centered in a header before printing. Other print options have already been set to print compressed to one page and to display the filename, sheet name, and current date in a footer.

If you need more than one work session to complete the desired exercises, continue working on *ee2-p5challenge* instead of starting over again on the original *ee2-0503* file.

1. Using HLOOKUP to Convert Text to Numbers

You would like to analyze data on contributions you have made to a variety of agencies and organizations. You have the agency names entered in a row above the data. Now you want to convert the agency names to unique numeric codes so that you can generate a frequency distribution. Because the names to convert are entered across a row instead of down a column, use HLOOKUP instead of VLOOKUP. To use the HLOOKUP function to convert text to numbers, follow these steps:

1. Open the *ee2-p5challenge* workbook, if necessary, and select the #1-HLOOKUP worksheet.
   The names of the agencies or organizations that have received your contributions are already in alphabetical order across row 3 in the range A3:J3.
2. Enter the numbers 1 through 10, one to a cell, in the range A4:J4—that is, the number 1 in cell A4, the number 2 in cell B4, and so forth.

3. Select cell D12, and enter an HLOOKUP function with the following arguments:

Lookup_value	C12
Table_array	$A$3:$J$4
Row_index_num	2

After entering the function, the number *2*—the code for Church—displays in cell D12.

4. Copy the contents of cell D12 to the range D13:D45.

5. Check the accuracy of number assignments in the Agency Code column D.

For example, verify that the number *4* displays in cell D20 and the number *8* displays in cell D30.

6. Save your changes to the *ee2-p5challenge* workbook.

2. Creating a Frequency Distribution

You want to count the number of times you made contributions within several ranges of declared value. Initially, you decide to set bins of $100, $500, $1,000, $1,500, $2,000, and $2,500. To summarize your contributions using the FREQUENCY function, follow these steps:

1. Open the *ee2-p5challenge* workbook, if necessary, and select the #2-FREQUENCY worksheet.

2. In cells D4 through D9, enter the values **100**, **500**, **1000**, **1500**, **2000**, and **2500** respectively. You may want to convert the values to currency with no decimal places for readability.

3. Select the cell range E4:E10.

You are working with data that seldom matches bin specifications, so remember to include one more cell in the frequency range than you defined in the bin range.

4. Enter the FREQUENCY function to count occurrences of Declared Value based on the bins you set up.

Excel provides counts of 28, 4, 0, 1, 0, 1, and 0 respectively. You have contributed items of declared value $100 or less 28 times, and items of declared value between $101 and $500 four times.

5. Add labels in column F to describe each of the frequency distribution ranges in column E.

6. Save your changes to the *ee2-p5challenge* workbook.

3. Using Nested IF Functions to Display Messages That Vary

You reviewed your worksheet and noted that the Receipt field has three messages: *No*, *Yes*, and *Pending*. To make sure your tax records are in order, you want to add a new field called Action Message and enter messages in the column. You have already entered two test conditions and two messages in the worksheet. By setting up conditions and messages on the worksheet, you can easily change them without editing complex formulas. To use a nested IF function to display messages that vary, follow these steps:

1. Open the *ee2-p5challenge* workbook, if necessary, and select the #3-Double IF worksheet. Test conditions *No* and *Pending* display in cells D5 and D6 respectively. Two messages display in the range F5:F6—*Contact the agency* and *Follow-up needed*.

2. Select cell G12 and then display the Function Arguments dialog box for the IF function.

3. Enter **E12=$D$5** in the Logical_test text box.

4. Enter **$F$5** in the Value_if_true text box.

5. Select the Value_if_false text box, and click the IF button at the left end of the formula bar. Excel temporarily hides the original IF dialog box and displays a new, blank IF dialog box.

6. In the Logical_test text box, enter a test condition that checks if the contents of cell E12 match the contents of cell D6 (make the reference to cell D6 absolute).

7. In the Value_if_true text box, specify cell F6 (make the reference to cell F6 absolute).

8. Enter " " in the Value_if_false text box—that is, type a quotation mark, press (Spacebar), and type another quotation mark.

This instruction tells Excel to display nothing if cell E12 contains an entry other than *No* or *Pending*. The only other entry is Yes, which means you already have a receipt and no action message is needed.

9. Click OK to accept your settings.

   The message *Contact the agency* displays in cell G12.

10. Copy the nested IF function in cell G12 to the range G13:G45, and make sure that copied results are accurate.

11. Save your changes to the *ee2-p5challenge* workbook.

4. Using COUNTIF and SUMIF to Summarize Data

You decide to analyze your contribution data by generating counts and totals specific to the type of contribution (Category) and the organization receiving the contribution (Agency). You have already set up the labels to describe calculations. Now you want to enter COUNTIF and SUMIF functions to produce the information you seek. To use COUNTIF and SUMIF to summarize selected categories of contributions, follow these steps:

1. Open the *ee2-p5challenge* workbook, if necessary, and select the #4-IFcalcs worksheet.
   Labels indicate that calculated results are to display in the range A3:A6, based on conditions you specify in the range G3:G6.

2. Enter data in cell G3 and a function in cell A3 so that the number of times you donated to Goodwill (**8**) displays in cell A3.

3. Enter data in cell G4 and a function in cell A4 so that the sum of cash contributions (**$2,265**) displays in cell A4.

4. Enter data in cell G5 and a function in cell A5 so that the total declared value contributed to the church (**$1,650**) displays in cell A5.

5. Enter data in cell G6 and a function in cell A6 so that the number of times a contribution exceeded $99.99 (**10**) displays in cell A6.

6. In row 7, set up one more COUNTIF or SUMIF function to display information of your choice.

7. Save your changes to the *ee2-p5challenge* workbook.

Discovery Zone exercises require advanced knowledge of topics presented in *essentials* lessons, application of skills from multiple lessons, or self-directed learning of new skills.

Before beginning your first Project 5 Discovery Zone exercise, complete the following steps:

1. Open the file named *ee2-0504*, and immediately save it as **ee2-p5discovery**.
   The *ee2-p5discovery* workbook contains three sheets: an overview, and two exercise sheets named #1-RentalDays, and #2-Charts.

2. Select the Overview worksheet to view the organization of the Project 5 Discovery Zone Exercises workbook.

Each exercise is independent of the other, so you may complete the exercises in any order. Be sure to save the workbook after completing each exercise. If you need a paper copy of the completed exercise, enter your name centered in a header before printing. Other print options have already been set to print compressed to one page and to display the filename, sheet name, and current date in a footer.

Be sure to save your changes, and close the workbook if you need more than one work session to complete the desired exercises. Continue working on *ee2-p5discovery* instead of starting over again on the original *ee2-0504* file.

1. Creating a Frequency Distribution for Selected Intervals

You are interested in finding out the number of rentals for 1 day, for 2 or 3 days, for 4 to 7 days, and for more than 7 days. Open the *ee2-p5discovery* workbook, and select the sheet named #1-RentalDays. Set up a frequency distribution to produce the information you want. Be sure to label results (2 one-day rentals, 11 rentals for two or three days, 9 rentals for four to seven days, and 8 rentals for more than seven days). Create another frequency distribution based on the same data, but set up different bins this time.

2. Using SUMIF to Create Data and Charting the Results

Your firm rents cars classified by size as truck, subcomp, compact, mid size, full size, and luxury. You want to compare the revenues generated from each category. Open the *ee2-p5discovery* workbook, and select the sheet named #2-Charts. Set up six SUMIF functions in adjacent cells to calculate total rental pre-discount, one for each size category (for example, rentals of compact cars sum to $142.40 and rentals of luxury cars sum to $1,300). Use the results to create a well-labeled column chart comparing the rental fee. Create a second chart based on the same data—a well-labeled pie chart. What conclusions can you draw from the charts? Does one chart seem more useful than the other? Why?

Guiding Cell Entry with Data Validation

Objectives

In this project, you learn how to

- ✔ Attach an Input Message to a Cell
- ✔ Restrict Cell Entries to Data from a List
- ✔ Restrict Cell Entries to Whole Numbers within Specified Limits
- ✔ Create a User-Specified Error Alert Message
- ✔ Copy Data Restrictions and Messages to Other Cells
- ✔ Find and Fix Invalid Data
- ✔ Find Cells That Have Data Restrictions or Messages
- ✔ Play Back Worksheet Data

Key terms in this project include

- ❑ data validation
- ❑ error alert message
- ❑ input message

Why Would I Do This?

You can introduce errors in a worksheet by entering the wrong data or by creating calculations that are not correct. Data in worksheets are used to make decisions. If the data or the calculations in a worksheet are not accurate, decisions based on that data are likely to be wrong—often with costly results. Excel provides a variety of data validation options to guide data entry and prevent common data entry errors.

Visual Summary

Data validation options enable you to set up data entry instructions, drop-down lists of allowable entries, and error messages. Figure 6.1 illustrates a common data validation technique—restricting data entry to an item on a drop-down list.

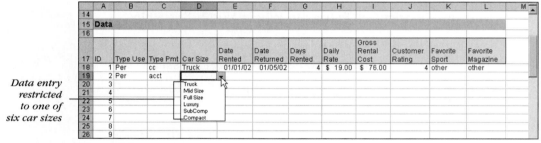

Data entry restricted to one of six car sizes

Figure 6.1

In this project, you use lists and limits to validate data entry, attach input messages to cells, specify error messages, and activate a feature to hear the contents of worksheet cells. Other topics include copying, editing, and deleting validation features. To make it easier to focus on individual validation techniques, the data for each lesson are set up on separate worksheets. Let's begin by setting up a message that displays whenever a cell is selected.

Lesson 1: Attaching an Input Message to a Cell

You are setting up a worksheet to hold survey data provided by customers who recently rented vehicles from Indy 500 Motor Works. Staff members will enter the data from the surveys, and you want to give them as much guidance as possible. You decide to include data validation features in the worksheet design.

To apply a validation method to a worksheet, select a cell and then open the Data Validation dialog box containing three tabs (see Figure 6.2). These tabs can be used individually or in combination to set up messages and apply a variety of restrictions to a cell.

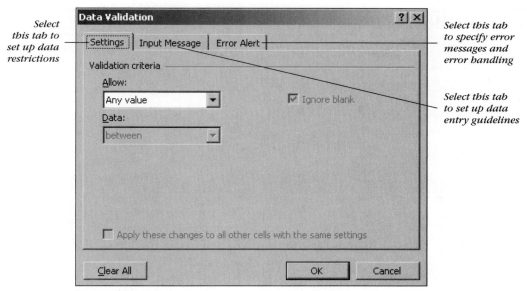

Select this tab to set up data restrictions

Select this tab to specify error messages and error handling

Select this tab to set up data entry guidelines

Figure 6.2

In this case, you want to set up an ***input message***, a convenient way to display instructions to users when they access a specific cell in a worksheet. The display can have two parts—the heading (optional) and the message itself. Clicking a cell formatted with an input message causes the predefined text to display in a box near the lower-right corner of the cell (or in the Office Assistant balloon, if that Help feature is active).

Use this feature now to provide instructions for entering one of two Type Use codes—*Per* and *Bus*. These codes denote that a rental was for *Personal* or *Business* use.

To Attach an Input Message to a Cell

1 **Open the *ee2-0601* file and save it as** `Indy500Validation`.
The workbook contains seven worksheets: Message, Drop-down List, Limits, Error Alert, Copy, FindFix, and Playback.

2 **Select the Message worksheet, and click cell B18.**
Cell B18 is the first cell in the Type Use column of the data area of the Message worksheet.

3 **Select Data, Validation.**
The Data Validation dialog box opens.

4 **Select the Input Message tab, and type** `Codes for Type Use` **in the Title text box.**

5 **Type** `Enter Per (personal) or Bus (business)` **in the Input message area (see Figure 6.3).**

(Continues)

To Attach an Input Message to a Cell (Continued)

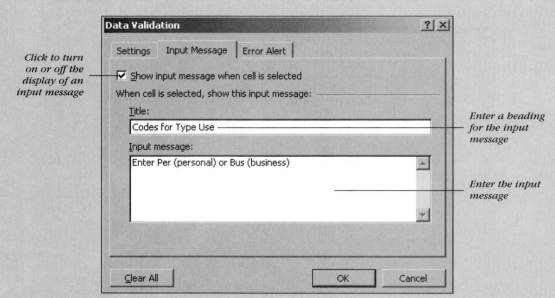

Click to turn on or off the display of an input message

Enter a heading for the input message

Enter the input message

Figure 6.3

6 **Click OK, and make sure that cell B18 is the current cell.**
The specified message displays near the lower-right corner of cell B18 if the Office Assistant is not active (see Figure 6.4). The message displays in the Office Assistant's balloon if that feature is active.

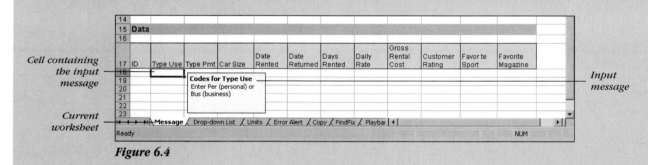

Cell containing the input message

Current worksheet

Input message

Figure 6.4

7 **Save your changes to the *Indy500Validation* workbook.**
Keep the *Indy500Validation* workbook open for the next lesson, or close the workbook and exit Excel.

To extend your knowledge...

Positioning an Input Message

If the Office Assistant is active, an input message displays in its balloon rather than as a box near the cell. If desired, you can drag the Assistant closer to the cells where you are entering data.

Lesson 2: Restricting Cell Entries to Data from a List

Options on the Settings tab of the Data Validation dialog box allow you to restrict the type of data that can be entered in a cell. Choices range from allowing any value to allowing only whole numbers, decimals, dates, times, values between two numbers, or values in a list.

The last option—values in a list—is the focus of this lesson. Selecting from a list instead of typing is likely to improve both the speed and the accuracy of data entry. You decide to use this feature to set up a list of car sizes. Figure 6.5 shows the options for restricting data entry to values in a list. You can create a list directly in the Source text box by typing allowable entries separated by commas; however, you may find it easier to type the allowable entries in another area of the worksheet and then refer to that range in the Source text box.

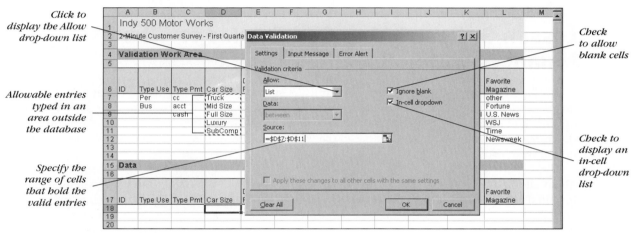

Figure 6.5

In this lesson, you apply a validation list to the first cell in the Car Size field. Users of the worksheet can then select among Truck, Mid Size, Full Size, Luxury, and SubComp instead of typing each entry. Those allowable entries are already set up for you in a separate area of the worksheet.

To Restrict Cell Entries to Data from a List

❶ Open the *Indy500Validation* workbook, if necessary, and select the Drop-down List worksheet.

❷ Click cell D18.
This selects the first cell below Car Size in the Data area of Indy 500 Motor Works.

❸ Choose Data, Validation, and select the Settings tab.

❹ Display the Allow drop-down list, and select List.

❺ Enter =$D$7:$D$11 in the Source text box.
Be sure to start the entry with an equal (=) sign. The dollar signs make the reference to range D7:D11 absolute—an essential specification if the data validation setting is copied to other cells.

❻ Check that your specifications match those shown in Figure 6.5, including the check mark in the In-cell drop-down check box.

(Continues)

To Restrict Cell Entries to Data from a List (Continued)

7   **Click OK.**

8   **Display the drop-down list in cell D18 (that is, click the small arrowhead at the right end of cell D18).**

9   **Select Luxury from the drop-down list.**
The word *Luxury* displays in cell D18.

10   **Save your changes to the *Indy500Validation* workbook.**
Keep the *Indy500Validation* workbook open for the next lesson, or close the workbook and exit Excel.

Lesson 3: Restricting Cell Entries to Whole Numbers within Specified Limits

Controlling data entry through a drop-down list is suitable for selecting among relatively few exact-match entries. Some data, such as whole numbers, decimals, dates, and times, normally would not be validated using a list. For example, if you wanted to allow any date in the year 2001 using a drop-down list, you would have to set up 365 dates. Selecting from such a list would take longer than if no list were used at all.

As an alternative, you can specify that data must fit specified criteria, and that any attempt to enter invalid data produces an ***error alert message*** in one of three styles—Stop, Warning, or Information. For example, you can require that data be above or below a stated value, within a range of values, or outside a range of values. While this form of validation is not as accurate as restricting entries to a list, it still prevents some errors.

As you continue working with Indy 500 Motor Works survey data, you decide to set up a validation limiting data entry for Customer Rating to a whole number between 1 and 5. Further, you decide to skip using an Input message because you know that Validation automatically generates an error message if an invalid entry is attempted.

To Restrict Cell Entries to Whole Numbers within Specified Limits

1   **Open the *Indy500Validation* workbook, if necessary, and select the Limits worksheet.**

2   **Click cell J18, and select Data, Validation.**

3   **Select the Settings tab in the Data Validation dialog box, and select Whole number from the Allow drop-down list.**
The phrase *Whole number* displays in the Allow text box, and the word *between* displays in the Data text box.

4   **Type 1 in the Minimum text box and 5 in the Maximum text box.**
Check that your specifications match those in Figure 6.6, and make changes as necessary.

To Restrict Cell Entries to Whole Numbers within Specified Limits

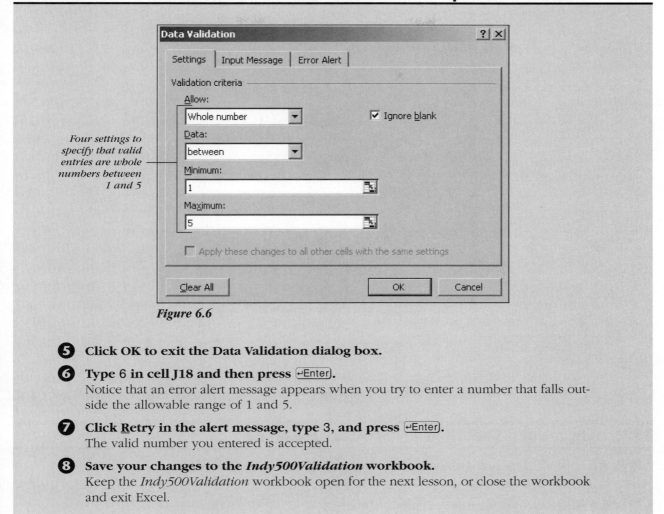

Four settings to specify that valid entries are whole numbers between 1 and 5

Figure 6.6

❺ Click OK to exit the Data Validation dialog box.

❻ Type 6 in cell J18 and then press ↵Enter.
Notice that an error alert message appears when you try to enter a number that falls outside the allowable range of 1 and 5.

❼ Click Retry in the alert message, type 3, and press ↵Enter.
The valid number you entered is accepted.

❽ Save your changes to the *Indy500Validation* workbook.
Keep the *Indy500Validation* workbook open for the next lesson, or close the workbook and exit Excel.

Lesson 4: Creating a User-Specified Error Alert Message

When validation settings have been specified, Excel displays an error alert message when invalid data are entered in the cell. This is a general message and does not explain how to correct the problem. You can specify an error alert message that replaces the one generated by Excel.

You can choose from three different levels of error alerts: Information, Warning, and Stop. Each style of error message offers different levels of protection. Information messages allow you to accept the invalid data or cancel entry. Warnings allow you to accept the invalid data, change your data, or cancel entry. Stop messages prevent invalid data from being entered.

Figure 6.7 illustrates the Error Alert tab of the Data Validation dialog box. Creating a message involves a three-step process. Select the style of error alert you want to use, compose your message, and check on the option to display your message.

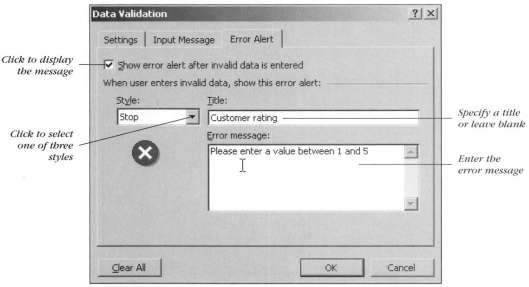

Figure 6.7

In this lesson, you are concerned about entering the Customer Rating code correctly. The setting has already been made to cell J18; however, the Excel-generated error message does not give the user enough information about what the correct data should be. You decide to use the Stop style and display your own message.

To Create a User-Specified Error Alert Message

❶ Open the *Indy500Validation* workbook, if necessary, and select the Error Alert tab.

❷ Click cell J18, and select Data, Validation.

❸ Select the Error Alert tab.
Stop displays in the Style text box. The Title and Error message text boxes are blank.

❹ Type Customer rating in the Title text box.

❺ Type Please enter a value between 1 and 5 in the Error message text box.
Check that your specifications match those in Figure 6.7, and make changes as necessary.

❻ Click OK to exit the Data Validation dialog box, type 6 in cell J18, and press ⏎Enter.
Notice that the error message is more helpful this time.

❼ Click Retry, type 3 in cell J18, and press ⏎Enter.
The valid number you entered is accepted.

❽ Save your changes to the *Indy500Validation* workbook.
Keep the *Indy500Validation* workbook open for the next lesson, or close the workbook and exit Excel.

Lesson 5: Copying Data Restrictions and Messages to Other Cells

You can apply validation settings and messages to a single cell or an entire range of cells. If you are designing a worksheet and have not yet entered data, you can apply one or more validation settings to the first blank cell of a range, and then copy the specifications to the rest of the range. To do this, copy the cell containing the validation restrictions using <u>C</u>opy and <u>P</u>aste commands or drag the fill handle.

You can also apply validation specifications to existing data by using Paste <u>S</u>pecial instead of <u>P</u>aste. Paste <u>S</u>pecial allows you to select from a variety of copy options, one of which is Validatio<u>n</u>.

The Favorite Sport column in the survey results for Indy 500 Motor Works already contains data. Now you want to create a drop-down list to control data entry for new records and to check the accuracy of records already entered.

To Copy Data Restrictions and Messages to Other Cells

❶ Open the *Indy500Validation* workbook, if necessary, and select the Copy worksheet.

❷ Click cell K18.
A small arrow indicating a drop-down list displays at the right end of the cell.

❸ Click several other cells in column K below cell K18.
A drop-down list has not been applied to remaining cells in the column.

❹ Click cell K18, and click the Copy button in the toolbar (or choose <u>E</u>dit, <u>C</u>opy).

❺ Select the range K19:K47.

❻ Right-click within the highlighted range K19:K47, and select Paste <u>S</u>pecial (or choose <u>E</u>dit, Paste <u>S</u>pecial).

❼ Select Validatio<u>n</u>, click OK, and press (Esc).
A validation drop-down list for Favorite Sport is copied to all remaining cells in the column that contain data. Pressing (Esc) removes the marquee from cell K18.

 ### If you have problems...

If *other* displays in all cells, you selected <u>P</u>aste instead of Paste <u>S</u>pecial. Use <u>U</u>ndo to reverse the paste results and start again with step 6.

---

❽ Display the drop-down list for cell K20.
Options on the copied drop-down list include *basketball* and *golf* (see Figure 6.8). Data already entered in column K include two errors in spelling—*basketbal* in cell K27 and *gulf* in cell K35. Do not correct the errors now. You learn to audit for such errors in Lesson 6.

(Continues)

To Copy Data Restrictions and Messages to Other Cells (Continued)

	A	B	C	D	E	F	G	H	I	J	K	L	M
16													
17	ID	Type Use	Type Pmt	Car Size	Date Rented	Date Returned	Days Rented	Daily Rate	Gross Rental Cost	Customer Rating	Favorite Sport	Favorite Magazine	
18	1	Per	cc	Truck	01/01/02	01/05/02	4	$ 19.00	$ 76.00	4	other	other	
19	2	Per	acct	Mid Size	03/04/02	03/16/02	12	$ 11.50	$138.00	3	tennis	Fortune	
20	3	Per	cc	Full Size	02/16/02	02/25/02	9	$ 14.00	$126.00	5	basketball	S. News	
21	4	Per	cash	Luxury	03/12/02	03/15/02	3	$ 26.00	$ 78.00	5	other	SJ	
22	5	Per	cc	SubComp	02/06/02	02/09/02	3	$ 7.50	$ 22.50	1	tennis	me	
23	6	Per	cc	Luxury	02/19/02	02/22/02	3	$ 26.00	$ 78.00	4	basketball	SJ	
24	7	Bus	acct	Mid Size	01/01/02	01/05/02	4	$ 11.50	$ 46.00	3	golf	rtune	
25	8	Bus	acct	Mid Size	01/12/02	01/13/02	1	$ 11.50	$ 11.50	1	football	rtune	
26	9	Bus	cc	Truck	02/01/02	02/07/02	6	$ 19.00	$114.00	4	baseball	other	
27	10	Bus	acct	Full Size	01/23/02	01/27/02	4	$ 14.00	$ 56.00	2	basketbal	U.S. News	
28	11	Per	cc	Luxury	03/02/02	03/09/02	7	$ 26.00	$182.00	2	golf	WSJ	
29	12	Per	cash	Mid Size	02/13/02	02/14/02	1	$ 11.50	$ 11.50	5	tennis	Fortune	
30	13	Bus	cc	Full Size	01/09/02	01/12/02	3	$ 14.00	$ 42.00	4	basketball	U.S. News	
31	14	Per	acct	Truck	02/06/02	02/21/02	15	$ 19.00	$285.00	4	other	other	
32	15	Bus	cc	Compact	03/03/02	03/05/02	2	$ 8.90	$ 17.80	1	baseball	Newsweek	
33	16	Bus	cc	Full Size	03/01/02	03/15/02	14	$ 14.00	$196.00	4	basketball	U.S. News	
34	17	Bus	cc	Truck	02/25/02	02/27/02	2	$ 19.00	$ 38.00	5	other	other	
35	18	Per	acct	Luxury	01/15/02	01/30/02	15	$ 26.00	$390.00	3	gulf	WSJ	
36	19	Bus	acct	Compact	03/14/02	03/16/02	2	$ 8.90	$ 17.80	4	baseball	Newsweek	

Drop-down list copied to cell K20

Pre-existing errors

Figure 6.8

9 **Save your changes to the *Indy500Validation* workbook.**

Keep the *Indy500Validation* workbook open for the next lesson, or close the workbook and exit Excel.

To extend your knowledge...

Applying Validation After Data Entry

Applying validation restrictions to worksheets after data are already entered is a common situation. Perhaps you entered data manually until you discovered all possible answers. Now you want to turn maintenance of the data over to other staff. It's also possible that you must now maintain a worksheet developed by someone else. If you do apply validation to cells that already contain data, just be sure to look for and correct any pre-existing errors.

Lesson 6: Finding and Fixing Invalid Data

Once validation restrictions are applied to a cell they are in effect whenever you enter data in that cell; however, if you apply validation to a cell that already contains data, the existing data are not automatically checked for validity. Excel offers a variety of auditing tools, one of which finds cells with errors.

The Formula Auditing toolbar contains a feature to circle invalid data that works in combination with validation. When you select the Circle Invalid Data button on the Formula Auditing toolbar, Excel places a red circle around cells whose contents don't meet the validation rule settings. Once you have identified errors in your data, you must investigate each one and make corrections. As you correct the data, the red circles disappear.

In this lesson, you find and correct the three types of errors described in Figure 6.9.

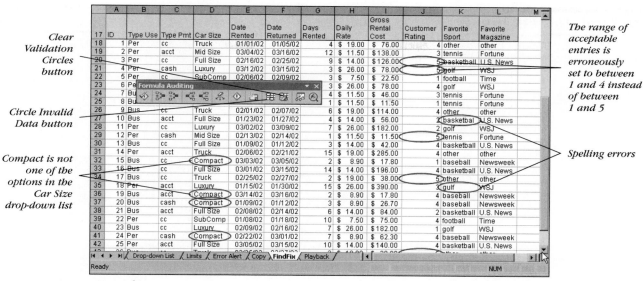

Clear Validation Circles button

Circle Invalid Data button

Compact is not one of the options in the Car Size drop-down list

The range of acceptable entries is erroneously set to between 1 and 4 instead of between 1 and 5

Spelling errors

Figure 6.9

In the Car Size field, each occurrence of Compact is circled, which suggests that the word Compact must be missing in the drop-down list set up in the range D7:D11. To correct this problem, you can add Compact to the list, thus increasing the defined range by one cell.

The validation setting for Customer Rating incorrectly limits data to a range of numbers 1 through 4, while the data contains numbers 1 through 5. To correct this problem, you must change the maximum allowed whole number to 5 instead of 4.

The third error involves misspellings in the Favorite Sport column. The data restrictions in the validation list (K7:K12) are correct. Because cells K18:K47 use a validation drop-down list, you can make corrections by dropping down the list in each cell with a red circle (one at a time) and selecting the correct entry.

To Find and Fix Invalid Data

❶ Open the *Indy500Validation* workbook, if necessary, and select the FindFix worksheet.

❷ Choose Tools, point to Formula Auditing, and select Show Formula Auditing Toolbar.

❸ Click the Circle Invalid Data button, and scroll to view records in rows 18 through 47.
All invalid data according to validation settings appear circled in red (refer to Figure 6.9).

❹ Click cell D12, and enter Compact.

❺ Select cells D18:D47, and choose Data, Validation.

❻ On the Settings tab, change the =$D$7:$D$11 entry in the Source text box to =$D$7:$D$12 (see Figure 6.10).

(Continues)

To Find and Fix Invalid Data (Continued)

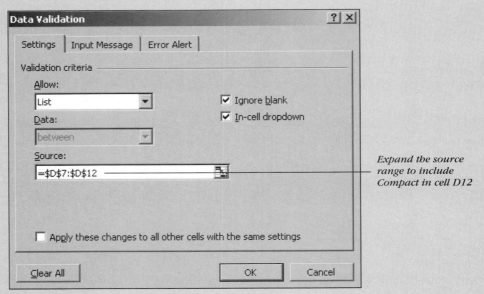

Figure 6.10

❼ **Click OK.**
   You corrected the range specifying the list to use in validating car size. The cells containing the word *Compact* are no longer circled in red.

❽ **Select the range J18:J47.**

❾ **Display the Data Validation dialog box, and select the Settings tab.**

❿ **Type 5 in the Maximum text box, and click OK.**
   You corrected the value specifying the maximum allowed for entering customer-rating data. The cells containing a customer rating of 5 are no longer circled in red.

⓫ **Display the drop-down list in cell K27, and select *basketball*; then display the drop-down list in cell K35, and select *golf*.**
   All errors in the worksheet are corrected. Note, however, that the red circles do not disappear after you make corrections from drop-down lists. You must reapply the Circle Invalid Data option to recheck for errors.

⓬ **Click the Circle Invalid Data button on the Formula Auditing toolbar.**
   There should be no cells circled in red.

⓭ **Close the Formula Auditing toolbar, and save your changes to the *Indy500Validation* workbook.**
   Keep the *Indy500Validation* workbook open for the next lesson, or close the workbook and exit Excel.

Lesson 7: Finding Cells That Have Data Restrictions or Messages

You may not know if the worksheet you are using contains data validation restrictions and messages. This is especially true if you are using a worksheet someone else has designed. You can use the Go To Special dialog box (see Figure 6.11) to highlight cells that contain validation restrictions and messages.

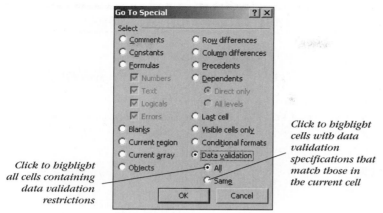

Figure 6.11

In this lesson, you display a worksheet containing survey data and look for cells that have data restrictions or messages.

To Find Cells That Have Data Restrictions or Messages

1 Open the *Indy500Validation* workbook, if necessary, and select the FindFix worksheet.

2 Select cell A1, and choose **E**dit, **G**o To.

3 Click the **S**pecial button.
The Go To Special dialog box displays.

4 Click the Data **v**alidation option in the lower-right corner, and click A**l**l.

5 Make sure that your settings match those in Figure 6.11, and click OK.
Use your mouse to scroll around the worksheet. Notice that the Type Use, Type Pmt, Car Size, Customer Rating, Favorite Sport, and Favorite Magazine fields are all selected (see Figure 6.12).

	A	B	C	D	E	F	G	H	I	J	K	L	M
16													
17	ID	Type Use	Type Pmt	Car Size	Date Rented	Date Returned	Days Rented	Daily Rate	Gross Rental Cost	Customer Rating	Favorite Sport	Favorite Magazine	
18	1	Per		Truck	01/01/02	01/05/02	4	$ 19.00	$ 76.00	4	other	other	
19	2	Per	acct	Mid Size	03/04/02	03/16/02	12	$ 11.50	$138.00	3	tennis	Fortune	
20	3	Per	cc	Full Size	02/16/02	02/25/02	9	$ 14.00	$126.00	5	basketball	U.S. News	
21	4	Per	cash	Luxury	03/12/02	03/15/02	3	$ 26.00	$ 78.00	5	golf	WSJ	
22	5	Per	cc	SubComp	02/06/02	02/09/02	3	$ 7.50	$ 22.50	1	football	Time	
23	6	Per	cc	Luxury	02/19/02	02/22/02	3	$ 26.00	$ 78.00	4	golf	WSJ	
24	7	Bus	acct	Mid Size	01/01/02	01/05/02	4	$ 11.50	$ 46.00	3	tennis	Fortune	
25	8	Bus	acct	Mid Size	01/12/02	01/13/02	1	$ 11.50	$ 11.50	1	tennis	Fortune	
26	9	Bus	cc	Truck	02/01/02	02/07/02	6	$ 19.00	$114.00	4	other	other	
27	10	Bus	acct	Full Size	01/23/02	01/27/02	4	$ 14.00	$ 56.00	2	basketbal	U.S. News	
28	11	Per	cc	Luxury	03/02/02	03/09/02	7	$ 26.00	$182.00	2	golf	WSJ	
29	12	Per	cash	Mid Size	02/13/02	02/14/02	1	$ 11.50	$ 11.50	5	tennis	Fortune	
30	13	Bus	cc	Full Size	01/09/02	01/12/02	3	$ 14.00	$ 42.00	4	basketball	U.S. News	
31	14	Per	acct	Truck	02/06/02	02/21/02	15	$ 19.00	$285.00	4	other	other	
32	15	Bus	cc	Compact	03/03/02	03/05/02	2	$ 8.90	$ 17.80	1	baseball	Newsweek	
33	16	Bus	cc	Full Size	03/01/02	03/15/02	14	$ 14.00	$196.00	4	basketball	U.S. News	
34	17	Bus	cc	Truck	02/25/02	02/27/02	2	$ 19.00	$ 38.00	5	other	other	
35	18	Per	acct	Luxury	01/15/02	01/30/02	15	$ 26.00	$390.00	3	gulf	WSJ	
36	19	Bus	acct	Compact	03/14/02	03/16/02	2	$ 8.90	$ 17.80	4	baseball	Newsweek	
37	20	Bus	cash	Compact	01/09/02	01/12/02	3	$ 8.90	$ 26.70	4	baseball	Newsweek	
38	21	Bus	acct	Full Size	02/08/02	02/14/02	6	$ 14.00	$ 84.00	2	basketball	U.S. News	
39	22	Per	cc	SubComp	01/08/02	01/18/02	10	$ 7.50	$ 75.00	4	football	Time	
40	23	Bus	cc	Luxury	02/09/02	02/16/02	7	$ 26.00	$182.00	1	golf	WSJ	
41	24	Per	cash	Compact	02/22/02	03/01/02	7	$ 8.90	$ 62.30	4	baseball	Newsweek	

Message / Drop-down List / Limits / Error Alert / Copy \ **FindFix** / Playback /

Ready   Sum=101   NUM

Figure 6.12

6 Click any cell that is not highlighted.

(Continues)

To Find Cells That Have Data Restrictions or Messages (Continued)

This deselects the highlighted cells.

7 **Click any cell in the range B18:B47, and display the Go To Special dialog box.**

8 **Click Data validation, click Same, and click OK.**
The entire Type Use data field displays highlighted, indicating that the data validation in cell B18 is used in all cells in that field.

9 **Save your changes to the *Indy500Validation* workbook.**
Keep the *Indy500Validation* workbook open for the last lesson in this project, or close the workbook and exit Excel.

 ## To extend your knowledge...

Impact of Saving or Closing on Circled Data

Saving or closing a workbook turns off the Circle Invalid Data feature and causes the red circles around incorrect data to disappear. To display the circles again, repeat the process to turn on the Formula Auditing toolbar and then select the Circle Invalid Data button.

Lesson 8: Playing Back Worksheet Data

If you have speakers installed on your computer system, Excel makes it possible to hear, as well as see, the contents of cells. Buttons on the Text To Speech toolbar enable you to listen to the contents of worksheet cells that are not hidden. If you select the Speak Cells button (see Figure 6.13), the computer audibly plays back the existing contents of the range you specify—one cell at a time. If you prefer to hear the value as soon as you enter data into a cell, you can select the Speak On Enter button.

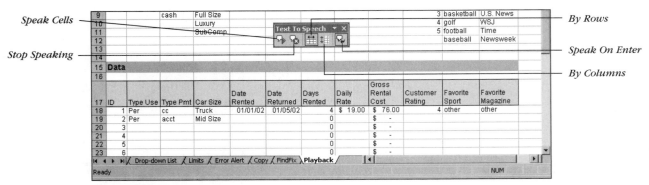

Figure 6.13

In this lesson, you first select a range of cells for the computer to read back to you. You also play back cell contents after every cell entry. You must have speakers installed to complete this lesson.

To Play Back Worksheet Data

❶ Open the *Indy500Validation* workbook, if necessary, and select the Playback worksheet.

❷ Choose <u>V</u>iew, <u>T</u>oolbars and then select Text To Speech.
The Text To Speech toolbar displays (refer to Figure 6.13).

❸ Select the range A18:L18, and click the Speak Cells button on the Text To Speech toolbar.
Excel plays back the contents of the specified range, one cell at a time. To stop the playback before Excel reads each cell in the range, click the Stop Speaking button.

❹ Click the Speak On Enter button on the Text To Speech toolbar.

❺ Click cell E19, type 01/05/02, and press Tab⇄.
If your speaker system is operating, the default computer voice plays back *January fifth zero two* as the contents of cell E19. Pressing Tab⇄ makes active the next unlocked cell in a protected worksheet—in this case, cell F19.

❻ Type 01/09/02 in cell F19, and press Tab⇄.
The default computer voice plays back *January ninth zero two* as the contents of cell F19. The active cell is H19. Pressing Tab⇄ skipped cell G19, a protected cell containing a formula that calculates days rented.

❼ Type 11.50 in cell H19, and press Tab⇄.
The default computer voice plays back *eleven dollars and fifty cents* as the contents of cell H19. The active cell is J19. Pressing Tab⇄ skipped cell I19, a protected cell containing a formula that calculates gross rental cost.

❽ Click the Speak On Enter button on the Text To Speech toolbar.
Clicking the Speak On Enter button again turns the feature off. If you do not click the button to turn off the feature, the computer voice continues to play back the contents of new cell entries even if the toolbar is not visible.

❾ Close the Text To Speech toolbar, save your changes to the *Indy500Validations* workbook, and close the workbook.
This concludes Project 6. You can exit Excel, or continue with the end-of-project exercises.

To extend your knowledge...

Changing the Default Computer Voice

You can select another computer voice and change the voice speed setting through Windows. Choose Start, <u>S</u>ettings, <u>C</u>ontrol Panel. Select the Speech icon, click the Text to Speech tab in the Speech Properties dialog box, and make the desired changes..

Summary

This project had a single focus—presenting ways to increase data accuracy by applying data validation techniques. Your experiences ranged from simply displaying a message upon selecting a cell to preventing the entry of data that did not meet predefined restrictions. You learned that you can apply validation settings to blank cells or cells containing data. Remaining topics included using the Formula Auditing toolbar to find invalid data, using the Go To Special dialog box to find cells that have data restrictions or messages, and selecting options to audibly play back the contents of worksheet cells.

You can expand your learning by experimenting with variations of data validation, such as restricting data entry to a time period or to text containing a specified number of characters. There are numerous onscreen Help topics related to data validation. Explore the speech recognition topics, too, and learn how to train the computer to recognize your voice.

Checking Concepts and Terms

Multiple Choice

Circle the letter of the correct answer for each of the following.

1. Which Data Validation tab would you use to restrict data entry to the values in a list? [L2]

   a. Settings
   b. Error Alert
   c. Input Message
   d. In-cell List

2. Which error alert style allows you to enter invalid data? [L4]

   a. Information
   b. Warning
   c. Stop
   d. Both a and b

3. Which Data Validation tab can be used to display a message? [L1, L4]

   a. Settings
   b. Input Message
   c. Error Alert
   d. Both b and c

4. Which of the following is an accurate statement? [L6]

   a. If you apply validation to a cell that already contains data, the existing data are automatically checked for validity.
   b. You can use a button on the Formula Auditing toolbar to highlight cells that contain validation restrictions and messages.
   c. When you select the Circle Invalid Data button on the Formula Auditing toolbar, Excel places a red circle around cells with contents that don't meet the validation rule settings.
   d. All of the above

5. Which of the following is true? [L2, L8]

   a. The List setting for data validation is used to restrict data to a range between two numbers.
   b. The Speak Cells button on the Text To Speech toolbar is a toggle button; click it once to turn the feature on, and again to turn the feature off.
   c. Both a and b
   d. Neither a nor b

Discussion

1. You are designing a worksheet to track your donations during a year (see Figure 6.14). Before you start to enter data, describe what validation technique(s) you might use to ensure that accurate dates are entered in column A (limit your discussion to options available through the Settings and/or Input Message tabs of the Data Validation dialog box). [L1-L3]

	A	B	C	D	E
1	Deductible Contributions - Year 2003				
2					
3	Date	Declared Value	Organization	Receipt	Category
4					
5					
6					
7					
8					

Figure 6.14

2. You are designing a worksheet to track your donations during a year (refer to Figure 6.14). You plan to limit your donations to five organizations. Before you start to enter data, describe what validation technique(s) you might use to ensure that each organization's name is entered quickly and accurately in column C (limit your discussion to options available through the Settings and/or Input Message tabs of the Data Validation dialog box). [L1-L3]

3. You are designing a worksheet to track your donations during a year (refer to Figure 6.14). You want to prevent all entries in the Receipt field (column D) except Y or N, for Yes or No respectively. Before you start to enter data, describe how you might use options on the Error Alert tab of the Data Validation dialog box to achieve the desired results. [L4]

Skill Drill

Skill Drill exercises reinforce project skills. Each skill that is reinforced is the same, or nearly the same, as a skill presented in the project. Detailed instructions are provided in a step-by-step format.

Before beginning your first Project 6 Skill Drill exercise, complete the following steps:

1. Open the file named *ee2-0602,* and immediately save it as **ee2-p6drill**.
   The workbook contains an overview sheet and six exercise sheets named #1-Message, #2-Data List, #3-Data Limits, #4-Warning, #5-Find Errors, and #6-Fix Errors.
2. Click the Overview sheet to view the organization and content of the Project 6 Skill Drill Exercises workbook.

There are six exercises. Each exercise is independent of the others, so you may complete the exercises in any order. Be sure to save the workbook after completing each exercise. If you need a paper copy of the completed exercise, enter your name centered in a header before printing. Other print options have already been set to print compressed and to display the filename, sheet name, and current date in a footer.

Be sure to save your changes and close the workbook, if you need more than one work session to complete the desired exercises; then, continue working on *ee2-p6drill* instead of starting over again on the original *ee2-0602* file.

1. Using Input Messages to Guide Data Entry

You are concerned about the accuracy of your tax data related to contributions, particularly the dates of contribution. Last year, you kept typing in the correct month and day, but the wrong year. To include a reminder in the worksheet, you decide to add a message in each date cell reminding you to type the correct year. To create an input message, follow these steps:

1. Open the *ee2-p6drill* workbook, if necessary, and select the #1-Message worksheet.
2. Select cell A19.
3. Choose <u>D</u>ata, Va<u>l</u>idation.
4. Select the Input Message tab.
5. Type `Contribution Date` in the <u>T</u>itle text box.
6. Type `Check that the date you enter is for the year 2002` in the <u>I</u>nput message text box, and click OK.

    Check cell A19 to see that your message is attached and is correct.
7. Save your changes to the *ee2-p6drill* workbook.

2. Restricting Data Entry to a List of Values

You decide to control data entry in the Receipt field. To restrict data entered in a cell to a list of values, follow these steps:

1. Open the *ee2-p6drill* workbook, if necessary, and select the #2-Data List worksheet.
2. Select cell D19.
3. Choose <u>D</u>ata, Va<u>l</u>idation, and select the Settings tab.
4. Select List from the <u>A</u>llow drop-down list.
5. Enter `=$D$5:$D$7` in the <u>S</u>ource text box, and click OK.
6. Type `Lost` in cell D19, and press `↵Enter`.

    An Excel Stop Error message appears advising you that the entry you just made is invalid.
7. Click Cancel.
8. Select No from the drop-down list attached to cell D19.

    The entry is accepted this time because No is one of the entries on the list.
9. Save your changes to the *ee2-p6drill* workbook.

3. Restricting Data to a Range of Dates

You are concerned that the dates of your contributions fall in the year 2002. Last year at an audit several of your contributions were dated wrong. The auditor listened doubtfully to your explanation about typing errors. This year you want to apply the Data Validation setting to the Date column to avoid this type of data entry error. You will restrict contribution dates to the year 2002. To do this you must refer to the first and last days in the year 2002.

To limit data to a range of dates, follow these steps:

1. Open the *ee2-p6drill* workbook, if necessary, and select the #3-Data Limits worksheet.
2. Select cell A19.
3. Choose <u>D</u>ata, Va<u>l</u>idation.
4. Select the Settings tab.
5. Select Date from the <u>A</u>llow drop-down list.
6. Type `01/01/2002` in the <u>S</u>tart date text box, and `12/31/2002` in the E<u>n</u>d date text box.
7. Click OK to exit the Data Validation dialog box.

    You should test your validation settings and messages by entering erroneous data.
8. Type `July 4, 3002` in cell A19, and press `↵Enter`.

Remember that you can type dates in several formats. In this case, you could have typed 7/4/3002. In this example, Excel displays a Stop Error Alert message.

9. Select Cancel, type `July 4, 2002`, and press <kbd>↵Enter</kbd>.

The entry is accepted this time because the date falls within the allowable range of dates.

10. Save your changes to the *ee2-p6drill* workbook.

4. Applying a Warning Error Alert Message

Earlier, you applied a validation setting to the Date field in your contributions database. After giving it some thought, you decide that you want to attach your own error alert message to the cell. The error message will advise users that they should enter a year 2002 date.

To add an error message to data validation, follow these steps:

1. Open the *ee2-p6drill* workbook, if necessary, and select the #4-Warning worksheet.
2. Select cell A19.
3. Choose Data, Validation and then select the Error Alert tab.
4. Select Warning from the Style drop-down list.
5. Type `Contribution Date` in the Title text box.
6. Type `Please enter a date between January 1, 2002 and December 31, 2002` in the Error message text box.
7. Click OK to exit the Data Validation dialog box.
8. In cell A19, enter an invalid date, and check that your validation message works correctly. Excel displays your message guiding data entry, followed by *Continue?*. You can choose one of three buttons: Yes, No, and Cancel. Clicking Yes enters the invalid date. You can also click No to correct the entry, or click Cancel to stop the data entry attempt.
9. Click No.
10. Enter a valid date.
11. Save your changes to the *ee2-p6drill* workbook.

5. Finding Errors in a Worksheet

You have just applied data validation restrictions and messages to your existing database of contributions. Now you realize that these restrictions only affect new entries to the database. You must use the Formula Auditing toolbar to circle all existing entries in the database that do not meet the validation restrictions.

To find errors in worksheets using validation, follow these steps:

1. Open the *ee2-p6drill* workbook, if necessary, and select the #5-Find Errors worksheet.
2. Choose Tools, point to Formula Auditing, and select Show Formula Auditing Toolbar.
3. Click the Circle Invalid Data button, and scroll down to view the errors circled in red.
4. Identify the reasons for the invalid data.
5. Click the Clear Validation Circles button.

6. Fixing Errors in a Worksheet

You identified errors in a worksheet by using the Formula Auditing toolbar. Now you must correct them. You notice that there are three common errors. Several dates have invalid years, the Receipt field's drop-down list allows an invalid entry, and the Category field contains misspellings.

To fix the errors in the worksheet, follow these steps:

1. Open the *ee2-p6drill* workbook, if necessary, and select the #6-Fix Errors worksheet.
2. Use the Circle Invalid Data button on the Formula Auditing toolbar to circle data errors.
3. Change the Year portion of the dates in cells A19 and A24 to `2002`.
4. Select cell D7, and enter `Pending`.

5. Select cells D19:D52. Choose <u>D</u>ata, Va<u>l</u>idation, and select the Settings tab.

6. In the <u>S</u>ource text box, edit as necessary to specify the range `=$D$5:$D$7` and then click OK.

7. Select cell E25 and then choose the correct entry *Electronics* from the drop-down list.

8. Repeat the previous step, and correct the error in cell E41.

9. Click the Circle Invalid Data button on the Formula Auditing toolbar to check that all errors are corrected, and close the Formula Auditing toolbar.

10. Save your changes to the *ee2-p6drill* workbook.

Challenge

Challenge exercises expand on or are somewhat related to skills that are presented in the lessons. Each exercise provides a brief narrative introduction, followed by instructions in a numbered-step format that are not as detailed as those in the Skill Drill section.

Before beginning your first Project 6 Challenge exercise, complete the following steps:

1. Open the file named *ee2-0603*, and immediately save it as `ee2-p6challenge`.
   The *ee2-p6challenge* workbook contains five sheets: an overview, and four exercise sheets named #1-Lists, #2-Messages, #3-Find and Copy, and #4-Find and Fix.

2. Click the Overview sheet to view the organization of the Project 6 Challenge Exercises workbook.

Each exercise is independent of the others, so you may complete the exercises in any order. Be sure to save the workbook after completing each exercise. If you need a paper copy of the completed exercise, enter your name centered in a header before printing. Other print options have already been set to print compressed to one page and to display the filename, sheet name, and current date in a footer.

If you need more than one work session to complete the desired exercises, continue working on *ee2-p6challenge* instead of starting over again on the original *ee2-0603* file.

1. Creating Drop-Down Lists and Input Messages

You have been experiencing keyboard errors entering data in the Position and Department fields. You decide to apply a drop-down list to these fields. The lists already exist in the Database Work Area. Apply drop-down lists and input messages to both fields. The input message should advise the user to select an entry from the drop-down list attached to the cell.

To apply drop-down lists and input messages, follow these steps:

1. Open the *ee2-p6challenge* workbook, if necessary, and select the #1-Lists worksheet.

2. Select all of the cells in the list that contain position data in column C (the range C32:C142).

3. Display the Data Validation dialog box.

4. Select the Settings tab, and apply the List option using A12:A25 as the <u>S</u>ource.

5. Specify the input message `Select an entry from the drop-down list`, and click OK.
   You specified data validation for the Position data field. You can check your specifications by selecting any cell in the field and displaying the drop-down list. Visually check that your message is correct.

6. Select all the cells in the list that contain department data (the range D32:D142), and open the Data Validation dialog box.

7. Select the Settings tab and then apply the List option using B12:B19 as the source.

8. Specify the input message `Select an entry from the drop-down list`, and click OK. Visually inspect the validations for the Department field in the same manner as you did the Position field.

9. Save your changes to the *ee2-p6challenge* workbook.

2. Applying Validations with Information and Warning Messages

You want to apply validation restrictions and error messages to the Shift and Hire Date fields. Shift data should be limited to whole numbers between 1 and 3, with an input message and an Information error alert. Hire Date should restrict entries to dates between August 1, 1988 and the current date, with an appropriate input message and a Warning error alert. This is a little different because you will use the =Today() function to determine the current date. The date settings will also be stored in cells rather than typed directly into the validation settings.

To apply validations with information and warning messages, follow these steps:

1. Open the *ee2-p6challenge* workbook, if necessary, and select the #2-Messages worksheet.

2. Select the Shift field data starting in row 32, and open the Data Validation dialog box.

3. Use the Settings tab to allow whole numbers between 1 and 3.

4. Select the Input Message tab, type `Shift` as the message Title, and type `Please enter 1, 2, or 3` as the Input message.

5. Use the Error Alert tab to display the Information message `You have entered an incorrect number. Please enter 1, 2, or 3.`

Check that your Input and Error messages display correctly. You can test your validation by entering an invalid shift, such as 0 or 4.

6. Enter `8-1-88` in cell C12, and enter `=TODAY()` in cell D12.

7. Select the Hire Date data starting in row 32, and open the Data Validation dialog box.

8. Use the Settings tab to allow Dates. Refer to cell C12 as the Start date and to cell D12 as the End date.

9. Use the Input Message tab to inform users that they must enter a date between August 1, 1988 and the current date.

10. Use the Error Alert tab to display a Warning message with two messages in the Error message box:

`Please enter a date between August 1, 1988 and the current date.`
`Select Yes to accept the date, No to enter another date, or Cancel to quit.`

When you return to the worksheet, you can test your Hire Date validation settings. Try entering the date `1-1-1980` or a date in the future.

11. Save your changes to the *ee2-p6challenge* workbook.

3. Finding and Copying Validation Restrictions and Messages

You have just looked at your worksheet for the first time in several days and can't remember if you finished entering validation restrictions and messages. The first thing to do is find all validations in the worksheet. You will find that validations are applied to the Position, Department, Shift, and Hire Date fields of the first record only.

To find and copy validation restrictions and messages, follow these steps:

1. Open the *ee2-p6challenge* workbook, if necessary, and select the #3-Find and Copy worksheet.

2. Choose Edit, Go To, and select the Special button.

3. Select the Data validation and All options, and click OK.

Cells C32, D32, E32, and G32 are highlighted. There are validation restrictions in the Position, Department, Shift, and Hire Date fields of the first record only.

4. Copy the entire first record (cells A32:G32) to the Clipboard.

5. Use the Paste Special command to paste only the validations to the remaining records in the database (cells A33:G142). Deselect all cells, and press Esc to clear the marquee.
6. Repeat steps 2 and 3 to check if the validation restrictions copied correctly.
7. Save your changes to the *ee2-p6challenge* workbook.

4. Finding and Fixing Errors Using the Formula Auditing Toolbar

Having applied validation restrictions and messages to the existing data in your worksheet, you need to check that there are no data that violate these restrictions.

To find and fix errors using the Formula Auditing toolbar, follow these steps:

1. Open the *ee2-p6challenge* workbook, if necessary, and select the #4-Find and Fix worksheet.
2. Display the Formula Auditing toolbar, click the Circle Invalid Data button, and scroll down to view errors in the database range (A32:G142).
   Red circles surround all *Marketing* entries in the Department field. There are two errors in Shift data (both employees should be on the first shift).
3. Click to display any drop-down list within the Department column.
   Marketing is not in the drop-down list, but it is entered in cell B19. Apparently the range is not defined correctly in the validation settings.
4. Select the Department data in column D starting in row 32.
5. Display the Data Validation dialog box, and edit the Source range on the Settings tab to include cell B19.
   The red circles around the *Marketing* entries disappear.
6. Click the Circle Invalid Data button.
   Check that all red circles in the Department field are turned off. If *Marketing* entries are still circled, check that you spelled Marketing correctly in the list. Also, test the drop-down list to make sure Marketing is one of the choices. If it isn't, check that the cell reference in the Source text box on the Settings tab is correct.
7. Change the data in each of the Shift fields circled in red to 1.
   As you correct each entry, the red circle disappears.
8. Save your changes to the *ee2-p6challenge* workbook.

D iscovery Zone

Discovery Zone exercises require advanced knowledge of topics presented in *essentials* lessons, application of skills from multiple lessons, or self-directed learning of new skills.

Before beginning your first Project 6 Discovery Zone exercise, complete the following steps:

1. Open the file named *ee2-0604*, and immediately save it as **ee2-p6discovery**.
   The *ee2-p6discovery* workbook contains four sheets: #1-Scenario and its related sheet #1-Analyze, and #2-Scenario and its related sheet #2-Validation.
2. Click the #1-Scenario and #2-Scenario worksheets, respectively, to read explanations of the related exercises.

Each exercise is independent of the other, so you may complete the exercises in any order. Be sure to save the workbook after completing each exercise. If you need a paper copy of the completed exercise, enter your name centered in a header before printing. Other print options have already been set to print compressed to one page and to display the filename, sheet name, and current date in a footer.

Be sure to save your changes and close the workbook if you need more than one work session to complete the desired exercises; then, continue working on *ee2-p6discovery* instead of starting over again on the original *ee2-0604* file.

1. Analyzing Validation Requirements for a Database

An important part of the process of creating and maintaining a database in Excel is to ensure the accuracy of its data. To practice the process of determining what validation restrictions to apply, select the #1-Analyze worksheet in the *ee2-p6discovery* workbook. Notice that there is a Database Work Area located just above the database. Column A contains a list of the field names from the database. Next to each field name is a blank cell. Analyze each field in the database carefully, and in the space next to the field name, describe the validation restriction, Input Message, and/or Error Alert you would apply to that field. Not every field requires validation. If no validation is required, enter **None**.

2. Applying Validation Restrictions to a Database

Once you know what validations you need to use, you must apply them to the database. To practice the process of applying validation restrictions, open the #2-Validation worksheet in the *ee2-p6discovery* workbook. Notice that there is a Validation Instructions area located just above the database. Column A contains a list of the field names from the database. Next to each field name is a description of the validation that should be applied to the field. Follow the instructions, and apply the recommended validation to each field.

Creating PivotTable and PivotChart Reports

Objectives

In this project, you learn how to

- ✔ Display Help on Pivot Tables and Related Charts
- ✔ Create a Pivot Table
- ✔ Expand a Pivot Table
- ✔ Remove, Hide, and Show Data
- ✔ Refresh a Pivot Table
- ✔ Create a Chart from Pivot Table Data
- ✔ Apply Predefined Formats to a Pivot Table

Key terms in this project include

- ❑ indented format
- ❑ nonindented format
- ❑ pivot table
- ❑ PivotTable and PivotChart Wizard
- ❑ refresh

Why Would I Do This?

Imagine that your responsibilities include maintaining employee data and generating reports based on that data. The annual budget review takes place early next month, and your supervisor has requested information based on current salary levels—total salaries for each department, average salary for each position, and so forth. You have a large amount of data available in an Excel list. Using Excel's powerful PivotTable and PivotChart Report Wizard, you can quickly create the summary information you need.

Visual Summary

A *pivot table* is an interactive table that quickly summarizes large amounts of data from a data source such as a list or another table. As its name suggests, you can rotate its rows and columns to see different comparisons of the source data. You can also expand or reduce the amount of detail shown in the table, and create a chart that plots the data in a pivot table. Figure 7.1 illustrates a data source, and a pivot table based on the data source.

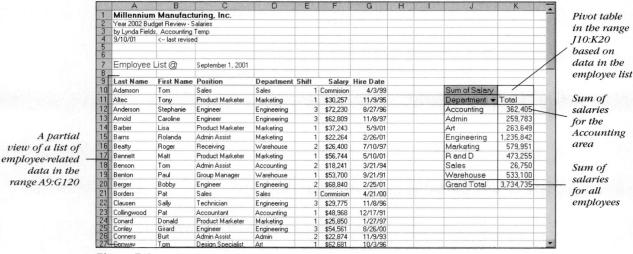

A partial view of a list of employee-related data in the range A9:G120

Pivot table in the range J10:K20 based on data in the employee list

Sum of salaries for the Accounting area

Sum of salaries for all employees

Figure 7.1

In this project, you create, expand, edit, and format a pivot table. You also create a chart based on pivot table data. Start by viewing related Help topics in Lesson 1.

Lesson 1: Displaying Help on Pivot Tables and Related Charts

Before you begin to create pivot tables and related charts, use Excel's onscreen Help to get an overview of analyzing data interactively. You can find out when to use a PivotTable report, what types of reports are available, and how to create a report.

To Get Help on Pivot Tables and Related Charts

1 **Start Excel and display a blank worksheet.**

2 **Type** pivot table **in the Ask a question box and then press** ⏎Enter.
Help topics associated with the phrase *pivot table* display in a drop-down list.

3 **Select the topic *About PivotTable reports*.**
Excel displays the selected topic in the right pane of the Microsoft Excel Help window as shown in Figure 7.2.

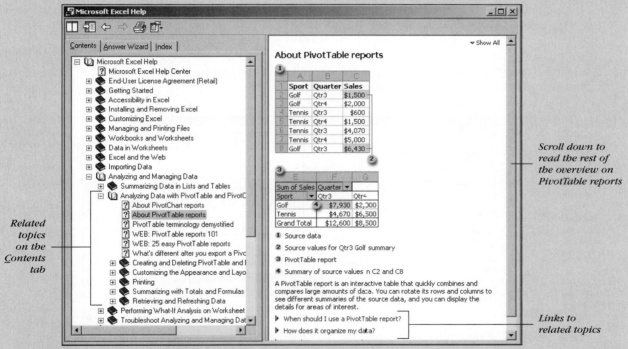

Related topics on the Contents tab

Scroll down to read the rest of the overview on PivotTable reports

Links to related topics

Figure 7.2

If you have problems...

If the Contents, Answer Wizard, and Index tabs are not visible, click the Show button on the Help window's toolbar.

4 **After reviewing the illustration of source data and a PivotTable report, click the link *When should I use a PivotTable report?* (refer to the bottom of the right pane in Figure 7.2) and then read the answer.**

5 **Find and open the topic *PivotTable terminology demystified* on the Contents tab in the left pane of the Help window, click Show All in the upper-right corner, and scroll to view numerous illustrations of related terms.**

(Continues)

To Get Help on Pivot Tables and Related Charts (Continued)

6 Click the topic *About PivotChart reports* on the Contents tab, and view the sample PivotChart report.

7 Read other topics of your choice—you must be connected to your Internet service provider to access topics that begin with *WEB*—and then close the Help window.

Lesson 2: Creating a Pivot Table

The **PivotTable and PivotChart Wizard** guides you through the steps to make a custom report from a list of data. The initial steps include specifying the data source, the type of report (PivotTable or PivotChart), and the location of the report (a new worksheet or the existing worksheet). At that point you have two options for completing the design of the pivot table: using a Layout dialog box or making selections directly on the worksheet.

You can easily set up a pivot table directly on the worksheet by dragging the names of fields listed in the PivotTable toolbar to the appropriate areas of a pivot table shell (see Figure 7.3). That way you can view the data while you arrange the fields.

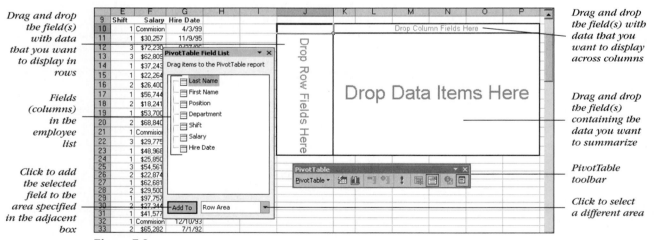

Figure 7.3

If the pivot table you have in mind is very large and complex, using the on-sheet layout illustrated in Figure 7.3 can be quite time-consuming because data updates each time you make a change. You may prefer to design the pivot table using the Layout dialog box (see Figure 7.4) and then display the results when you are done.

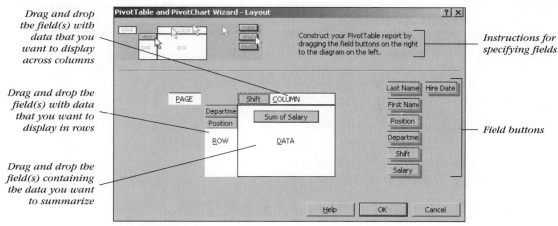

Drag and drop the field(s) with data that you want to display across columns

Drag and drop the field(s) with data that you want to display in rows

Drag and drop the field(s) containing the data you want to summarize

Instructions for specifying fields

Field buttons

Figure 7.4

In this lesson you design a pivot table directly on the worksheet. You create a simple table that totals salaries by department for Millennium Manufacturing.

To Create a Pivot Table

① **Open the *ee2-0701* workbook, and save it as salarypivots.**
The workbook is comprised of a worksheet named Employees, which contains employee-related data organized as an Excel list.

② **Click any cell within the list range A9:G120, and choose Data, PivotTable and PivotChart Report.**
The PivotTable and PivotChart Wizard – Step 1 of 3 dialog box opens, as shown in Figure 7.5.

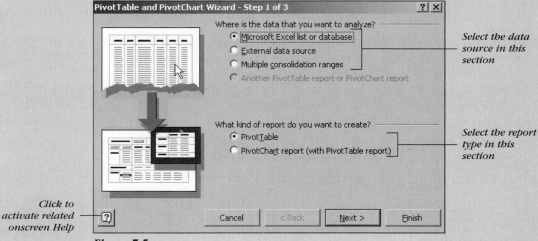

Select the data source in this section

Select the report type in this section

Click to activate related onscreen Help

Figure 7.5

③ **Select *Microsoft Excel list or database* as the data source.**

④ **Select PivotTable as the report type, and click the Next button.**

(Continues)

To Create a Pivot Table (Continued)

The PivotTable and PivotChart Wizard – Step 2 of 3 dialog box opens. Because you clicked within the list before activating the Wizard, Excel automatically selects the entire list and displays $A$9:$G$120 in the Range window.

⑤ Click Next.
The PivotTable and PivotChart Wizard – Step 3 of 3 dialog box opens. Use this dialog box to specify creating the pivot table in a new worksheet or in the existing worksheet.

⑥ Select Existing worksheet, and click cell J10.
This tells Excel to position the upper-left cell of the pivot table in cell J10 in the active worksheet. Employees!$J$10 displays in the window below the Existing worksheet option (see Figure 7.6).

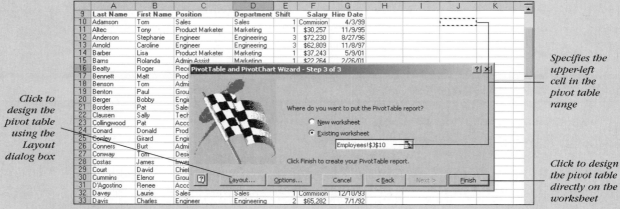

Click to design the pivot table using the Layout dialog box

Specifies the upper-left cell in the pivot table range

Click to design the pivot table directly on the worksheet

Figure 7.6

⑦ Click the Finish button.
Excel creates a shell for a pivot table (refer to Figure 7.3).

⑧ Click Department in the PivotTable Field List box, make sure that Row Area is selected in the lower-right corner of the PivotTable Field List box, and click the Add To button.
Excel adds the Department field as a row in the pivot table (see Figure 7.7). You can also drag the Department field to the *Drop Row Fields Here* section in the pivot table shell. Now specify that you want to view salary data.

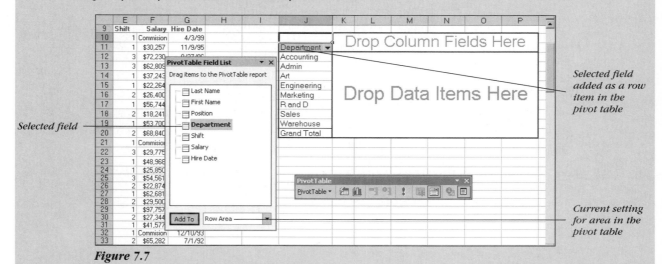

Selected field

Selected field added as a row item in the pivot table

Current setting for area in the pivot table

Figure 7.7

To Create a Pivot Table

9 **Click Salary in the PivotTable Field List box. Display the area drop-down list to the right of the Add To button, select Data Area, and click the Add To button.**

Excel adds salary data to the pivot table (see Figure 7.8). You can also drag the Salary field to the *Drop Data Items Here* section in the pivot table shell. By default, the summary calculation on salary data is a count. Now change the calculation to a sum.

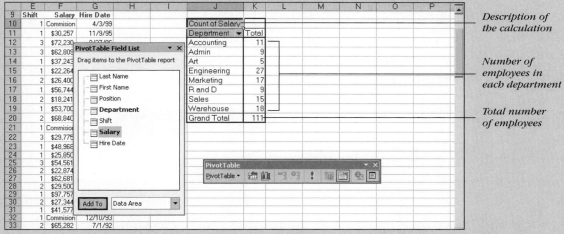

Figure 7.8

10 **Double-click Count of Salary (cell J10).**

The PivotTable Field dialog box opens.

11 **Select Sum in the Summarize by list box (see Figure 7.9).**

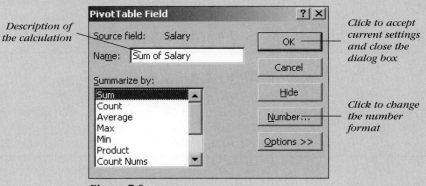

Figure 7.9

Sum of Salary replaces *Count of Salary* in the Name text box.

12 **Click the Number button to open the Format Cells dialog box. Specify Currency format without the $ sign and with zero decimal places.**

13 **Click OK twice to close the Format Cells and PivotTable Field dialog boxes respectively.**

(Continues)

To Create a Pivot Table (Continued)

The pivot table reflects the changes in type of summary and number formatting (see Figure 7.10).

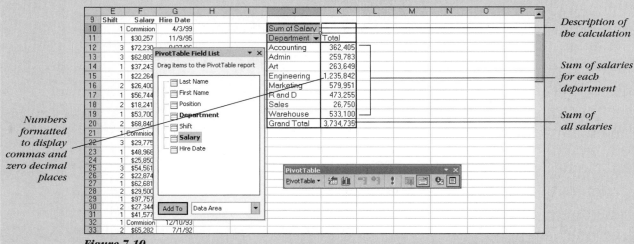

Numbers formatted to display commas and zero decimal places

Description of the calculation

Sum of salaries for each department

Sum of all salaries

Figure 7.10

14 **Close the PivotTable Field List box by clicking the Close button—a large X—in the upper-right corner of that box.**

15 **Use a similar process to close the PivotTable toolbar, and save your changes to the *salarypivots* workbook.**

Keep the *salarypivots* workbook open for the next lesson, or close the workbook and exit Excel.

To extend your knowledge...

Deleting a Pivot Table

Before you can delete a pivot table, you must select it using a three-step process. Right-click within the pivot table, choose <u>S</u>elect from the shortcut menu, and click Entire <u>T</u>able. After selecting the table, choose <u>E</u>dit, Clear, <u>A</u>ll. When you delete a pivot table, the source data are not affected.

Lesson 3: Expanding a Pivot Table

You can greatly expand a pivot table by adding more fields to a pivot table on the worksheet or to the row, column, and data areas of the Layout dialog box. For example, instead of displaying a single column with total salary for each Millennium Manufacturing department, you can add columns that provide totals for each shift within a department. You can also add rows that provide totals for each position within a department. In this lesson, you make these changes directly on the worksheet.

To Expand a Pivot Table Using the Layout Dialog Box

1 **Open the *salarypivots* workbook, if necessary.**
A pivot table showing salaries by department and in total displays in the range J10:K20.

2 **If you do not see the Pivot Table Field List box, right-click within the pivot table and then select Show Field List.**

3 **Click Position in the PivotTable Field List box. Display the area drop-down list to the right of the Add To button, select Row Area, and click the Add To button.**
Excel adds position data to the pivot table.

4 **Click Shift in the PivotTable Field List box. Display the area drop-down list to the right of the Add To button, select Column Area, and click the Add To button.**
Excel adds Shift data to the pivot table (see Figure 7.11). The summary information in the table has more than doubled as a result of adding data from two fields.

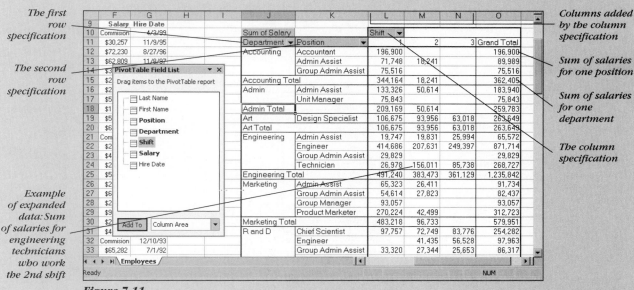

The first row specification

The second row specification

Example of expanded data: Sum of salaries for engineering technicians who work the 2nd shift

Columns added by the column specification

Sum of salaries for one position

Sum of salaries for one department

The column specification

Figure 7.11

5 **Save your changes to the *salarypivots* workbook.**
Keep the *salarypivots* workbook open for the next lesson, or close the workbook and exit Excel.

Lesson 4: Removing, Hiding, and Showing Data

As your information needs change, you may want to display more or less summary data in a pivot table. The process for removing a field is opposite that of adding a field—drag the field away from the pivot table on the worksheet or drag the field away from the Row, Column, or Data area in the Layout dialog box. Showing or hiding detail in a field is as easy as pulling down a list of items in a field on the pivot table and checking or un-checking the field.

In this lesson, you modify the pivot table in preparation for creating a chart. You remove the Shift field, and then hide data for the Engineering, R and D, and Warehouse departments. When you are done, only the Accounting, Administration, Art, Marketing, and Sales summary data display.

To Remove, Hide, and Show Data

❶ Open the *salarypivots* workbook, if necessary.

❷ Click the Shift button in the pivot table (cell L10), and drag it upward off the pivot table.
The three columns of Shift summary data are removed from the pivot table. Excel keeps the removed field button accessible by positioning it just above the pivot table.

❸ Display the Department drop-down list (cell J11).
Check marks in front of department names indicate the pivot table currently displays summary data for all departments (see Figure 7.12). Clicking a check mark deselects the box and temporarily hides the related data in the pivot table.

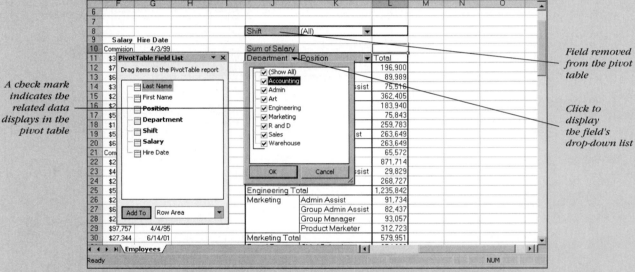

Figure 7.12

❹ Uncheck the Engineering, R and D, and Warehouse items in the Department drop-down list.

❺ Click OK.
Summary data for the Engineering, R and D, and Warehouse departments does not display in the pivot table (see Figure 7.13).

To Remove, Hide, and Show Data

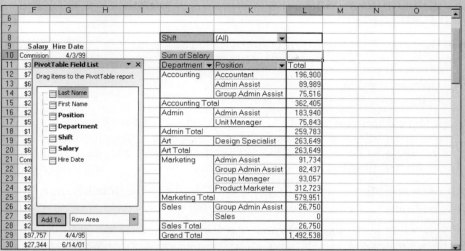

Figure 7.13

 6   **Save your changes to the *salarypivots* workbook.**

Keep the *salarypivots* workbook open for the next lesson, or close the workbook and exit Excel.

To extend your knowledge...

Displaying the Top or Bottom Items in a Field

You can display a user-specified number of top or bottom items in a pivot table field. Click within the pivot table, click P̲ivotTable on the PivotTable toolbar, and select *Sort a̲nd Top 10*. Under *Top 10 AutoShow*, click O̲n. In the S̲how box, select Top or Bottom, and in the box to the right, specify the number of items to display. In the U̲sing field box, click the data field to use for calculating the top or bottom items and then click OK.

Lesson 5: Refreshing a Pivot Table

If you change data in a worksheet and that data impacts a summary calculation in a pivot table, Excel does not automatically update the pivot table. After making changes to the worksheet, you must ***refresh*** (recalculate) the pivot table.

A word of caution is in order to avoid using invalid data to make decisions. Because you are so used to Excel recalculating a worksheet automatically, it's easy to overlook refreshing any pivot tables that incorporate the changed data. In complex pivot tables, errors in summary amounts are difficult to detect visually; therefore, acquire the habit of refreshing pivot tables after any change in worksheet data.

In this lesson you change worksheet data, check for changes in pivot table amounts, refresh the pivot table, and check amounts again.

To Refresh a Pivot Table

❶ Open the *salarypivots* workbook, if necessary. Close the PivotTable Field List box, if it displays.

❷ Scroll the worksheet to display column A, starting with row 7.
Currently the salary for accountant Pat Collingwood is $48,968 (cell F23).

❸ Scroll right as needed to display the entire pivot table.
The sum of salaries for accountants is $196,900 (cell L12).

❹ Change the contents of cell F23 to $50,968 instead of *$48,968*.
You changed the salary of an accountant, but the sum of salaries for accountants in the pivot table did not change ($196,900 in cell L12). Just looking at the summary data, it is not apparent that the pivot table contains an error.

❺ Right-click anywhere within the pivot table, and choose Refresh Data.
The sum of salaries for accountants increases from $196,900 to $198,900 in cell L12.

❻ Save your changes to the *salarypivots* workbook.
Keep the *salarypivots* workbook open for the next lesson, or close the workbook and exit Excel.

To extend your knowledge...

Other Ways to Select Refresh

Refresh Data is an option on the shortcut menu that displays when you right-click within a pivot table. You can also choose the menu sequence Data, Refresh Data or click the Refresh Data button on the PivotTable toolbar.

Lesson 6: Creating a Chart from Pivot Table Data

A pivot table provides informative summary data in rows and columns. Creating a chart based on pivot table data can be an effective means to interpret that data. You can create a chart quickly by right-clicking within an existing pivot table and then selecting PivotChart from the shortcut menu. You can also use the PivotTable and PivotChart Wizard to create both a chart and its related table at the same time.

For either method, Excel automatically creates a column chart on a separate sheet. You can then edit the PivotChart report just as you would any Excel chart—adding and deleting data points, changing chart type, applying number formats, and so forth. You can use any chart type except XY (scatter), bubble, and stock.

In this lesson, you create a column chart based on the pivot table in the *salarypivots* workbook. You then hide the Art department salary data, which limits the chart to Accounting, Admin, Marketing, and Sales salaries. You also convert the chart type to Line so you can compare the effectiveness of the two chart types.

To Create and Modify a Chart Based on Pivot Table Data

❶ Open the *salarypivots* workbook, if necessary.

❷ Right-click any cell in the pivot table (J10:L29), and select PivotChart on the shortcut menu.

To Create and Modify a Chart Based on Pivot Table Data

Excel creates a column chart based on the visible data in the pivot table (see Figure 7.14). Department and Position buttons display centered below the chart.

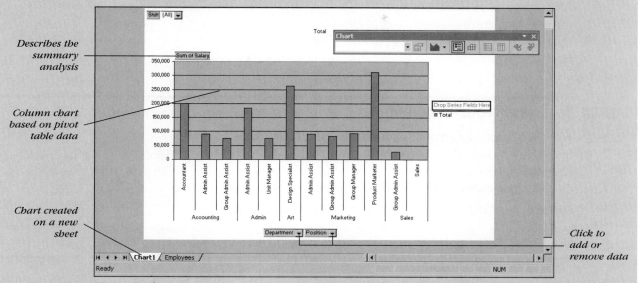

Describes the summary analysis

Column chart based on pivot table data

Chart created on a new sheet

Click to add or remove data

Figure 7.14

❸ **Display the Department drop-down list, uncheck Art, and click OK.**
The column depicting Art department data disappears from the chart.

❹ **Right-click a blank area within the chart, and select Chart Type from the shortcut menu.**
The Chart Type dialog box opens.

❺ **Select Line in the Chart type section of the dialog box, and click OK.**
A line chart replaces the column chart (see Figure 7.15).

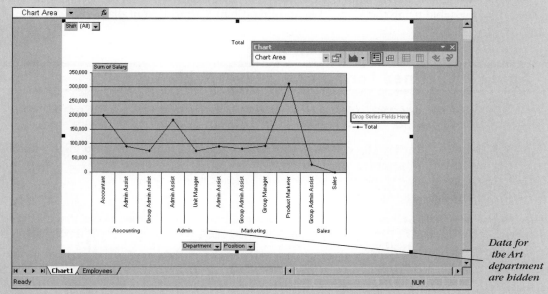

Data for the Art department are hidden

Figure 7.15

(Continues)

To Create and Modify a Chart Based on Pivot Table Data (Continued)

6 **Click outside the chart to deselect it, and save your changes to the *salarypivots* workbook.**
Keep the *salarypivots* workbook open for the next lesson, or close the workbook and exit Excel.

 ## To extend your knowledge...

How Changes in Pivot Table Data Affect a Related Chart

If a chart is based on pivot table data—which in turn summarizes worksheet data—you should understand the impact on the chart of a change in underlying worksheet data. Such a chart will only be updated when its associated pivot table is refreshed.

Creating a Static Chart Based on Pivot Table Data

You can convert an existing PivotChart report to a static chart—also known as a nonpivoting chart— by deleting the associated PivotTable report. You cannot change the charted data in a static chart.

Lesson 7: Applying Predefined Formats to a Pivot Table

A variety of predefined formats can be applied to pivot tables. These formats not only improve the aesthetics of a table, they focus the reader's attention on different areas of the table. Some formats work better than others, depending on the layout and complexity of the pivot table. You should experiment with different types of formats to see which best presents your data.

In this lesson, you apply a table format to a pivot table, switch to a report format, and then add a field to the table using the PivotTable and PivotChart Wizard Layout dialog box.

To Apply Predefined Formats to a Pivot Table

1 **Open the *salarypivots* workbook, if necessary, and select the Employees worksheet.**

2 **Scroll to display the entire pivot table in the range J10:L27, and click any cell within this range.**
The pivot table displays in the PivotTable Classic format—the default format automatically assigned to new pivot tables.

3 **Click the Format Report button on the PivotTable toolbar. If the PivotTable toolbar is not in view, right-click within the pivot table and then select Show PivotTable Toolbar.**
The AutoFormat dialog box opens (see Figure 7.16). Report formats—the indented formats—display first. An ***indented format*** supports the presentation of pivot table data in categories and subcategories. Each subcategory is offset to the right from its main category.

To Apply Predefined Formats to a Pivot Table

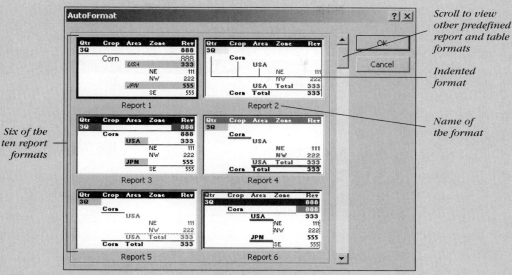

Figure 7.16

4 **Scroll down to view the remaining report formats and the table formats.**
Ten table formats—the nonindented formats—display after the report formats. A ***nonindented format*** does not offset subcategories within categories in a PivotTable report. The last two choices are PivotTable Classic (the default) and None.

5 **Double-click the Table 1 format (the description displays below the associated format), click anywhere outside the table to deselect it, and scroll to view the entire pivot table.**
The pivot table displays in the Table 1 format (see Figure 7.17).

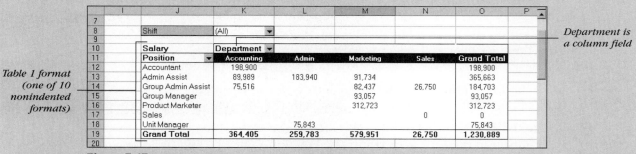

Figure 7.17

6 **Click a cell within the pivot table, and click the Format Report button on the PivotTable toolbar.**

7 **Double-click the Report 1 format, and click anywhere outside the table to deselect it.**
The pivot table displays in the Report 1 format (see Figure 7.18).

(Continues)

To Apply Predefined Formats to a Pivot Table (Continued)

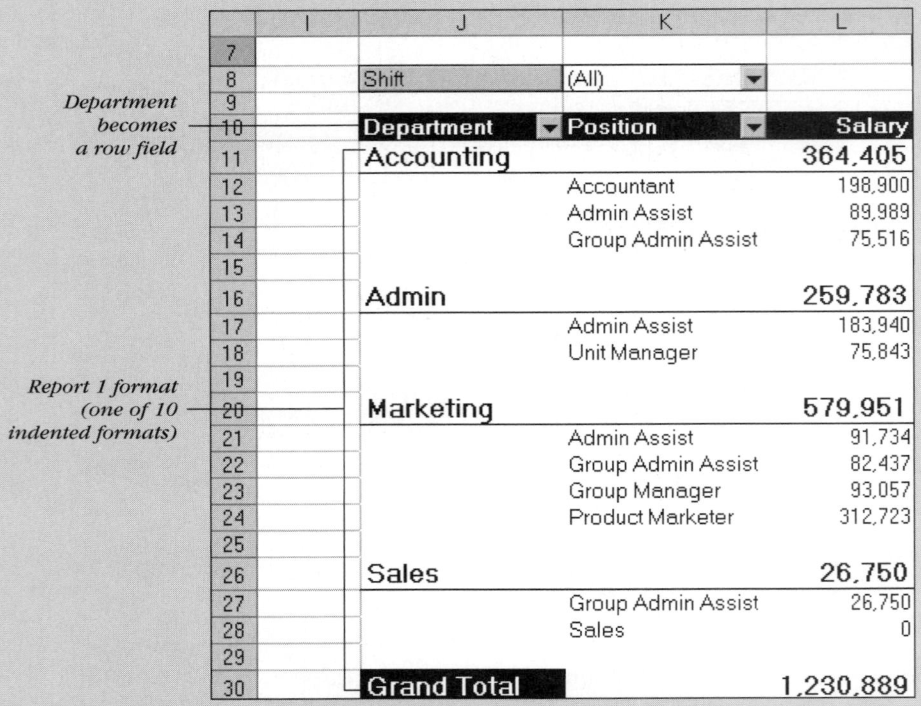

Department becomes a row field

Report 1 format (one of 10 indented formats)

	I	J	K	L
7				
8		Shift	(All) ▼	
9				
10		**Department** ▼	**Position** ▼	**Salary**
11		Accounting		364,405
12			Accountant	198,900
13			Admin Assist	89,989
14			Group Admin Assist	75,516
15				
16		Admin		259,783
17			Admin Assist	183,940
18			Unit Manager	75,843
19				
20		Marketing		579,951
21			Admin Assist	91,734
22			Group Admin Assist	82,437
23			Group Manager	93,057
24			Product Marketer	312,723
25				
26		Sales		26,750
27			Group Admin Assist	26,750
28			Sales	0
29				
30		Grand Total		1,230,889

Figure 7.18

8 Display the Department drop-down list (cell J10), and uncheck the four fields currently in the pivot table—Accounting, Admin, Marketing, and Sales.

9 Check two fields, Engineering and R and D, and click OK.
The pivot table continues to display the Report 1 format.

10 Click within the pivot table, display the PivotTable drop-down list in the PivotTable toolbar, and select Wizard.
The PivotTable and PivotChart Wizard – Step 3 of 3 dialog box opens.

11 Click the Layout button in the lower-left corner of the dialog box.
Now add the Shift data as a row item in the PivotTable report.

12 Locate the field buttons on the right side of the dialog box, and drag the Shift field button to the Row area below the Position field (see Figure 7.19).

To Apply Predefined Formats to a Pivot Table

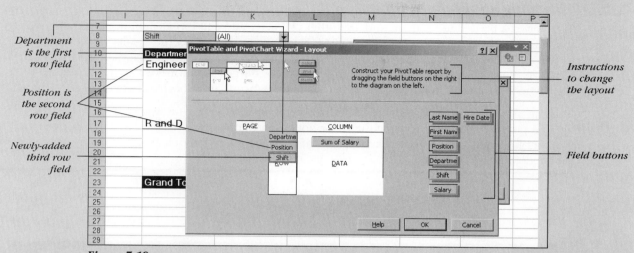

Department is the first row field

Position is the second row field

Newly-added third row field

Instructions to change the layout

Field buttons

Figure 7.19

Three field buttons are now in the row area in the order—from top to bottom—Department, Position, and Shift.

13 **Click OK, and click Finish.**

14 **Close the PivotTable Field List box and the PivotTable toolbar.**
The report displays the layered (indented) layout shown in Figure 7.20.

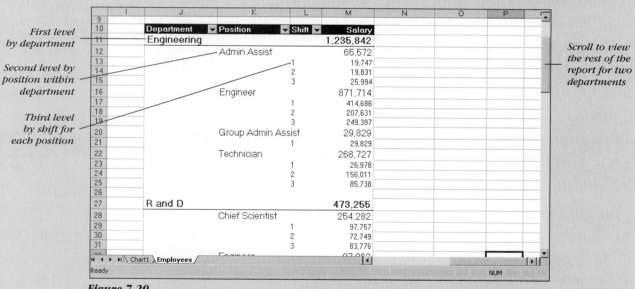

First level by department

Second level by position within department

Third level by shift for each position

Scroll to view the rest of the report for two departments

Figure 7.20

15 **Save your changes to the *salarypivots* workbook.**
This concludes Project 7. Continue with end-of-project exercises or exit Excel.

To extend your knowledge...

Removing a Predefined Format

To remove a predefined format, and any other character and cell formats applied manually, display the gallery of predefined formats and choose None. You may not get the results you want, however, because Excel simply removes effects such as borders, shading, italics, and changes in font size. Because cell contents remain in place, the action does not move any fields, change display to indented or nonindented format, or remove blank lines inserted between items in rows.

You can also reproduce the original layout of a pivot table by saving the workbook just before you apply a predefined format. If using the None option produces unwanted effects, you can close the workbook without saving your changes, and then reopen the workbook as it was before you applied the predefined format.

Summary

You began this project by viewing onscreen Help on creating pivot tables and related charts, followed by creating a pivot table directly on the worksheet. In subsequent lessons you learned how to add and remove fields, hide and show fields, refresh a pivot table, and create a chart from pivot table data. You completed the project by applying predefined formats. These experiences provided only a glimpse of the power of pivot tables.

You can reinforce and extend your learning by exploring the many onscreen Help topics on creating PivotTable and PivotChart reports, and experimenting with those features. For example, try displaying the top or bottom items for a field. Learn how to use page fields and sort the data in a pivot table. Find out about grouping and ungrouping data in PivotTable and PivotChart reports.

Checking Concepts and Terms

Multiple Choice

1. Which of the following is a true statement? [L2]

   a. To delete a pivot table, right-click within it and then select <u>D</u>elete from the shortcut menu.

   b. To delete a pivot table, click within the pivot table to select it and then press Del.

   c. Both a and b

   d. Neither a nor b

2. Which of the following chart types cannot be used to chart pivot table data? [L6]

   a. line

   b. XY (scatter)

   c. column

   d. all of the above

3. If you wanted to apply an indented format, which of the following predefined formats would you choose? [L7]

   a. PivotTable Classic

   b. Report 1

   c. Table 1

   d. none of the above

4. Which of the following is a summary calculation available in a pivot table? [L2]

   a. Max

   b. Average

   c. both a and b

   d. neither a nor b

5. Which of the following is a term associated with updating the data in a pivot table after a change in the data source for the table? [L5]

   a. recalculate

   b. redo

   c. refresh

   d. none of the above

Discussion

1. An Excel list contains data on volunteer activities of students in the current year. Fields in the list include the name of the volunteer, month and day the volunteer activity occurred, number of hours contributed, and name of the volunteer organization. Describe three variations of pivot tables you could create to summarize data in the list. Be specific as to the type of summary calculation and which fields you would set up as column and row fields. [L2]

2. An Excel list contains data on sales of musical instruments in the current year. Fields in the list include month and day of sale, type of instrument, make and model, salesperson, selling price, and store number. Describe three variations of charts based on data in pivot tables you could create to interpret data in the list. Be specific as to the type of chart and the data shown along the Y and X axes. [L6]

3. Use onscreen Help to learn about a Page field in an Excel PivotTable report. Describe how you might use that feature in a pivot table based on the employee data used for lessons in this project. [L1]

Skill Drill

Skill Drill exercises reinforce project skills. Each skill that is reinforced is the same, or nearly the same, as a skill presented in the project. Detailed instructions are provided in a step-by-step format.

Before beginning your first Project 7 Skill Drill exercise, complete the following steps:

   1. Open the file named *ee2-0702,* and immediately save it as **ee2-p7drill**.
      The workbook contains an overview sheet and six exercise sheets named #1-New Table, #2-Expand Table, #3-Add Counts, #4-Refresh, #5-AutoFormat, and #6-PivotChart.

   2. Click the Overview sheet to view the organization and content of the Project 7 Skill Drill Exercises workbook.

Each exercise is independent of the others, so you may complete the exercises in any order. Be sure to save the workbook after completing each exercise. If you need a paper copy of the completed exercise, enter your name centered in a header before printing. Other print options have already been set to print compressed and to display the filename, sheet name, and current date in a footer.

Be sure to save your changes and close the workbook if you need more than one work session to complete the desired exercises. Continue working on *ee2-p7drill* instead of starting over again on the original *ee2-0702* file.

1. Creating a Pivot Table

You keep track of your contributions in an Excel list. Now you would like to find out how much you gave to each agency during the year. To get the information you need by creating a pivot table, follow these steps:

1. Open the *ee2-p7drill* workbook, if necessary, and select the #1-New Table worksheet.
2. Click any cell in the list range A13:E42.
3. Choose <u>D</u>ata, <u>P</u>ivotTable and PivotChart Report, and click the <u>N</u>ext button.
   This accepts the default settings for data and type of report—a pivot table based on an Excel list.
4. Verify that the specified range is $A$13:$E$42, and click the <u>N</u>ext button.
5. Click <u>E</u>xisting worksheet, click G14, and click <u>F</u>inish.
   Excel creates a shell for a pivot table on the worksheet.
6. Click *Agency* in the PivotTable Field List box, make sure that Row Area is selected in the lower-right corner of the PivotTable Field List box, and click the Add To button.
   Excel adds the Agency field as a row in the pivot table.
7. Click *Declared Value* in the PivotTable Field List box. Display the area drop-down list to the right of the Add To button, select Data Area, and click the Add To button.
   A pivot table displaying a summary of contributions by agency displays in the range G14:H22. The Grand Total of contributions is **4685**.
8. Click outside the table to deselect it, and save your changes to the *ee2-p7drill* workbook.

2. Expanding a Pivot Table

You can expand a pivot table by adding one or more column, row, and data fields. Assume that you created a simple pivot table to sum contributions by agency. Now expand that table to show subtotals by agency based on whether or not a receipt was provided. To expand a pivot table, follow these steps:

1. Open the *ee2-p7drill* workbook, if necessary, and select the #2-Expand Table worksheet.
2. Click within the pivot table.
   The PivotTable Field List box displays.
3. Click *Receipt* in the PivotTable Field List box.
4. Display the area drop-down list to the right of the Add To button in the PivotTable Field List box, select Column Area, and click the Add To button.
   Two new columns display between the Agency and Grand Total columns. The total of contributions for which no receipt was provided is **685**. Contributions confirmed by receipts total **4000**.
5. Save your changes to the *ee2-p7drill* workbook.

3. Displaying Counts in a Pivot Table

As you analyze your contributions during the past year, you want to know how many times you made a contribution to each agency. To display counts in a pivot table, follow these steps:

1. Open the *ee2-p7drill* workbook, if necessary, and select the #3-Add Counts worksheet.
2. Right-click any cell in the pivot table, and select <u>W</u>izard from the shortcut menu.
3. Click the <u>L</u>ayout button.
4. Drag the Declared field button onto the <u>D</u>ATA area.
   Two *Sum of Declared Value* buttons display in the <u>D</u>ATA area.

5. Double-click the upper of the two *Sum of Declared Value* buttons.

The PivotTable Field dialog box displays.

6. Select Count, and click OK.

Count of Declared Value displays in the <u>D</u>ATA area above *Sum of Declared Value*.

7. Click OK and then click <u>F</u>inish.

The table expands to include counts of contributions. You made three contributions to the Salvation Army with a total declared value of **135**. You made seven contributions to Goodwill with a total declared value of **2660**.

8. Save your changes to the *ee2-p7drill* workbook.

4. Refreshing a Pivot Table

After creating a pivot table, you discover an error in the amount of a contribution to the Girl Scouts. You need to edit the worksheet data and refresh the pivot table. To create a pivot table, change data, and refresh the pivot table, follow these steps:

1. Open the *ee2-p7drill* workbook, if necessary, and select the #4-Refresh worksheet.
2. Click any cell in the list range A13:E42.
3. Choose <u>D</u>ata, <u>P</u>ivotTable and PivotChart Report, and click the <u>N</u>ext button.
4. Verify that the specified range is $A$13:$E$42, and click the <u>N</u>ext button.
5. Click <u>E</u>xisting worksheet, click cell G14, and click <u>F</u>inish.
6. Click *Agency* in the PivotTable Field List box, make sure that Row Area is selected in the lower-right corner of the PivotTable Field List box, and click the Add To button.
7. Click *Declared Value* in the PivotTable Field List box. Display the area drop-down list to the right of the Add To button, select Data Area, and click the Add To button.

The total for contributions to the Girl Scouts (**100**) displays in cell H18 of the pivot table.

8. Click cell B16 in the list of contributions, and change *100* to **200**.

Note that cell H18 still displays *100* as the total for contributions to the Girl Scouts organization.

9. Right-click any cell in the pivot table, and select <u>R</u>efresh Data from the shortcut menu. Alternatively, click within the pivot table and then click the Refresh Data button on the PivotTable toolbar.

Now cell H18 displays the correct amount—*200*.

10. Save your changes to the *ee2-p7drill* workbook.

5. Applying a Predefined Format to a Pivot Table

Your pivot table format is acceptable for your personal or inter-office use; however, to prepare your table for use with presentation graphics, you want to apply one of Excel's AutoFormats. To apply a predefined format to a pivot table, follow these steps:

1. Open the *ee2-p7drill* workbook, if necessary, and select the #5-AutoFormat worksheet.
2. Set zoom level to 75%, and scroll to view the pivot table to the right of the data.

The pivot table is wider than it is tall, displaying agencies in columns and categories in rows. Now apply a report format to produce an indented effect that is easier to view and print.

3. Click any cell in the pivot table, and click the Format Report button on the PivotTable toolbar. If the PivotTable toolbar is not in view, right-click within the pivot table and select Show PivotTable <u>T</u>oolbar.
4. Select Report 4, click OK, and click outside the pivot table to deselect it.

Data are now displayed in three columns, with indenting that clearly defines the levels of detail in rows.

5. Save your changes to the *ee2-p7drill* workbook.

6. Creating a Chart Based on Pivot Table Data

You think it might be easier to compare the amounts donated to various agencies if you see the data in a column chart. To create a chart based on data in a pivot table, follow these steps:

1. Open the *ee2-p7drill* workbook, if necessary, and select the #6-PivotChart worksheet.

2. Right-click any cell in the pivot table.

3. Choose PivotChart.

A column chart displays on a new worksheet named Chart1. Much higher amounts were contributed in total to Church and Goodwill than to the other four categories.

4. Display the field drop-down list for Agency at the bottom of the chart.

5. Uncheck the Church and Goodwill agencies, and click OK.

Excel hides the data for the two agencies receiving the largest contributions. The Y-axis scale shifts to illustrate more clearly the differences between amounts contributed to the other four agencies.

6. Select the #6-PivotChart worksheet.

Hiding data in a chart also hides the data in the associated pivot table.

7. Save your changes to the *ee2-p7drill* workbook.

Challenge

Challenge exercises expand on or are somewhat related to skills that are presented in the lessons. Each exercise provides a brief narrative introduction, followed by instructions in a numbered-step format that are not as detailed as those in the Skill Drill section.

Before beginning your first Project 7 Challenge exercise, complete the following steps:

1. Open the file named *ee2-0703*, and immediately save it as `ee2-p7challenge`.

The *ee2-p7challenge* workbook contains five sheets: an overview, and four exercise sheets named #1-MaxMin, #2-Modify, #3-PivotChart, and #4-MultiCalc.

2. Click the Overview sheet to view the organization of the Project 7 Challenge Exercises workbook.

Each exercise is independent of the others, so you may complete the exercises in any order. Be sure to save the workbook after completing each exercise. If you need a paper copy of the completed exercise, enter your name centered in a header before printing. Other print options have already been set to print compressed to one page and to display the filename, sheet name, and current date in a footer.

If you need more than one work session to complete the desired exercises, continue working on *ee2-p7challenge* instead of starting over again on the original *ee2-0703* file.

1. Creating Summary Data Using MAX or MIN

As you analyze current residential real estate listings, you decide to display the highest selling price for a home in each area. Next you want to switch the display to the lowest price at which someone could buy into each area. To do this, you can use Max and Min summary calculations respectively. To create summary data using Max or Min, and format the results to Currency with zero decimal places, follow these steps:

1. Open the *ee2-p7challenge* workbook, if necessary, and select the #1-MaxMin worksheet.

2. Click any cell within the database, and activate the PivotTable and PivotChart Wizard.

3. Specify that you want to create a pivot table in the current worksheet starting in cell K5.

4. Lay out the pivot table to include Area as a row field and Price as the Data item.

5. Specify Max as the summary calculation on Price.

Max of Price displays in cell K5. The second column displays the highest asking price for a home in the corresponding area. For example, the highest asking price for a home in Champions Village is *156400*.

6. Change the summary calculation from Max to Min.

Excel replaces the prices in the second column with the lowest asking price for a home in each corresponding area. For example, the lowest asking price for a home in Champions Village is *102900*.

7. Double-click Min of Price in cell K5, and click the <u>N</u>umber button in the PivotTable Field dialog box.

8. Specify Currency with $ sign and zero decimal places as the number format.

Numbers display with the specified format. The Grand Total (in this case, the minimum of the listed values) is *$74,500*.

9. Deselect the pivot table, and save your changes to the *ee2-p7challenge* workbook.

2. Changing the Number and Location of Fields

You created a pivot table that displays the counts of homes in each area—the list of areas in one column, and the counts in the adjacent column to the right. Now you want to add counts for type of heat, and number of bedrooms within each type of heat. That way you can easily answer a question such as "How many of the three bedroom homes in Glenn Lakes have electric heat?" To change the number and location of fields in a pivot table, follow these steps:

1. Open the *ee2-p7challenge* workbook, if necessary, and select the #2-Modify worksheet.

2. Click within the pivot table (K5:L17). Use the PivotTable Field List box to add two fields to the Row area—first Heat; then Bed.

3. Click Area in the PivotTable Field List box and then add it to the Column area.

Adding the Area field to the Column area removes it from the Row area. Excel computes the requested counts in a pivot table that extends across many columns. Scroll to view counts at a detailed level. For example, there are five 3-bedroom homes with electric heat in the Glenn Lakes area.

4. Apply the Report 6 AutoFormat to the pivot table.

5. Deselect the pivot table, and save your changes to the *ee2-p7challenge* workbook.

3. Creating a PivotChart Report Using the Wizard

You know how to create a chart from an existing pivot table. Now you want to create a chart and its associated pivot table at the same time. To create a PivotChart report, follow these steps:

1. Open the *ee2-p7challenge* workbook, if necessary, and select the #3-PivotChart worksheet.

2. Click any cell in the list range A5:I40, and activate the PivotTable and PivotChart Wizard.

3. Specify that you want to create a PivotCha<u>r</u>t report with the corresponding pivot table located at cell K5.

Excel creates a blank Chart1 worksheet.

4. Use the PivotTable Field List box in the Chart1 worksheet to set up two fields: *Price* in the Data Area of the chart, and *Area* as the Category Axis.

5. Change *Sum of Price* to *Average of Price*.

6. Click the worksheet tab named #3-PivotChart.

Excel automatically created the pivot table on which the chart is based.

7. Format the numbers in the pivot table to Comma, zero decimal places, and deselect the pivot table.

8. Switch back to the Chart1 worksheet. Add titles and other documentation as appropriate, and change display of Y-axis values to include commas and dollar signs with zero decimal places.

9. Close the Chart toolbar, close the PivotTable Field List box, and save your changes to the *ee2-p7challenge* workbook.

4. Specifying More Than One Summary Calculation

For each area in the residential listings database, you want to know the number of homes available for sale and the average price of homes. To specify more than one summary calculation, follow these steps:

1. Open the *ee2-p7challenge* workbook, if necessary, and select the #4-MultiCalc worksheet.

2. Click any cell within the database, and activate the PivotTable and PivotChart Wizard.

3. Specify that you want to create a pivot table in the current worksheet starting in cell K5, and access the PivotTable and PivotChart Wizard – Layout dialog box.

4. Lay out the pivot table to include Area as a <u>R</u>OW field and Price as a <u>D</u>ATA item two times.

5. Specify Count as the summary calculation on the first Price data item, and specify Average as the summary calculation on the second Price data item.

6. Close or exit as needed to generate the pivot table.

7. Widen column K as desired, and change the format of numbers in the pivot table to comma, zero decimal places.

The table displays in PivotTable Classic format. Eight houses are listed for sale in Glenn Lakes, at an average price of *159,975*.

8. Apply a Table 6 predefined format.

Notice that Excel does not retain number formatting when you apply a predefined format.

9. Change the display of numbers to comma, zero decimal places.

10. Deselect the pivot table and save your changes to the *ee2-p7challenge* workbook.

iscovery Zone

Discovery Zone exercises require advanced knowledge of topics presented in *essentials* lessons, application of skills from multiple lessons, or self-directed learning of new skills.

Before beginning your first Project 7 Discovery Zone exercise, complete the following steps:

1. Open the file named *ee2-0704*, and immediately save it as `ee2-p7discovery`.

The *ee2-p7discovery* workbook contains three sheets: an overview, and two exercise sheets named #1-MultiPivot, and #2-Page.

2. Select the Overview worksheet to view the organization of the Project 7 Discovery Zone Exercises workbook.

Each exercise is independent of the other, so you may complete the exercises in any order. Be sure to save the workbook after completing each exercise. If you need a paper copy of the completed exercise, enter your name centered in a header before printing. Other print options have already been set to print compressed to one page and to display the filename, sheet name, and current date in a footer.

Be sure to save your changes, and close the workbook if you need more than one work session to complete the desired exercises. Continue working on *ee2-p7discovery* instead of starting over again on the original *ee2-0704* file.

1. Creating Multiple Pivot Tables

Your supervisor has asked you to review the shipping data for Great Wilderness Outfitters, Inc. (GWO). This analysis already contains a great deal of information about GWO's shipping performance. The list begins in row 10 on the #1-MultiPivot sheet of the *ee2-p7discovery* workbook. It contains data on the day of the week an order was taken and which shift processed the order.

Through PivotTable and PivotChart reports you can determine in more detail the day of the week and which shift has the best or worst performance. Generate and save as many variations of pivot tables and associated charts as you need to identify the problem areas.

2. Including a Page Field in a Pivot Table

You know how to create two-dimensional pivot tables by setting up row and column fields. Your data analysis can take on a third dimension if you set up a page field. For example, if you are analyzing employees' salary data, you can set up a pivot table to view summary analysis by Position (row) and Shift (column) for each Department (page).

Use onscreen Help to learn about Page fields and then display the #2-Page worksheet in the *ee2-p7discovery* workbook. Create the three-dimensional pivot table described in the first paragraph (sum on the Salary field). After you create the pivot table, use the Page pull-down button to page through each department's salary data.

Creating Hyperlinks and Using Collaborative Tools

Objectives

In this project, you learn how to

- ✔ Create a Hyperlink between Worksheets in an Excel Workbook
- ✔ Create a Hyperlink between a Word Document and an Excel Worksheet
- ✔ Create a Hyperlink between a PowerPoint Slide and an Excel Worksheet
- ✔ Track Changes in a Workbook
- ✔ Accept or Reject Changes
- ✔ Edit a Shared Workbook
- ✔ Work with Discussion Comments

Key terms in this project include

- ❑ change tracking
- ❑ discussion comment
- ❑ History worksheet
- ❑ hyperlink
- ❑ shared workbook

Why Would I Do This?

While working with multiple applications and collaborating with others on end products, you are likely to encounter a ***hyperlink***—a link from a document that you can click to jump to another location, open another file, or start a process—such as sending an e-mail or transferring a file. Hyperlinks in Web pages enable you to link to other locations in the current Web site as well as to other Web sites. You can create your own hyperlinks in Microsoft Office applications that can link you to other application files, other locations within the current file, or Internet links.

Excel also provides a variety of collaborative tools. You can, for example, track changes that you and others make to a workbook, and accept or reject each change. You can create, edit, and delete discussion comments associated with a workbook that is stored on a discussion server, and you can reply to the discussion comments written by others. These features support a dynamic collaborative process that promotes working smarter by sharing ideas and information.

Visual Summary

You start this project by creating and using three hyperlinks—a hyperlink to another worksheet in the current Excel workbook (see Figure 8.1), a hyperlink from a Word document to an Excel worksheet, and a hyperlink from a PowerPoint slide to an Excel worksheet.

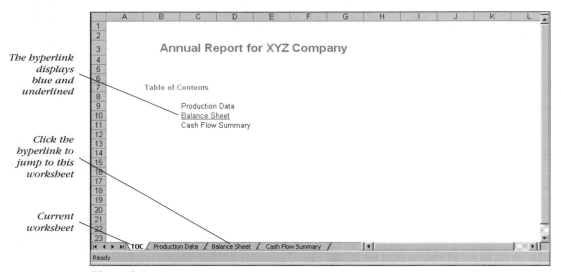

Figure 8.1

You also turn on and use a feature to track changes in a workbook. Each change can be accepted or rejected. Excel automatically attaches a note that identifies the user who made the change, specifies the date and time the change was made, and provides a description of the change (see Figure 8.2).

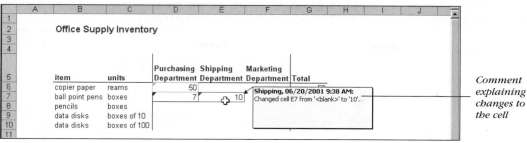

Figure 8.2

You also edit a shared workbook and learn to work with discussion comments.

Lesson 1: Creating a Hyperlink between Worksheets in an Excel Workbook

A hyperlink can be text—which generally displays blue and underlined—or a picture. When you position the pointer on a hyperlink, the pointer changes to a hand, which indicates that the text or picture is an item you can click to be moved to a related location.

You can set up a hyperlink to provide a quick means of moving from one location to another by clicking on the link. If the hyperlink is set up in an Excel worksheet, the connection can be to a position within the same worksheet, to another worksheet in the same workbook, to another workbook, to another application, or to a place within a Web site.

In this lesson, you open a workbook containing a preliminary design for a company's annual report. You then set up hyperlinks between two worksheets.

To Create a Hyperlink between Worksheets

1 **Open the *ee2-0801* workbook, and save it as** Annual Report.
The workbook contains the beginnings of a layout for an annual report. The first worksheet, named *TOC*, is the Table of Contents. Now create a hyperlink to jump to the start of the Balance Sheet and another link to jump back to the top of the TOC worksheet.

2 **Click cell A1 in the TOC worksheet, and name the cell** TOC.
Although you can jump to specific cells, it is easier and less confusing to jump to named cells. Remember, you can quickly name the current cell by clicking the Name box and then typing a name for the cell.

3 **Click cell A3 in the Balance Sheet worksheet, name the cell** BalSheet, **and save the workbook.**

4 **Click cell C10 in the TOC worksheet, and select Insert, Hyperlink.**
The Insert Hyperlink dialog box displays.

5 **In the Link to area—a column along the left side of the dialog box—click P**la**ce in This Document.**
An outline of cell references and defined names displays in the Insert Hyperlink dialog box (see Figure 8.3).

(Continues)

To Create a Hyperlink between Worksheets (Continued)

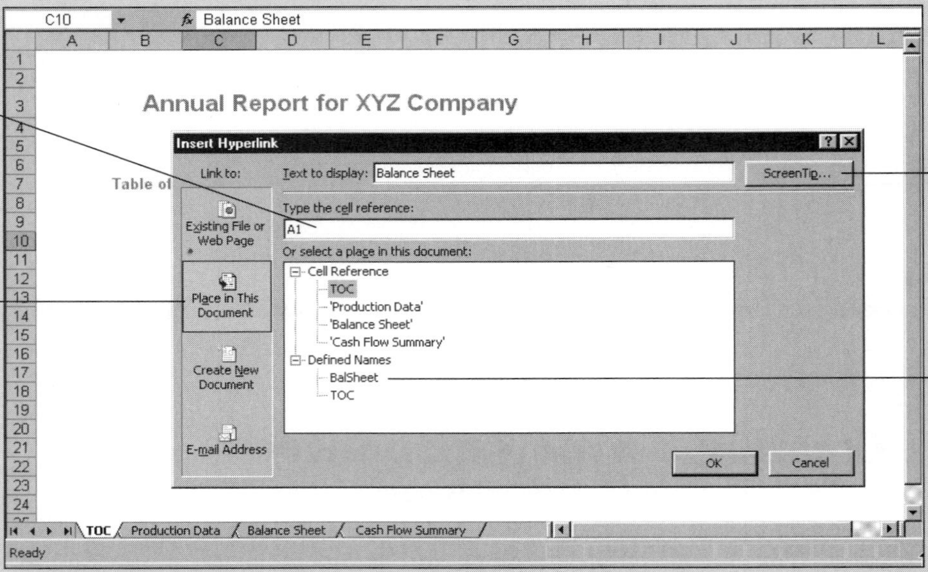

Type the location to jump to here, or select from the list below this text box

Click to place the hyperlink in the current worksheet

Click to set up a ScreenTip

Click to establish a link to cell A3 in the Balance Sheet worksheet

Figure 8.3

6 **Click BalSheet, the first name listed under Defined Names.**

> ### If you have problems...
>
> If you do not see BalSheet, you may need to expand the Defined Names outline by clicking the "+" outline symbol next to it.

7 **Click the ScreenTip button in the upper-right corner of the dialog box, and enter** Click to view the Balance Sheet **in the ScreenTip text box.**

8 **Click OK to close the Set Hyperlink ScreenTip dialog box; then click OK to close the Insert Hyperlink dialog box.**
Balance Sheet in cell C10 displays blue and underlined, indicating it is a hyperlink (refer to Figure 8.1). Now test the link.

9 **Position the pointer on the blue underlined text in cell C10.**
The pointer changes to a hand, and the ScreenTip *Click to view the Balance Sheet* displays.

10 **Click the hyperlinked text in cell C10.**
Excel jumps to the destination for the hyperlink, which is cell A3 in the Balance Sheet worksheet.

11 **Click cell E1 in the Balance Sheet worksheet, enter** TOC, **and then create a hyperlink in cell E1 to the cell named TOC in the Table of Contents worksheet. (Include a ScreenTip** Click to view the Table of Contents.**)**
The steps to complete this step are similar to those described in steps 4 through 8.

12 **Click the new hyperlink.**
If the TOC hyperlink is set up properly, cell A1 in the TOC worksheet becomes the active cell.

13 **Save your changes to the *Annual Report* workbook, and close the workbook.**
Continue with the next lesson, or exit Excel.

To extend your knowledge…

Removing and Restoring a Hyperlink

To remove a hyperlink, right-click the cell containing the hyperlink and then select <u>R</u>emove Hyperlink from the shortcut menu. If you remove a hyperlink in error, you can immediately choose <u>E</u>dit, <u>U</u>ndo Remove Hyperlink to restore the link.

Changing the Appearance of Hyperlinks

Hyperlinks initially display as blue and underlined, which tends to be a standard for links on Web sites, links within e-mail, and so forth; however, the appearance of a hyperlink you create is entirely under your control, and you can apply any formatting—font, color, size, shading, and so on—to it. To change the formatting of a hyperlink, right-click it, and choose <u>F</u>ormat Cells from the shortcut menu. Make your desired selections from the Format Cells dialog box, and click OK.

Lesson 2: Creating a Hyperlink between a Word Document and an Excel Worksheet

You can easily set up hyperlinks between Microsoft Office applications. For example, you can create a hyperlink in an Excel worksheet that jumps to a specific location in a Word document. You can also create a hyperlink in a Word document that jumps to an Excel worksheet.

Assume you are writing a sales report in Microsoft Word, and you want its readers to be able to quickly see data in an Excel worksheet that supports statements made in the report. If the report is a formal one, to be distributed widely throughout the organization, you would probably copy or link the worksheet data to the Word document. Its readers could then view the worksheet data as they read the report online or in hardcopy format; however, if the report is not yet final, or is intended strictly for internal use among a few readers, you might prefer to shorten the word-processed report by only placing hyperlinks to worksheet data within it. If you choose the hyperlink approach, the workbook referenced in the hyperlink must continue to be stored in the location captured in the hyperlink.

In this lesson, you open a Word document that contains the initial lines in a sales report, and create a hyperlink in that report to supporting data stored in an Excel workbook. You then test the hyperlink.

To Create a Hyperlink between a Word Document and an Excel Worksheet

1 In Word, open *ee2-0802.doc* and save it as `wordlink.doc`.

2 Select the phrase *(Click to view the Excel data)*.
Now create the hyperlink to an Excel worksheet.

3 Choose <u>I</u>nsert, Hyper<u>l</u>ink.

4 In the Link to area on the left side of the dialog box, click E<u>x</u>isting File or Web Page.

5 Select the Excel workbook *ee2-0803* from the location in which you are storing the student files that accompany this text.

6 Click the ScreenTi<u>p</u> button, type `Click to view the associated Excel file`, and click OK.

7 Click OK to close the Insert Hyperlink dialog box.
The hyperlinked text *(Click to view the Excel data)* displays blue and underlined. Now test the hyperlink.

(Continues)

To Create a Hyperlink between a Word Document and an Excel Worksheet (Continued)

8 **Position the pointer on the hyperlink.**
The ScreenTip that you defined displays. You also see the message *CTRL + click to follow link* in bold.

9 **Press and hold** Ctrl **and then click the hyperlink in the Word document.**
The Sales Data worksheet displays (see Figure 8.4). When Excel is accessed through a hyperlink, the Web toolbar displays automatically.

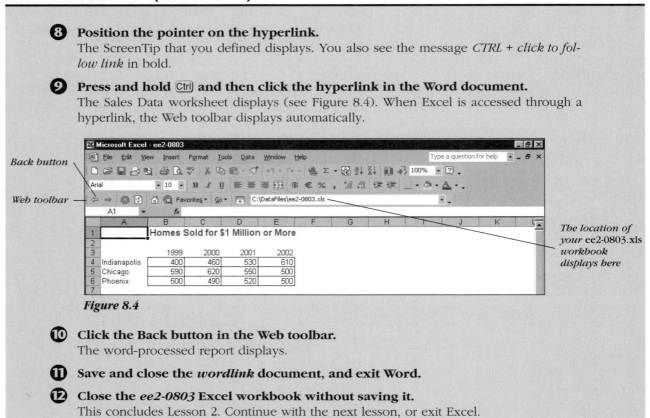

Back button

Web toolbar

The location of your ee2-0803.xls workbook displays here

Figure 8.4

10 **Click the Back button in the Web toolbar.**
The word-processed report displays.

11 **Save and close the** *wordlink* **document, and exit Word.**

12 **Close the** *ee2-0803* **Excel workbook without saving it.**
This concludes Lesson 2. Continue with the next lesson, or exit Excel.

To extend your knowledge...

Setting a Hyperlink to Excel Data

When you set a hyperlink to an Excel worksheet from another Office application, the link accesses the first worksheet of the workbook. Make sure that the Excel data you want to display is in the first worksheet or store it in its own workbook.

Lesson 3: Creating a Hyperlink between a PowerPoint Slide and an Excel Worksheet

You can create a hyperlink in Excel that jumps to a specific slide in a PowerPoint presentation. You can also create a hyperlink in a PowerPoint presentation that jumps to a worksheet cell in an Excel workbook. The latter situation is far more common. Creating the hyperlink in PowerPoint makes it possible for you to reference Excel data without making it a primary focus of a slide. The worksheet data would not be visible on the slide, but you could activate the hyperlink during the presentation and display the associated worksheet data in Excel.

In this lesson, you open a PowerPoint presentation file containing a single slide with a chart based on Excel data. The chart is not linked to the corresponding Excel file. You create a hyperlink between the chart on the PowerPoint slide and the Excel worksheet on which the chart is based, and test the link.

To Create a Hyperlink between a PowerPoint Slide and an Excel Worksheet

1 **In PowerPoint, open the *ee2-0804.ppt* file and save it as** pplink.ppt.
The PowerPoint presentation consists of a single slide—a chart based on data in the *ee2-0805* Excel workbook. There are no links between the two files.

2 **Click the PowerPoint chart to select it, and choose Insert, Hyperlink.**

3 **In the Link to area on the left side of the dialog box, click Existing File or Web Page.**

4 **Select the Excel workbook *ee2-0805* from the location in which you are storing the student files that accompany this text.**

5 **Click the ScreenTip button, enter** Click the chart to view the associated Excel data, **and click OK.**

6 **Click OK to close the Insert Hyperlink dialog box, and click outside the chart to deselect it.**
Now verify that the hyperlink works as intended.

7 **Click the Slide Show button near the lower-left corner of the screen.**
The single slide containing a chart displays in Slide Show view.

8 **Click within the chart on the slide.**
Clicking the chart opens Excel and displays the first worksheet in the *ee2-0805* workbook.

9 **Click the Back button on the Web toolbar to jump back to the PowerPoint presentation.**

10 **Press Esc to end the slide show.**

11 **Close the Web toolbar, and close the *ee2-0805* workbook without saving it.**

12 **Save your changes to *pplink.ppt*, and exit PowerPoint.**
This concludes Lesson 3, the third of three lessons on hyperlinks. Continue with the next lesson, or exit Excel.

Lesson 4: Tracking Changes in a Workbook

Excel enables you to track the changes in a workbook, whether you make all of the changes yourself or multiple changes are made by multiple users. In a work environment, it is common practice for two or more people to collaborate on developing or editing a workbook. Each user needs to know what changes the others have made.

Change tracking records row and column insertions and deletions, moves and copies, and changes to cell contents. The feature does not track formatting changes to cells or data, hiding or unhiding rows or columns, and adding or changing comments.

You can only track changes in a shared workbook. A ***shared workbook*** is a workbook that is set up to enable multiple users to make changes. When the track changes setting is active, the word *[Shared]* displays to the right of the filename in the title bar. While in shared mode, certain operations are not available. For example, you cannot delete a worksheet while a workbook is shared.

In this lesson, you work with an office supply inventory model. Imagine that the workbook is available to many users on a network. After opening the workbook, you save it using a different name. You then turn on the track changes feature and prepare to monitor changes made by different users.

To Track Changes in a Workbook

① **Open the *ee2-0806* workbook, and save it as** inventory.

② **Choose Tools, Track Changes, Highlight Changes.**
The Highlight Changes dialog box displays (see Figure 8.5).

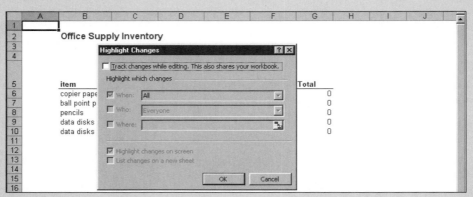

Figure 8.5

③ **Click the *Track changes while editing* check box at the top of the dialog box.**

④ **Check the When check box and then select All from the drop-down list, if necessary.**
The *When* check box determines the extent of tracking changes. Selecting All (the default) causes all changes to be tracked. Other options include *Since I last saved*, *Not yet reviewed*, and *Since date*. If you select the last option, Excel provides a prompt to enter the date.

⑤ **Check the Who check box, and select Everyone from the drop-down list.**
Options on the Who drop-down list include *Everyone* and *Everyone but Me*. The latter might be used if you were a supervisor or wanted to monitor only changes other people in your workgroup made to the workbook.

⑥ **Leave the Where check box unchecked.**
If you check Where, you can select specific cells to be monitored.

⑦ **Check the *Highlight changes on screen* check box, if necessary.**
When the *Highlight changes on screen* check box is selected, Excel creates a cell comment for every cell that is changed.

⑧ **Click OK. If a message box appears asking if you want to continue the save operation, click OK.**
The word *[Shared]* displays in the title bar. Tracking changes automatically shares the workbook, even though you may be the only one making changes.

⑨ **Save your changes to the *inventory* workbook.**
This concludes Lesson 4, the first of three lessons on change tracking. Continue with the next lesson, or close the workbook and exit Excel.

To extend your knowledge...

Setting the Number of Days to Track Changes

When you turn on change tracking, the history is kept for 30 days. When you turn off change tracking or stop sharing the workbook, all change history is deleted.

You can increase or decrease the number of days that changes are tracked. Choose Tools, Share Workbook and then select the Advanced tab in the Share Workbook dialog box. Type the desired number of days in the *Keep change history for* spinner box, and click OK.

Lesson 5: Accepting or Rejecting Changes

Excel provides three ways to view tracked changes—onscreen highlighting, a History worksheet, and a dialog box in which you can accept or reject each change. You are using the first method when you view a shared workbook onscreen. Excel outlines changes with a different color for each user, and displays a note when you position the pointer on a changed cell. The note includes the name of the user who made the change, the date and time of the change, and a description of the change.

A **History worksheet** is a separate worksheet that provides detailed information about changes in a list form—one change per row. You can print the list of changes. You can also analyze changes by filtering records in the list.

You can also view each change in sequence in a dialog box that enables you to accept or reject each change. When multiple users revise a tracked document, generally one person makes the final decision on whether to keep or discard the suggested changes. It is a good idea to accept or reject changes on a regular basis, so as to keep the display of changes made to other changes at a minimum.

In this lesson you use the first and third methods to view tracked changes. You make a change in the Office Supply model, and view information about the change onscreen. You then make a second change, and use the Accept or Reject Changes dialog box to accept one change and reject another.

To Accept or Reject Changes

1 Open the *inventory* workbook, if necessary, and make sure that Highlight Changes is active for all changes.

2 Enter the number 7 in cell D7.
Excel automatically displays a border around the cell and inserts a comment, as evidenced by the small triangular comment indicator in the upper-left corner of the cell.

3 Position the pointer on cell D7.
The attached comment displays. It identifies the user—by name or computer number—that made the change, specifies the date and time the change was made, and provides a description of the change (see Figure 8.6).

(Continues)

To Accept or Reject Changes (Continued)

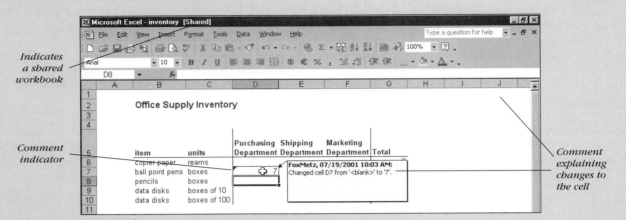

Figure 8.6

4 **Enter the number 5 in cell D9.**

5 **Choose Tools, Track Changes, Accept or Reject Changes.**
A message box displays with the following text: *This action will now save the workbook. Do you want to continue?*

6 **Click OK.**
The Select Changes to Accept or Reject dialog box displays (see Figure 8.7).

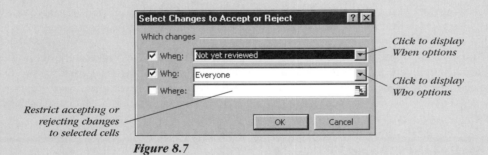

Figure 8.7

7 **If necessary, check the When box, and select *Not yet reviewed* from the drop-down list.**

8 **If necessary, check the Who box, and select Everyone from the drop-down list.**

9 **Click OK.**
The Accept or Reject Changes dialog box displays (see Figure 8.8).

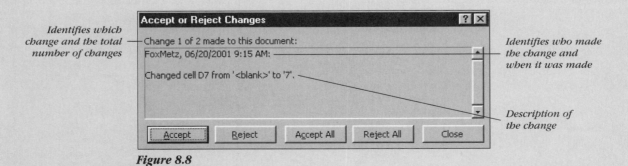

Figure 8.8

To Accept or Reject Changes

⑩ Click the <u>A</u>ccept button to accept the first change.
Information about the second change displays in the Accept or Reject Changes dialog box.

⑪ Click the <u>R</u>eject button to reject the second change.

⑫ Save your changes to the *inventory* workbook.
This concludes Lesson 5. Continue with the next lesson, or close the workbook and exit Excel.

To extend your knowledge...

Removing a Workbook from Shared Use

To remove a workbook from shared use, choose <u>T</u>ools, Sha<u>r</u>e Workbook and then select the Editing tab. Make sure that you are the only person listed in the *<u>W</u>ho has this workbook open now* section. Remove the check mark from the *<u>A</u>llow changes by more than one user at the same time* check box, and click OK. Click <u>Y</u>es in response to the prompt about effects on other users.

Lesson 6: Editing a Shared Workbook

In the previous lesson, you learned the process to accept or reject changes by evaluating changes made by a single user in one workbook. In this lesson, you simulate changes made by two users—the Purchasing department and the Shipping department—in the same workbook. You view the changes and end the simulation of multiple users.

At the end of the lesson, a "To extend your knowledge..." section explains how to merge workbooks if multiple users make changes to separate copies of the same workbook.

To Edit a Shared Workbook

❶ Open the *inventory* workbook, if necessary. Make sure that its status is still shared, and that <u>H</u>ighlight Changes is still active for all changes.
If the file is shared, the word *[Shared]* displays after the filename in the title bar. Now create the simulation by revising the User name on the General tab in the Options dialog box.

If you have problems...

If the workbook is not currently shared, choose Sha<u>r</u>e Workbook on the <u>T</u>ools menu, click the Editing tab, and check that the *<u>A</u>llow changes by more than one user at the same time* check box is selected.

❷ Choose <u>T</u>ools, <u>O</u>ptions.

❸ Click the General tab, and make note of the current entry in the User <u>n</u>ame text box.
You restore the User name to the current entry near the end of this lesson.

❹ Change the User <u>n</u>ame to Purchasing, and click OK.

(Continues)

To Edit a Shared Workbook (Continued)

If you have problems...

If you are working in a computer lab or networked environment, you may not be able to change the user name on your system and complete this lesson. Instead, read the remaining steps and the "To extend your knowledge..." sections at the end of this lesson to gain an understanding of related processes.

5 **Enter the number 50 in cell D6, save the workbook, and position the pointer on cell D6.**

The comment indicates that *Purchasing* made the change. The borders around cells D6 and D7 are different colors, indicating the changes were made by different users.

6 **Choose Tools, Options; click the General tab, change the User name to** Shipping, **and click OK.**

7 **Enter the number 10 in cell E7, save the workbook, and position the pointer on cell E7.**

Changes are detected only after a file is saved. The comment indicates that *Shipping* made the change. The borders around the three changed cells all have a different color assigned, indicating that three users made the changes.

8 **Choose Tools, Track Changes, Accept or Reject Changes, and then click OK.**

The Accept or Reject Changes dialog box displays (see Figure 8.9).

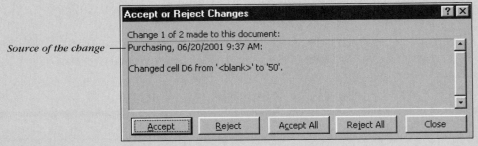

Source of the change

Figure 8.9

At this point, you could proceed to accept or reject changes made by multiple users the same way you accepted or rejected changes made by a single user in the previous lesson. Instead, restore the appropriate user name and save your changes to the shared workbook.

9 **Click Close.**

The Accept or Reject Changes dialog box closes without accepting or rejecting any change. Now end the simulation of multiple users by restoring the original user name and saving your changes.

10 **Choose Tools, Options, and select the General tab.**

11 **Change the User name to its original specification, and click OK.**

12 **Save your changes to the *inventory* workbook, and close the workbook.**

This concludes Lesson 6. You can continue with the last lesson, or exit Excel.

To extend your knowledge...

Conflicting Changes to a Shared Workbook

When change tracking is active, Excel displays a Resolve Conflicts dialog box if you try to save changes to a cell that has already been changed by another user. After you read the information about each change and the conflicting changes made by others, you can select Accept Mine, Accept All Mine, Accept Other, and Accept All Others. You can see how you and others resolved past conflicts by viewing the History worksheet.

Merging Workbooks

In this lesson, you worked with changes made by multiple users in a single file. Often two or more people collaborate on the development of a workbook by working on different copies of the file. If you want to merge copies of a shared workbook in which users have made changes, Excel requires that each copy be set up to maintain the history of changes.

If you intend to merge workbooks, set up Shared mode in the original workbook and make copies for others to edit. All copies of the workbook must remain in the Shared mode while being modified. Collaborators can work on their copies from remote locations on a network or download them to their computers. When editing is complete, all of the workbooks must be merged into one before accepting or rejecting changes.

Merging copies of a shared workbook takes only a few steps. Choose Compare and Merge Workbooks from the Tools menu and then save the shared workbook if prompted. Hold down Ctrl, click the name of each copy of the shared workbook listed in the *Select Files to Merge Into Current Workbook* dialog box that you want to merge, and click OK. You can then accept or reject changes as usual.

Lesson 7: Working with Discussion Comments

Microsoft Office also supports collaborative efforts through its discussion comments feature. A **discussion comment** is a remark associated with a Web page or Office application file that is stored on a discussion server. When you are a participant in a discussion, you can reply to comments made by others. You can also create, edit, and delete your own comments.

Comments are stored separately from the Web page or application document under discussion. Moving or renaming a document breaks the links between the document and the discussion comments.

To use discussion comments, you must have access to a discussion server and permission to participate in the discussion. A server administrator sets up a subscription process and sets permissions to read and create discussion comments. The server may be on the Internet or part of an organization's intranet.

The requirement to have an organization-specific discussion server limits the hands-on component on this topic. In this lesson, you turn on the Web Discussions toolbar, and view related buttons and dialog boxes.

To Use Discussion Comments

❶ **Launch Excel, if necessary.**

❷ **Select Tools, Online Collaboration, Web Discussions.**
   The Web Discussions toolbar displays at the bottom of the screen (see Figure 8.10).

(Continues)

To Use Discussion Comments (Continued)

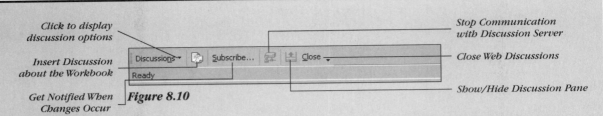

Click to display discussion options

Insert Discussion about the Workbook

Get Notified When Changes Occur

Stop Communication with Discussion Server

Close Web Discussions

Show/Hide Discussion Pane

Figure 8.10

③ **Position the pointer on the Subscribe button.**
The ScreenTip *Get Notified When Changes Occur* displays.

④ **Click the Subscribe button.**
Microsoft displays the Internet Explorer dialog box shown in Figure 8.11.

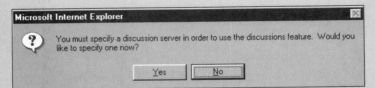

Figure 8.11

⑤ **Click No to close the dialog box.**

⑥ **Click the small arrow at the right end of the Discussions button on the Web Discussions toolbar.**
A pop-up menu with five options displays. The options to refresh, filter, and print discussions are not available unless you are connected to a discussion.

⑦ **Choose Discussion Options from the pop-up menu.**
The Discussion Options dialog box displays (see Figure 8.12).

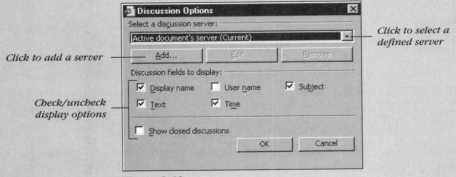

Click to add a server

Check/uncheck display options

Click to select a defined server

Figure 8.12

⑧ **Click the Add button.**
The Add or Edit Discussion Servers dialog box displays (see Figure 8.13).

To Use Discussion Comments

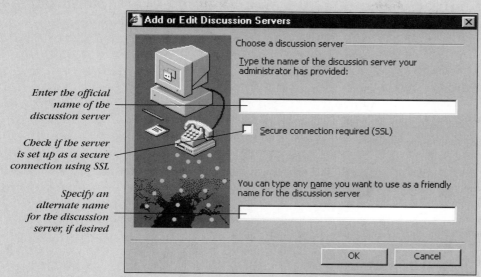

Enter the official name of the discussion server

Check if the server is set up as a secure connection using SSL

Specify an alternate name for the discussion server, if desired

Figure 8.13

⑨ Click Cancel to close the Add or Edit Discussion Servers dialog box, and click Cancel to close the Discussion Options dialog box.

⑩ Click the Close button on the Web Discussions toolbar.
This concludes Project 8. You can continue with end-of-project exercises, or exit Excel.

Summary

The initial three lessons on hyperlinks focused on how to set up connections between one location and another within a workbook and between Excel and other Microsoft applications. Subsequent lessons focused on features that support the collaborative process. You explored using features that enable a workbook to be edited by more than one person at a time. Topics included designating a workbook as shared, tracking changes, accepting or rejecting tracked changes, and editing a shared workbook. You also learned the purpose of discussion comments, and viewed options on the Web Discussions toolbar. To expand your knowledge of features that support the collaborative process, review the many related onscreen Help pages.

Checking Concepts and Terms

Multiple Choice

Circle the letter of the correct answer for each of the following.

1. Which of the following is true? [L4]

   a. Tracking automatically sets up a shared workbook.

   b. You can delete a worksheet if its workbook is currently in shared mode.

   c. Both a and b

   d. Neither a nor b

2. Which of the following is not an option when determining the extent of change tracking? [L4]

   a. All

   b. Since I last saved

   c. Not yet reviewed

   d. Between these dates

3. Which of the following is not captured by change tracking? [L4]

   a. Formatting changes

   b. Row and column insertions and deletions

   c. Moves and copies

   d. Changes to cell contents

4. A hyperlink set up in Excel can be a link to _____. [L1]

   a. a Web page

   b. another worksheet in the same workbook

   c. another application, such as Microsoft Word

   d. All of the above

5. Which of the following is true? [L6 and L7]

   a. A discussion comment is a remark associated with a Web page of an Office application file that is stored on a discussion server.

   b. If you are subscribed to a discussion, you can edit and delete discussion comments made by anyone participating in the discussion.

   c. Both a and b

   d. Neither a nor b

Discussion

1. A History worksheet summarizes the changes made when Excel's change tracking feature is active. Describe the process of viewing a History worksheet. (Onscreen Help provides the information you need to answer the question.)

2. Some changes are not tracked when Excel's change tracking is active, such as formatting changes to cells or data, hiding or unhiding rows or columns, and any changes to features unavailable in shared workbooks. List at least six unavailable features in shared workbooks. (Onscreen Help provides the information you need to answer the question.)

3. Excel provides the capability to filter discussion comments. Explain what types of filtering can be selected. (Onscreen Help provides the information you need to answer the question.)

Skill Drill exercises reinforce project skills. Each skill that is reinforced is the same, or nearly the same, as a skill presented in the project. Detailed instructions are provided in a step-by-step format.

Before beginning your first Project 8 Skill Drill exercise, complete the following steps:

1. Open the file named *ee2-0807*, and immediately save the workbook as `ee2-p8drill`.
   The workbook contains an overview sheet and four sheets: #1-Create Link, #2-Edit Link, #3-Remove Link, and #4-Track.
2. Click the Overview sheet to view the organization and content of the Project 8 Skill Drill Exercises workbook.

There are six exercises. You use worksheets in the *ee2-p8drill* workbook to complete the first four exercises. For exercises 5 and 6, you use onscreen Help. The exercises can be worked in any order. Be sure to save the workbook after completing each exercise. If you need a paper copy of the completed exercise, enter your name centered in a header before printing. Other print options have already been set to print compressed and to display the filename, sheet name, and current date in a footer.

Be sure to save your changes, and close the workbook if you need more than one work session to complete the desired exercises. Continue working on *ee2-p8drill* instead of starting over again on the original *ee2-0807* file.

1. Creating a Hyperlink in a Worksheet

You work for Real Estate for Tomorrow, Inc., and you manage a listing of residential real estate for sale. You want to create a hyperlink within the worksheet to the mailing address for the firm. To create the hyperlink, follow these steps:

1. Open the *ee2-p8drill* workbook, if necessary, and select the #1-Create Link worksheet.
2. Enter `Mailing Address` in cell A6.
3. Click cell M3, name the cell `address`, and save the workbook.
4. Click cell A6, and select Insert, Hyperlink.
5. In the Link to area—a column along the left side of the dialog box—click Place in This Document.
   An outline of cell references and defined names displays in the Insert Hyperlink dialog box.
6. Click *address* under Defined Names.
7. Click the ScreenTip button in the upper-right corner of the dialog box, and enter `Click to view the firm's mailing address` in the ScreenTip text box.
8. Click OK to close the Set Hyperlink ScreenTip dialog box and then click OK to close the Insert Hyperlink dialog box.
   Mailing Address in cell A6 displays blue and underlined, indicating it is a hyperlink. Now test the link.
9. Position the pointer on the blue underlined text in cell A6.
   The pointer changes to a hand, and the ScreenTip *Click to view the firm's mailing address* displays.
10. Click the hyperlinked text in cell A6.
    Excel jumps to cell M3, the destination for the hyperlink.
11. Save your changes to the *ee2-p8drill* workbook.

2. Editing a Hyperlink

You work for Real Estate for Tomorrow, Inc., and you manage a listing of residential real estate for sale. You want to improve the display of data by changing the destination cell in a hyperlink. To edit a hyperlink, follow these steps:

1. Open the *ee2-p8drill* workbook, if necessary, and select the #2-Edit Link worksheet.
2. Click the *Contact us!* hyperlink in cell A5.

    Excel jumps to cell M3. Depending on your display settings, you may not be able to see the complete phone and fax numbers.
3. Right-click the *Contact us!* hyperlink in cell A5, and select Edit Hyperlink from the shortcut menu.
4. In the *Type the cell reference* text box, change *M3* to **O3** (be sure to type the letter *O* instead of a zero).
5. Click OK, and then click the edited link in cell A5.

    Excel jumps to cell O3. You see the complete phone and fax numbers.
6. Save your changes to the *ee2-p8drill* workbook.

3. Removing a Hyperlink

You work for Real Estate for Tomorrow, Inc., and you manage a listing of residential real estate for sale. You want to delete data about real estate agents from the worksheet. To remove a hyperlink to agent names, and delete the associated data, follow these steps:

1. Open the *ee2-p8drill* workbook, if necessary, and select the #3-Remove Link worksheet.
2. Right-click the *Agent List* hyperlink in cell A5, and select Remove Hyperlink from the shortcut menu.

    The hyperlink is removed. The text *Agent List* no longer displays blue and underlined.
3. Delete the contents of cell A5 and the range M3:M7.
4. Save your changes to the *ee2-p8drill* workbook.

4. Tracking Changes in a Worksheet

You work for Real Estate for Tomorrow, Inc., and you manage a listing of residential real estate for sale. You want to track changes in the selling prices of several homes so that a co-worker can easily double-check your work. To turn on the change tracking feature and make a change, follow these steps:

1. Open the *ee2-p8drill* workbook, if necessary, and select the #4-Track worksheet.
2. Choose Tools, Track Changes, Highlight Changes.

    The Highlight Changes dialog box displays.
3. Click the *Track changes while editing* check box at the top of the dialog box.
4. Check the When check box and then select All from the drop-down list, if necessary.
5. Check the Who check box, and select Everyone from the drop-down list.
6. Leave the Where check box unchecked.
7. Check the *Highlight changes on screen* check box, if necessary, and click OK.
8. Click OK if a message box appears asking if you want to continue the save operation.

    The word *[Shared]* displays in the title bar. The change tracking feature is active.
9. Change the amount in cell B22 from *225,000* to **219,900**.

    Excel automatically displays a border around the cell and inserts a comment, as evidenced by the small triangular comment indicator in the upper-left corner of the cell.
10. Position the pointer on cell B22.

    The attached comment displays. It identifies the user—by name or computer number—that made the change, specifies the date and time the change was made, and provides a description of the change.
11. Save your changes to the *ee2-p8drill* workbook.

5. Getting Help on Merging Workbooks

You work for Real Estate for Tomorrow, Inc., and you manage a listing of residential real estate for sale. You want to learn more about merging workbooks. To view information about merging workbooks in onscreen Help, follow these steps:

1. Launch Excel, if necessary, and enter `merge workbooks` in the Ask a Question box in the upper-right corner of the screen.
2. Select the topic *Merge workbooks*, read the related information, and close the Microsoft Excel Help window.
3. Click the small down arrow at the right end of the Ask a Question box, and select *merge workbooks* from the list of recently requested Help topics.
4. Select the topic *Troubleshoot merging workbooks*.
5. Click the Show All button in the right pane, if necessary, and read the extensive information on dealing with merge problems.
6. Close the Microsoft Excel Help window.

6. Getting Help on Discussion Comments

You work for Real Estate for Tomorrow, Inc., and you manage a listing of residential real estate for sale. You want to learn more about discussion comments. To view information about discussion comments in onscreen Help, follow these steps:

1. Launch Excel, if necessary, and enter `discussion comments` in the Ask a Question box.
2. Select the topic *About Web Discussions*, and read the related information.
3. Display the Contents, Answer Wizard, and Index tabs, if necessary.
4. Click the Index tab, type `discussion` in the Type keywords text box, and click the Search button.

   Excel finds and lists 17 topics related to discussions.
5. Read the topics of your choice.

   Make sure that you are connected to the Internet before you select either Help topic that begins with WEB.
6. Close the Microsoft Excel Help window.

Challenge exercises expand on or are somewhat related to skills that are presented in the lessons. Each exercise provides a brief narrative introduction, followed by instructions in a numbered-step format that are not as detailed as those in the Skill Drill section.

Before beginning your first Project 8 Challenge exercise, complete the following steps:

1. Open the file named *ee2-0808*, and immediately save the workbook as `ee2-p8challenge`. The *ee2-p8challenge* workbook contains five sheets: an overview, and sheets named #1-SetLinks, #2-AcceptReject, #3-Web, and #4-Send.
2. Click the Overview sheet to view the organization of the Project 8 Challenge Exercises workbook.

There are four exercises, and you may work the exercises in any order. Be sure to save the workbook after completing each exercise. If you need a paper copy of the completed exercise, enter your name centered in a header before printing. Other print options have already been set to print compressed to one page and to display the filename, sheet name, and current date in a footer.

If you need more than one work session to complete the desired exercises, continue working on *ee2-p8challenge* instead of starting over again on the original *ee2-0808* file.

1. Creating Hyperlinks with a Large Worksheet

You are managing an employee database in an Excel worksheet. You want to set up hyperlinks to various areas within the worksheet. To create and test the links, follow these steps:

1. Open the *ee2-p8challenge* workbook, if necessary, and select the #1-SetLinks worksheet.
2. Set up four hyperlinks in the worksheet using the following range names and cell references:
   Criteria in cell F3, jumping to cell C12
   Database in cell F4, jumping to cell C21
   Drop-down lists in cell F5, jumping to cell T1
   Extract in cell F6, jumping to cell K134
3. Enter List of hyperlinks in cell A131, and set a hyperlink jumping to cell F3.
4. Copy the hyperlink in cell A131 to cells K136 and R1.
5. Make sure that each link in the range F3:F6 jumps to the appropriate area in the worksheet, and that each *List of hyperlinks* link jumps to cell F3.
6. Save your changes to the *ee2-p8challenge* workbook.

2. Accepting or Rejecting Tracked Changes

You are managing a Transportation Model worksheet. You want to track changes in that worksheet as you make them, followed by accepting or rejecting each change when you are done. To activate Excel's change tracking feature, make changes, and accept or reject each change, follow these steps:

1. Open the *ee2-p8challenge* workbook, if necessary, and select the #2-AcceptReject worksheet.
2. Turn on tracking of all changes by everyone.
3. Change the shipping cost per unit in cell H8 to 3.40.
4. Replace all occurrences of Chicago with St. Louis.
5. Change the capacity value in cell J17 from *20,000* to 22,000.
6. Activate accepting and rejecting changes for changes by everyone not yet reviewed.
7. Accept the change in city and shipping cost per unit, but reject the change in capacity.
8. Disable tracking changes while editing, which removes the workbook from shared use.
9. Save your changes to the *ee2-p8challenge* workbook.

3. Creating a Hyperlink to a Web Site

You developed a worksheet to track annual revenues for three cities over a four-year period. Now you want to create a hyperlink to a Web site for the first city. To create the hyperlink to a Web site, follow these steps:

1. Open the *ee2-p8challenge* workbook, if necessary, and select the #3-Web worksheet.
2. Click cell A13, and start the process to insert a hyperlink in the current document.
3. Select the E_xisting File or Web Page option in the Insert Hyperlink dialog box.
4. Type www.indy.org in the Add_ress text box, and click OK.
5. Save your changes to the *ee2-p8challenge* workbook.
6. Connect to the Internet, if necessary, and click the link to the Indianapolis Web site.
7. Use the Back button in your browser to return to Excel.

4. Creating an E-mail Hyperlink

You developed a worksheet to track annual revenues for three cities over a four-year period. Now you want to create a hyperlink to your e-mail address. To create the hyperlink, follow these steps:

1. Open the *ee2-p8challenge* workbook, if necessary, and select the #4-Send worksheet.
2. Click cell A13, and start the process to insert a hyperlink in the current document.

3. Select the E-mail Address option in the Insert Hyperlink dialog box.

4. Enter your personal e-mail address in the E-mail address text box, and click OK.

5. Save your changes to the *ee2-p8challenge* workbook.

Discovery Zone exercises require advanced knowledge of topics presented in *essentials* lessons, application of skills from multiple lessons, or self-directed learning of new skills.

There are two exercises, each based on a separate data file. Each exercise is independent of the other, so you may complete the exercises in any order. The second exercise on merging workbooks requires working with one other person.

1. Displaying and Printing a History Worksheet

You want to make several changes in a workbook and view the changes in a History worksheet. Open the *ee2-0809* workbook and save it as `ee2-p8discovery1`. Turn on change tracking, and make the following changes:

- Center the column headings in row 3
- Change the contents of cell B4 from *145,000* to `150,000`
- Change the name of the worksheet from *GlennLakes GC* to `Year 2002`
- Insert a row between *Golf Lessons* (row 5) and *Other Revenue* (row 6)

Save your changes to the *ee2-p8discovery1* workbook. Display and print a History worksheet, and note that centering the column headings in row 3—a formatting change—is not listed. Close the workbook.

Note: Whether you save the file or not as you close it, Excel does not retain the History worksheet.

2. Merging Workbooks

You (Person #1) are going to make changes to a workbook. Select someone else (Person #2) to make changes to a copy of the same workbook. After all changes are made, merge the workbooks. Follow the instructions below in three stages—prepare to edit, make changes, and merge the workbooks.

Prepare to Edit (Person #1): Open the *ee2-0810* workbook, enable change tracking, and save the workbook as `edit1`. Make a copy of the *edit1* workbook, change the name of the copy to *edit2*, and distribute the copy to Person #2.

Make Changes (Person #1): Open the *edit1* workbook, and make sure that change tracking is enabled. Change the contents of cell B4 from *145,000* to `150,000`, and save your change.

Make Changes (Person #2): Open the *edit2* workbook, and make sure that change tracking is enabled. Insert a row between *Golf Lessons* (row 5) and *Other Revenue* (row 6). Enter `Pro Shop Sales` in column A of the newly inserted row. Save your changes to the *edit2* workbook, and return a copy of the revised workbook to Person #1.

Merge Workbooks (Person #1): Make sure that the revised workbooks *edit1* and *edit 2* are in the same folder, and open the *edit1* workbook, if necessary. Select the option on the Tools menu to merge workbooks, and select the *edit2* workbook to merge into the current workbook. Complete the merge, and save the result as *ee2-p8discovery2*.

*T*ask Guide

A book in the *essentials* series is designed to be kept as a handy reference beside your computer even after you have completed all the projects and exercises. Any time you have difficulty recalling the sequence of steps or a shortcut needed to achieve a result, look up the general category in the alphabetized listing below, and then quickly find your task. If you have difficulty performing a task, turn to the page number listed in the third column to locate the step-by-step exercise or other detailed description. For the greatest efficiency in using this Task Guide, take a few minutes to familiarize yourself with the main categories and keywords before you begin your search.

To Do This	Use This Command	Page Number
	Data Validation	
Audit tools, find invalid data	Choose Tools, Formula Auditing. Select Show Formula Auditing Toolbar, and click the Circle Invalid Data button.	139
In-cell drop-down list, create	Choose Data, Validation; then select the Settings tab, and select List in the Allow text box. In the Source text box, enter an absolute reference to cells containing allowable entries (or select the cell range using the mouse). Be sure a check mark displays in the In-cell drop-down check box and then click OK.	133
In-cell drop-down list, use	Click a cell and then click the down arrow at the right end of the cell. Select the desired data from the list.	133
Message, create error alert	Choose Data, Validation and then select the Error Alert tab. Select the Stop, Warning, or Information style, and then enter a message in the Title and Error message text boxes. Click OK.	136
Message, create input message	Select the cell to which you want to attach an input message. Choose Data, Validation, and select the Input Message tab. Enter messages in the Title and Input message text boxes and then click OK.	131
Playback, selecting a voice	Choose Start, Settings, Control Panel, and click Speech. Select the desired voice and voice speed on the Text To Speech tab and then click OK.	143
Playback, speak on enter	Choose View, Toolbars and then select Text To Speech. Click the Speak On Enter button on the Text To Speech toolbar, enter data in a cell, and press ↵Enter or Tab⇆.	143
Playback, worksheet data	Choose View, Toolbars, and select Text To Speech. Select the range of cells to be played back, and click the Speak Cells button on the Text To Speech toolbar.	143

Continues ▶

To Do This	Use This Command	Page Number
Restricting data, whole numbers within a range	Select Data, Validation and then select the Settings tab in the Data Validation dialog box. Select Whole number from the Allow drop-down list; then enter a value in the Minimum text box and a value in the Maximum text box. Add appropriate error messages and then close the Data Validation dialog box.	134
Validation, copy	Select the cells containing the restrictions and messages to be copied; then click the Copy button, and select the destination. Choose Edit, Paste Special, and click Validation. Click OK.	137
Validation, find	Select Edit, Go To and then select the Special button. Click Data Validation, click All, and click OK.	141
Validation, range of values	Select Data, Validation and then select the Settings tab. Select Whole number from the Allow drop-down list, and select between from the Data drop-down list. Enter values in the Minimum and Maximum boxes and then click OK.	134

Documenting

To Do This	Use This Command	Page Number
Comment, attach	Select the cell to contain a comment, and choose Insert, Comment. Type a message in the comment box and then click outside the box.	63
Comment, delete	Right-click a cell with an attached comment, and select Delete Comment.	64
Comment, edit	Right-click a cell with an attached comment, and select Edit Comment.	64
Comment, print	Choose File, Page Setup, and click the Sheet tab. Display the Comments drop-down list, select *At end of sheet* or *As displayed on sheet*, and click OK.	64
Comment, turn on indicator only	Choose Tools, Options, select the View tab, and select *Comment indicator only* in the Comments section.	63
Comment, view all	Choose View, Comments.	63
Comment, view one	Position the mouse pointer on a cell displaying a red comment indicator in the upper-right corner.	63
File properties, view and set	Choose File, Properties. To view current settings, select among the General, Summary, Statistics, Contents, and Custom tabs. Make changes as desired on the Summary or Custom tabs and then click OK.	69
Range name, create	Select the range to be named, click the Name box at the left end of the Formula bar, type the range name, and press ↵Enter.	61
Range name, delete	Choose Insert, Name, Define. Select the name to delete, click the Delete button, and click OK.	63
Range name, display	Select Insert, Name, Define, and select the name. Click OK.	61

To Do This	Use This Command	Page Number
Range names, list	In a blank area of the worksheet, select a cell to be the upper-left corner of a two-column list. Choose Insert, Name, Paste and then select the Paste List button.	63

Formatting

AutoFormat, apply	Select cells, choose Format, AutoFormat, and click the Options button in the AutoFormat dialog box. Uncheck the Font check box near the bottom of the dialog box to keep the current font. Scroll down, click the desired format when it appears (format descriptions display below the related format), and click OK.	40
AutoFormat, remove	Select formatted cells, and choose Format, AutoFormat. Scroll down, click the None format, and click OK.	42
Cells, delete	Select cells and then choose Edit, Delete. Make sure that Shift cells left or Shift cells up is selected, and click OK.	33
Cells, insert	Select cells and then choose Insert, Cells. Make sure that Shift cells right or Shift cells down is selected, and click OK.	33
Custom format, create	Click the cell to be formatted, and choose Format, Cells. Select the Number tab, and click Custom in the Category list. Delete the contents, if any, currently in the Type text box, type the desired custom format in the Type text box, and click OK.	37
Format(s), replace	Click cell A1, and choose Edit, Replace. Click the Options button to display Format buttons and associated Preview boxes in the Find and Replace dialog box. Display the *Find what* Format drop-down list and then specify the desired format(s), or click a cell that already contains the desired formatting. Display the *Replace with* Format drop-down list and then specify the desired format(s), or click a cell that already contains the desired formatting. Click Replace All or Replace to complete the operation.	35
Special formats, apply	Select the cell(s) to be formatted, and choose Format, Cells. Select the Number tab, and click Special in the Category list. Select the language in the Locale (location) drop-down list, select a special format in the Type list, and click OK.	40
Styles, copy between workbooks	Open both workbooks and then select the workbook to copy styles to. Choose Format, Style, and click the Merge button to display the Merge Styles dialog box. In the *Merge styles from* list, double-click the name of the workbook that contains the styles you want to copy. If the two workbooks contain styles with the same names, you must confirm whether or not you want to replace the styles. Click OK.	44

Continues ▶

To Do This	Use This Command	Page Number
Styles, create	Select cells and then choose Format, Cells. Select the Font tab in the Format Cells dialog box, specify the combination of font attributes desired, and click OK.	43
Template, create	Choose File, Save As and then select Template from the Save as type drop-down list. Click Save, and choose File, Close.	46
Template, using a built-in	Choose File, New, and click General Templates in the New Workbook task pane. Select the Spreadsheet Solutions tab, click the desired template, and click OK.	48
Template, using a custom	Choose File, New, and click General Templates in the New Workbook task pane. Click the General tab in the Templates dialog box, click the desired template, and click OK.	46
Text, replace	Click cell A1 and then choose Edit, Replace. Type the character or phrase to be found in the Find what text box and then type the replacement character or phrase to be substituted in the Replace with text box. Click the Replace All button, click OK, and click Close.	35
Text, rotate	Select cells with text to be rotated, choose Format, Cells, and click the Alignment tab in the Format Cells dialog box. Type angle of rotation (in degrees) in the Degrees text box and then click OK.	35
Worksheet, copy and move	Select the sheet to be copied or moved. Choose Edit, Move or Copy Sheet, and click the *(move to end)* option in the Before sheet list box. Click the Create a copy check box (to move the worksheet uncheck this box), and then click OK.	45

Functions

COUNTIF	Click the Insert Function button on the formula bar, select the COUNTIF function from the Statistical category, and click OK. In the Range text box, enter the cell reference indicating the location of the data to be counted; in the Criteria text box, enter the criteria that must be met for a cell to be counted. Click OK.	115
FREQUENCY	Click the Insert Function button on the formula bar, select the FREQUENCY function from the Statistical category, and click OK. Type the Data_array cell reference indicating the data to be counted; type the Bins_array cell reference indicating the bins or groups to be tallied. If you have problems, type the function instead of using the Function Arguments dialog box, and press the three-key combination Ctrl+⇧Shift+↵Enter. (Do not click OK or press ↵Enter.)	112
Frequency Distribution, remove	Select all cells in the frequency array and then press Del.	112

To Do This	Use This Command	Page Number
IF, embedded within an IF	Click the Insert Function button on the formula bar, select the IF function from the Logical category, and click OK. Enter a Logical_test in the text box; enter a value in the Value_if_true text box, or choose IF from the left end of the formula bar. (If you choose IF, complete the empty IF dialog box that appears.) Enter a value in the Value_if_false text box or choose IF from the left end of the formula bar. (If you choose IF, complete the empty IF dialog box that appears.) Click OK.	118
Insert Function	Choose Insert, Function, or click the Insert Function button on the formula bar. Select a function category, select a function name, and click OK.	108
SUMIF	Click the Insert Function button on the formula bar, select the SUMIF function from the Math & Trig category, and click OK. In the Range text box, enter the cell reference indicating the location of the data to be evaluated; in the Criteria text box, enter the criteria that must be met for a cell to be summed. In the Sum_range text box, enter the cell reference indicating the location of the data to be summed and then click OK.	117
VLOOKUP	Click the Insert Function button on the formula bar, select the VLOOKUP function from the Lookup & Reference category, and click OK. Complete the Lookup_value, Table_array (this cell reference must be absolute), and Col_index_num text boxes; then click OK.	108
VLOOKUP, exact matches	Click the Insert Function button on the formula bar, select the VLOOKUP function from the Lookup & Reference category, and click OK. Complete the Lookup_value, Table_array (this cell reference must be absolute), and Col_index_num text boxes. Specify False as the Range_lookup and then click OK.	109

Hyperlinks

To Do This	Use This Command	Page Number
Create	Choose Insert, Hyperlink. Make a selection in the Link to section, such as Existing File or Web Page. Specify other settings as needed such as Text to display, ScreenTip, Look in, and/or Address, and then click OK.	181
Create, between a PowerPoint slide and an Excel worksheet	Open a PowerPoint slide show, select a phrase or object, and choose Insert, Hyperlink. Click Existing File or Web Page, select the destination Excel worksheet, add a ScreenTip if desired, and then click OK.	185
Create, between a Word document and an Excel worksheet	Open a Word document, select a phrase or object, and choose Insert, Hyperlink. Click Existing File or Web Page, select the destination Word document, add a ScreenTip if desired, and then click OK.	183

Continues ▶

To Do This	Use This Command	Page Number
Create, between worksheets	Open an Excel workbook, select the worksheet in which to place the hyperlink, specify a location for the link by clicking a cell, and choose Insert, Hyperlink. Select Place in this document, specify the destination cell in another worksheet, add a ScreenTip if desired, and then click OK.	181
Modify appearance	Right-click the hyperlink and select Format Cells. Specify the desired changes in the Format Cells dialog box, and click OK.	183
Remove	Right-click the hyperlink, and select Remove Hyperlink.	183

Integrating Applications

To Do This	Use This Command	Page Number
Embed data, from Excel to Word	Open the Excel file, select the appropriate cells, and choose Edit, Copy. Open the Word document, place the insertion point where you want to embed the data, and choose Edit, Paste Special. In the Paste Special dialog box, click the Paste option and then click Microsoft Excel Worksheet Object in the As list. Leave the Display as icon option unchecked, and click OK.	87
Import data, from Access to Excel	Open the appropriate workbook. Choose Data, Import External Data, and select New Database Query. Select MS Access Database, check *Use the Query Wizard to create/edit queries*, and click OK. Select the appropriate database and then click OK. Select the appropriate table and then click the > button. Follow Query Wizard prompts to select the desired table data. Select *Return Data to Microsoft Excel*, and click Finish. Specify *Existing worksheet*, click the upper left-most cell where the imported data should be stored, and click OK.	93
Import data, from Excel to Access	Make sure that the Excel data is in list format and there are no blank rows or columns within the list and then make sure that the Excel workbook is closed. Open the Excel workbook in Access, and follow the directions in the Link Spreadsheet Wizard.	97
Import data, from text file	Open a new workbook in Excel, and choose File, Open. In the Files of type list, select Text Files, and open the appropriate text file. Select Delimited as the original data type and then click Next. In the Delimiters area, check the appropriate type delimiter, click Next, and click Finish. Choose File, Save As, and select *Microsoft Excel Workbook* from the Save as type drop-down list. Change the filename as appropriate, click Save, and close the workbook.	91
Link chart, from Excel to PowerPoint	Open the Excel workbook, click within a blank area of the chart to select it, and choose Edit, Copy. Open the PowerPoint file and then select the appropriate slide to link the chart. Choose Edit, Paste Special, and click Paste link. Select Microsoft Excel Chart Object in the As list box, and click OK. Resize and move the chart as necessary.	90

To Do This	**Use This Command**	**Page Number**
Link data, from Excel to PowerPoint	Open Excel, select the cells to be linked, and choose Edit, Copy. Open the PowerPoint presentation, select the appropriate slide, and choose Edit, Paste Special. Click Paste link, and specify Microsoft Excel Worksheet Object in the As list box. Click OK.	89
Link data, from Excel to Word	Open the appropriate Excel workbook and then select cells to be linked. Choose Edit, Copy, and open the appropriate Word document. Place the insertion point where the worksheet data will be displayed, choose Edit, Paste Special; then click the Paste link option, and click Microsoft Excel Worksheet Object in the As list box. Leave the Display as icon option unchecked, and click OK.	85

Objects: Drawing

AutoShape, add fill color	Select the shape, click the down arrow attached to the Fill Color button in the Drawing toolbar, click the desired color, and click outside the object to deselect it.	7
AutoShape, add formatting	Right-click a shape and then select Format AutoShape from the shortcut menu. Make the desired formatting changes, and click OK.	6
AutoShape, add text	Right-click the object and then select Add Text from the shortcut menu. Type the text, and click outside the object to deselect it.	7
AutoShape, create	Click the AutoShapes button on the Drawing toolbar and then select a category, such as Block Arrows. Click the desired shape, click a cell to place the shape on the worksheet, and move and size as necessary.	5
AutoShape, flip or rotate	Select the AutoShape and then click Draw on the Drawing toolbar. Select Rotate or Flip, select the desired action, and deselect the object.	5
Callout, add 3-D and Shadow effect	Select the shape, click the Shadow Style button (or the 3-D Style button) in the Drawing toolbar, and click the desired style.	15
Callout, create	Click the AutoShapes button on the Drawing toolbar and then select Callouts. Select a callout style, click a cell to specify the upper-left corner of the callout, and click within the callout. Enter text; then move, size, and format the callout as necessary.	14
Clip art, insert	Select the cell where the upper-left corner of the graphic should appear. Click the Insert Clip Art button on the Drawing toolbar, or choose Insert, Picture, and select Clip Art. Type text in the Search text box, and click the Search button. Point to the desired clip, click the down arrow beside it, and choose Insert. Close the Insert Clip Art task pane and then move and size the object as necessary.	16
Drawing toolbar, show	Choose View, Toolbars and then click Drawing.	3

Continues ▶

To Do This	Use This Command	Page Number
Lines and arrows, add	Click the Line or Arrow button on the Drawing toolbar. Click and hold down the mouse button at the start point for the object, drag to the end point, and release the mouse button.	11
Lines and arrows, draw straight lines	Press and hold down Shift before releasing the mouse button.	12
Lines and arrows, format	Select the line or arrow. Select the Line Style, Dash Style, Arrow Style, or Line Color buttons on the Drawing toolbar, and apply the desired formatting.	13
Lines and arrows, move and size	Select the line or arrow. Use sizing handles to lengthen or shorten and to rotate. Click and drag the line between the sizing handles to move the object.	11
Object, copy	Select the object, such as a line or arrow, and then click the Copy button. Select the destination, and click the Paste button.	12
Objects, group	Hold down Shift and then select each object to be grouped. Click Draw on the Drawing toolbar, and select Group.	9
Objects, regroup	Click a previously grouped object, click Draw on the Drawing toolbar, and select Regroup.	10
Objects, reorder stacked objects	Select an object and then press Tab, or Shift+Tab.	10
Objects, ungroup	Click an object in the group, click Draw on the Drawing toolbar, and select Ungroup.	10
Predefined diagram, insert	Choose Insert, Diagram. Select the desired type of diagram, and click OK.	19
Text box, create	Click the Text Box button on the Drawing toolbar and then drag to create the text box. Click within the text box, and enter text.	7
Text box, edit text	Click within the box to display the flashing insertion point and then modify text as necessary.	7
Text box, fill with color	Select the text box border, click the down arrow to the right of the Fill Color button in the Drawing or Formatting toolbars, and click the desired color.	8
Text box, link text	Click within the text box or shape and then click the formula bar. Type an equal sign, click the cell containing the desired text, and press Enter.	8
WordArt, delete	Click within the object to select it, and press Del.	5
WordArt, format	Select the WordArt object. Click Format WordArt on the WordArt toolbar, specify the desired formatting, click OK, and deselect the object.	5
WordArt, insert	Click the Insert WordArt button, select a style, and click OK. Replace the *Your Text Here* message with the desired text and then click OK.	3
WordArt, resize	Select the WordArt object, click a sizing handle, and drag to increase or decrease the object's size.	3

To Do This	Use This Command	Page Number

PivotTable and PivotChart Reports

To Do This	Use This Command	Page Number
PivotChart, create from pivot table	Right-click any cell in the pivot table and then select PivotChart from the shortcut menu.	165
PivotChart, hide data series	Select the chart, click the drop-down arrow next to the data series, uncheck the field to be hidden, and click OK. Reverse the process to unhide the element.	165
PivotTable, change summary calculation	Double-click an existing summary button in the pivot table (for example, Sum of Salary), select the desired calculation from the Summarize by list in the PivotTable Field dialog box, and click OK.	157
PivotTable, create	Click any cell in the list, and choose Data, PivotTable and PivotChart Report. Specify the location of data and the type of report, and click Next. Enter the list range and then click Next. Specify the location for the report, click Finish, and drag items from the PivotTable Field List to the appropriate areas of the PivotTable report.	157
PivotTable, delete	Right-click within the pivot table, choose Select from the shortcut menu, and click Entire Table. Choose Edit, Clear, All.	160
PivotTable, expand	If you do not see the Pivot Table Field List box, right-click within the pivot table and then select Show Field List. Click a field name in the PivotTable Field List box, and display the area drop-down list to the right of the Add To button. Select Row Area, and click the Add To button. Click a field name in the PivotTable Field List box, display the area drop-down list to the right of the Add To button, select Column Area, and click the Add To button.	161
PivotTable, hide/show summary data	Display the field name drop-down list and then check the names of data to be shown; uncheck the names of data to be hidden.	162
PivotTable, predefined format—applying	Right-click any cell in the pivot table and select Show PivotTable Toolbar, if necessary. Click the Format Report button on the PivotTable toolbar, scroll the gallery of formats, select the desired format, and click OK. Deselect the pivot table.	166
PivotTable, predefined format—removing	Click any cell within the pivot table, and click the Format Report button on the PivotTable toolbar. Display the gallery of predefined formats, choose None, and click OK.	170
PivotTable, refresh	Right-click anywhere in the pivot table and then choose Refresh Data from the shortcut menu; or choose Data, Refresh Data; or click the Refresh Data button on the PivotTable toolbar.	164
PivotTable, remove summary data	Click the field button in the pivot table to be removed and then drag it off the pivot table.	162

Continues ▶

To Do This	Use This Command	Page Number
PivotTable, set user-specified top or bottom numbers	Click within the pivot table, click PivotTable on the PivotTable toolbar, and select *Sort and Top 10*. Under *Top 10 AutoShow*, click On. In the Show box, select Top or Bottom; in the box to the right, specify the number of items to display. In the Using field box, click the data field to use for calculating the top or bottom items, and click OK.	163

Protection

Password, create for a workbook	Choose File, Save As; display the Tools drop-down list and then select General Options. Enter a password to open or to modify the workbook, and click OK. Type the password(s) again to confirm them, and click OK.	73
Password, create for a worksheet range	Select Tools, Protection, Allow Users to Edit Ranges. Click the New button in the dialog box. Type a name in the Title text box, type a password in the Range password text box, and click OK. Type the new password in the Reenter password to proceed text box, and click OK twice.	70
Password, delete	Choose File, Save As; display the Tools drop-down list, and select General Options. Select the existing password, press ⌦Del, and click OK.	74
Password, open workbook	Choose File, Open and then select the password-protected file. Type the password when prompted, and click OK.	73
Protection, turn off	Select Tools, Protection, Unprotect Sheet.	66
Protection, turn on	Select Tools, Protection, Protect Sheet, and click OK.	66
Protection, unlock cell(s)	Select the cell(s) to unlock, choose Format, Cells, and click the Protection tab. Click the Locked check box to remove the check mark, and click OK.	67
Protection, unlock object	Select the object to unlock (picture, AutoShape, WordArt, and so forth). Choose Format and then select the description of the object. Click the Protection tab, click the Locked check box to remove the check mark, and click OK.	67

Tracking Changes

Accept or reject changes	Choose Tools, Track Changes, Accept or Reject Changes, and click OK if prompted to save the workbook. Check on/off the When, Who, and Where check boxes, select from associated drop-down lists or specify a range as needed, and click OK. Click Accept or Reject for each change found.	187
Change tracking, turn off	Choose Tools, Track Changes, Highlight Changes; uncheck Track changes while editing, click OK, and then click Yes.	186

To Do This	Use This Command	Page Number
Change tracking, turn on	Choose Tools, Track Changes, Highlight Changes, and then check Track changes while editing. Check on/off the When, Who, and Where check boxes, select from associated drop-down lists or specify a range as needed, click OK, and save the workbook.	186
Discussion comment, add	Select Tools, Online Collaboration, Web Discussions. If the Add or Edit Discussion Servers dialog box appears, select a discussion server. Click the Insert Discussion about the Workbook button on the Web Discussions toolbar, enter the discussion subject and discussion text, and click OK.	191
Discussion comment, delete	At the end of the discussion comment, click the Show a menu of actions button, and click Delete.	191
Discussion comment, edit	At the end of the discussion comment, click the Show a menu of actions button, click Edit, and edit the comment.	191
Discussion comment, reply	At the end of the discussion comment, click the S how a menu of actions button, click Reply, and enter your response.	191
Merge workbooks	Prior to merging, set up Shared mode in the original workbook and make copies for others to edit. To merge workbooks, place edited copies in the same folder, and then choose Tools, Compare and Merge Workbooks. Save the shared workbook if prompted, hold down Ctrl, click the name of each copy of the shared workbook listed in the Select Files to Merge Into Current Workbook dialog box that you want to merge, and click OK.	191
Share a workbook	Turn on change tracking, or choose Tools, Share Workbook and check Allow changes by more than one user at a time.	189

Glossary

adjustment handle A yellow diamond-shaped handle used to adjust the appearance, but not the size, of most AutoShapes. [p. 14]

array constant A group of constants arranged in a special way and used as an argument in a formula. [p. 108]

array formula A formula that you must enter by pressing the three-key combination Ctrl+⬆Shift+⏎Enter. The FREQUENCY function is an array formula. [p. 112]

array range A rectangular area of cells that share a common formula such as the FREQUENCY function, which counts the occurrences of values in a range of cells and creates an array range to display results. [p. 111]

AutoFormat A feature that enables you to apply one of 16 predefined formats to lists and cell ranges. [p. 40]

AutoShape A predefined shape that you create using the Drawing toolbar. [p. 5]

bin A predetermined category used to analyze data, such as the number of respondents in each age range (20-29, 30-39, and so forth). [p. 111]

built-in template A template provided by Excel that contains content and formatting designed to meet a common business need. [p. 48]

callout A text-filled object that points to other text or another object. [p. 13]

change tracking An Excel feature that records row and column insertions and deletions, moves and copies, and changes to cell contents. [pg. 185]

clip A drawing, photograph, or other media type such as sound, animation, or movies. [p. 15]

clip art Drawings as well as photographs and sound files. [p. 16]

Clip Organizer A Microsoft Office program you can use to find, add, and organize media clips. [p. 15]

comment An annotation attached to a cell that displays within a box whenever the mouse pointer rests on the cell. [p. 63]

comment indicator A small red triangle in the cell's upper-right corner indicating that supplementary information is stored in the cell, but is not visible unless the comment is opened. [p. 63]

COUNTIF function A function used to count the number of cells within a range that meet your specified criteria. [p. 115]

custom format A format designed for a unique purpose when a predefined format will not work. [p. 37]

custom template A workbook that you create and save with your preferred content and/or formatting in one or more worksheets. *See also* **template.** [p. 46]

data validation A feature that ensures the accuracy of data entered in a workbook using options that enable you to set up data entry instructions, drop-down lists of allowable entries, and error messages. [p. 130]

default workbook template The workbook that opens when you start Excel or open a new workbook without specifying a template. [p. 47]

default worksheet template Excel uses the default worksheet template when you insert a worksheet in a workbook. [p. 47]

destination file A file that contains linked or embedded data. [p. 85]

diagram A drawing that generally illustrates relationships. [p. 18]

discussion comment A remark associated with a Web page or Office application file that is stored on a discussion server. [pg. 191]

embedded object An object in a destination file that does not update when the data in the source file changes. [p. 85]

error alert message   A data validation means that allows you to specify that data must fit specified criteria, and that any attempt to enter invalid data produces an error alert message in one of three styles—Stop, Warning, or Information. [p. 134]

file property   A characteristic of a file, such as file type, file size, storage location, author's name, and date last revised. [p. 69]

frequency distribution   The counts of how often specific values occur within a set of values. [p. 111]

FREQUENCY function   A function that calculates how many times values occur within a range. [p. 106]

grouped objects   Two or more objects that can be manipulated as a single object. [p. 8]

History worksheet   A separate worksheet that provides—in a list, one change per row—detailed information about tracked changes. [pg. 187]

hyperlink   Text or an object that you can click to jump to another location, open another file, or start a process—such as sending an e-mail or transferring a file. [pg. 180]

indented format   A format that supports the presentation of pivot table data in categories and subcategories. [p. 166]

input message   A convenient data validation means to display instructions to users when they access a specific cell in a worksheet. [p. 131]

linked object   An object in a destination file that updates whenever the data in the source file changes. [p. 85]

nested IF   An IF function within an IF function. [p. 118]

nonindented format   A format that doesn't offset subcategories within categories in a PivotTable report. [p. 167]

object   A workbook, worksheet, range of cells, chart, clip art, or WordArt element that has properties, and can be referenced and used by another program. [p. 84]

Object Linking and Embedding (OLE)   A method of sharing data that is supported by many different programs, including all Office XP applications. [p. 84]

password   A collection of up to 255 case-sensitive characters that must be known to use a password-protected range, worksheet, or workbook. [p. 70]

pivot table   An interactive table that quickly summarizes large amounts of data from a data source such as a list or another table. [p. 154]

PivotTable and PivotChart Wizard   A wizard that guides you through the steps to make a custom report from a list of data. [p. 156]

range name   A name applied to a cell or range of cells. [p. 60]

read-only   A file attribute that enables you to view, but not change, a file that you save under the same name. [p. 73]

refresh   To recalculate data in a pivot table if you change data in a worksheet and that data impacts a summary calculation in a pivot table. [p. 163]

shared workbook   An Excel file that is set up to enable multiple users to make changes. [pg. 185]

source file   The file providing the data to link or embed. [p. 85]

style   A means of combining more than one format, such as font type, size, and color, into a single definition that can be applied to one or more cells. [p. 42]

SUMIF function   A function that adds the contents of cells within a range that meet your specified criteria. [p. 116]

template   A workbook (or worksheet) containing standardized content and/or formatting that you can use as the basis for other workbooks (or worksheets). [p. 46]

text box   An object that contains words and is shaped like a square or rectangle. [p. 7]

thumbnail   A miniature representation of an image. [p. 15]

unlock   To remove the default locked setting that prevents change to a cell or object when worksheet protection is active. [p. 67]

VLOOKUP function   A function that is used to search for a value in the leftmost column of a table. If found, the function displays the contents of a cell in that same row for the column you specify. [p. 106]

WordArt   A user-specified text in one of 30 predefined styles. [p. 3]

write access   The capability to modify a file. *See also* **read-only.** [p. 74]

Index